The South WEST
COAST PATH

2001 GUIDE

THE COMPLETE GUIDE
TO THE LONGEST NATIONAL TRAIL
BY THE
SOUTH WEST COAST PATH
ASSOCIATION

(FORMERLY THE SOUTH WEST WAY ASSOCIATION)

THE SOUTH WEST COAST PATH ASSOCIATION

Registered as a charity (No. 266754)

The Association formed to promote the interest of users of the South West Coast Path

Visit our Website at www.swcp.org.uk

CHAIRMAN
Brian Panton, 5 Nicholas Gardens, Ensbury Park,
Bournemouth BH10 4BA
Tel/Fax: (01202) 526954

TREASURER
David Richardson, J.P.
44 Whitchurch Avenue
Exeter EX2 5NT
Tel/Fax: (01392) 430985

SECRETARY
Eric Wallis
'Windlestraw', Penquit, Ermington,
Devon PL21 0LU
Tel/Fax: (01752) 896237
e-mail: wallispenquit@beeb.net

ADMINISTRATOR
Sarah Vincent
25 Clobells, South Brent,
Devon TQ10 9JW
Tel/Fax: (01364) 73859
e-mail: coastpath.swcpa@virgin.net

Published by:
The South West Coast Path Association

Trade Sales and Distribution:
Halsgrove Publishing, Halsgrove House, Lower Moor Way,
Tiverton Business Park, Tiverton, Devon. EX16 6SS
Contact: Marie Lewis 01884 243242

© South West Coast Path Association 2001

Printed in England by Swift Print, Dawlish

ISBN 0 907055 03 6

Jacket photograph: Morte Point, North Devon by Alan Winlow

This project is supported through
the European Agricultural
Guidance and Guarantee Fund

South West
Coast Path

CONTENTS

INTRODUCTION

The South West Coast Path is a 'National Trail' funded by the Countryside Agency (formerly the Countryside Commission) and maintained on its behalf by County Councils and National Park authorities. The route is waymarked by the distinctive acorn symbol. It is by far the longest of all the Long Distance trails; it runs from Minehead in Somerset right round the South West Peninsula to South Haven Point on the south side of Poole Harbour in Dorset. As a result of the 1999/2000 survey of the Coast Path end to end using a Global Positioning System, we now have access to very precise distances - the Coast Path is 630 miles (1014 km) long. The survey, carried out by the South West Coast Path Team, included the Isle of Portland. It is interesting to note that in a contour count undertaken by this Association, it was calculated that the walker will climb over 91,000 feet (27,737 m), which is three times Mount Everest.

This Guide attempts to provide in one single unit all the basic information you need to walk the path. The information is updated annually and members are advised by newsletters of important changes during the year. We try to provide the basic information in just one small book.

A survey established that one of the chief joys of those accomplishing the Pennine Way was the sense of achievement; of a challenge met. What of our path which is twice as long and requiring far more total effort? Because of its length, few will be able to undertake to walk it as a whole. That is why as much as possible of this guide is written to be just as useful to those who only wish to walk parts of the path.

The splendid idea of making this old path around the South West Peninsula one of the first of a series of Long Distance Paths came from a war-time committee of the Ramblers' Association. The idea was put into effect by being included in the National Park and Access to the Countryside Act of 1949. Some long distance paths have now been designated as National Trails, and now have an equal basis in law with the much better known National Parks. Unfortunately, however, being authorised by Act of Parliament so long ago and despite several Opening Ceremonies, the South West Coast Path is still UNFINISHED.

The South West Coast Path Association was formed after some months' preliminary work in May 1973. It is an independent body but works in co-operation with the Ramblers' Association. The South West Coast Path Association's first aim is to secure completion of the path, and we do believe we have been responsible for many path alignment improvements, better maintenance and waymarking during our 28 year existence.

Furthermore, the South West Coast Path Association believes the Countryside Agency has been in error in two respects. Firstly it has not made it a continuous path despite its own words: 'There should be a continuous right of way along the entire length of the path.' (Countryside Agency's National Long Distance Path - Some Questions Answered.)

Secondly, in several places, the Path has been diverted from the coast for no apparent good reason, even on occasions onto main roads with no pavement. Our Association believes it would be scenically more beautiful, less hindrance to agriculture and physically safer if kept on the coast. Experience has shown that diversions away from it are on the whole unsatisfactory.

It seems that no local walking organisations were ever consulted about the path until our Association came into being. Being reasonable people we cannot expect to have everything our own way - in fact there are many legitimate interests to consider. However, to establish a path without discussing it with the people who know it best, which is exactly what the Countryside Agency was apparently trying to do, seems altogether wrong.

Our Association believes that, in a tourist-orientated area such as the South West, a continuous coastal path will be a major asset. It hopes the Path will bring more business to less frequented places and relieve some of the pressure on the South West National Parks. There is a great number of bodies interested in various parts of the Path. Our Association believes it is important that it should represent all sections, and view the Path as a whole.

The path passes along some of the finest coastal scenery in Europe, and with its enormous variety and contrast between bustling resort and quiet cove is a never-ceasing source of delight.

This path is the longest National Trail in the country. We think it is the finest, and hope you will too. We certainly know of no other that has as much contrast and variety as ours; try it!

Members receive a free Annual Guide and two Newsletters a year with up-to-date information on the state of the path.

Enquiries to: The Administrator, (see page 2)

Subscriptions: Single: £9.50;   Joint: £10.50;   Associations & Local Authorities: £16.00; Life Membership: £140.00;   Joint Life Membership: £160.00;   Non-UK Membership: £14.00.

Both the Bournemouth Coast Path and the Solent Way link in with the end of the South West Coast Path at Sandbanks, thus providing a continuous path from Minehead to Emsworth. Guide books for those trails are out of print but for those who wish to continue along the south coast, this Association has produced a fact sheet. This is priced £1 including post and packaging - contact the Administrator.

LIABILITY DISCLAIMER

Information included or available through the South West Coast Path Association (SWCPA) is given in good faith and is believed to be accurate and correct at the time of going to print - however it cannot be guaranteed not to include inaccuracies or typographical errors.

Advice received via the SWCPA should not be relied upon for personal decisions and you should take into account the weather and your own capabilities before following the walks set out in this Guide. It is for the individual concerned to weigh up the risks of each of the walks described in this book.

The SWCPA makes no representations about the suitability of walks to any one person and will accept no liability for any loss or damage suffered as a result of relying on this book: it should be used for guidance only.

In no event shall the SWCPA be liable for any personal injury or any loss suffered as a result of using this publication.

THE REVERSE GUIDE

The Association has written a description of the Trail for those walking in the Poole to Minehead direction. It deals only with the path so this annual guide will be necessary for all the other information. The 'Reverse Guide' supplement is available from the Administrator at £3.50 including postage.

WEATHER

The South West Coast Path is more exposed to wind than any other Long Distance Trail, so please pay attention to gale forecasts as well as rain. Along some sections, strong winds can be dangerous, especially when rounding exposed headlands and crossing bridges; a high backpack can act like a sail. Detailed forecasts are available on 09068 400105 for Somerset, 09068 400104 for Devon and Cornwall, and on 09068 400103 for Dorset.

A WORD TO BEGINNERS

Long Distance Path Walking

These words are not for those hardy veterans who have all the gear, have done several paths already, and know all about it. We will only say to them at least read the second paragraph of 'Grading' near the beginning of the 'Trail Description' section. However, we do get a number of letters each year from those who have not ventured before on Long Distance Paths and need some advice. This we are pleased to try and provide and we do hope those who read this will find it helpful. However, it is easy to miss out things that folk wish to know, so if you who are new read this, and are still baffled, please write to us and we will try to provide the answers. As well as perhaps helping you, it will enable us to improve this section for another year and so be of help to more people.

For Those Who Have Never Been Walking

Have you been walking at all before? If the answer is no, do not for heaven's sake try and plan several days' continuous walking. You need to do some day walks - there are some very good ones on the coast. Better still, look for the sections marked 'Easy' - start at one end and stop and turn back before you have half had enough. We say before half because it is always better to do a bit less and really enjoy it.

You can soon progress to setting out to walk a whole section either by using two cars or using public transport. One point here - if possible use the public transport to go out and walk back to your car or base. This means that you do not get yourself in a position of having to race the clock if you should take a bit more time than you thought.

If you are walking on your own, do please take additional care for, as you will appreciate, if you fall or twist an ankle there can be problems. If you are on your own therefore, you should leave a note with someone to make sure that you arrive at your destination. Not everyone is happy walking on their own and can feel lonely. There is also an added problem that you may try to do too much, so please bear this in mind.

There is no need to buy expensive equipment for the easy sections at the start; a pair of stout shoes and a rainproof is all you need. As you progress, a small rucksack or haversack for 'eats' will be needed next.

Obviously if you can join a walking club and go out with them you will collect lots of friendly advice on all sorts of gear you may care to purchase as you become more serious about walking. Maps, guides, etc., are all listed in their appropriate sections.

For Those Who Have Walked, But Not On Long Distance Trails

Day walking on long distance trails is really no different from any other kind of day walking. It is only when you contemplate several days' continuous walking that other considerations arise and there are some pitfalls which even quite experienced day walkers often overlook.

Do not be too ambitious in the mileage you plan. Do not carry too much weight of gear.

Having stated the two big points, we will elaborate. You will not be able to accomplish in daily mileage the same amount you normally cover in a day walk; you will have to settle for less. The first reason is that you will be carrying more equipment; you must for instance, have a complete change of clothing and footwear, possibly nightwear and toilet kit. For this you need a bigger rucksack so you will be carrying quite a bit more weight than you normally do. Secondly, there is what we call the 'wear' factor. For the first few days until you are really fit, it is just simply more tiring having to walk each day. The last point could be called the 'interest' factor. Usually, if you are walking a long distance path, you are further from your home base, in fresh fields and pastures new; there is more to see so you will need more time to look around.

If you usually accomplish 15 miles (24 km) a day, aim, say, for 12 (19 km). This is particularly important if you are booking ahead. You can find yourself tied to a treadmill which you cannot get off. Booking ahead has the advantage that you know there is a bed ahead. On the other hand, it does mean even if you are tired, have developed blisters, and the weather is diabolical, you have to go on. Be guided too by our `Trail Description' section and the terrain you are tackling. 6 miles (10 km), say, of a `Severe' section can equal in effort 10-12 miles (16-19 km) of an 'Easy' one.

We have stated you must carry more gear and this is true. Having said that, think long and hard about every item you imagine you may need. You will be surprised - you may find you will not want it at all. Watch particularly those extras such as cameras and binoculars - they are often a source of considerable weight. One little additional point, many rucksacks, even modern ones, are not as waterproof as you think. A plastic liner, which can be obtained quite cheaply from rambling shops, etc., as an additional inner layer, may save you that most unpleasant discovery after a long day spent in the rain that your only change of clothing is no longer dry. We would also recommend that in addition to this liner, your dry clothing should then be enclosed in further plastic bags to ensure dryness. Trainer shoes are useful for wearing at the end of the day and can be worn on some parts of the path.

A sensible idea before undertaking a long walking holiday is to take, say, a weekend of two or three days first, walking continuously as a practice.

We are sometimes asked if you require a map as well as a guide book and our advice is certainly yes. One does not get as badly lost on the Coast Path as you can on inland ones but nonetheless a map is an asset. Furthermore many walkers derive much interest from looking at their route in relation to the rest of the countryside on ordinary walks and the same applies just as much, if not more so, on our Coast Path. The National Trail Guides offer a partial solution with their maps, but even these are not as useful as a Map Sheet.

Another point to watch especially on our Coast Path is the availability of refreshment. At main holiday times, you will get it nearly everywhere, except for the few places we especially mention in our 'Trail Description' section. Out of season, you will find it in surprisingly few places on long stretches of coast. The usual remarks about carrying stand-by supplies, therefore, certainly apply; better to carry an extra couple of bars of chocolate than to go hungry.

Walking Alone

The Association has a scheme that enables single female members who are a little nervous about walking alone to team up with other single female members. Contact the Administrator for information.

Easing The Load

On long trips it is a good idea to:

a)   Send guides, maps etc. ahead to larger post offices Poste Restante. The only snag is if you arrive on a Saturday evening.

b)   Start out with a few map-sized envelopes and the smallest available roll of sellotape so that you can despatch finished guides, maps, books etc. home.

SOUTH WEST COAST PATH ASSOCIATION PUBLICATIONS

Path Descriptions by our Association are detailed accounts on all aspects of short sections of the coast path and include maps and illustrations. They cover in great detail what cannot be included in the guide book.

These Path Descriptions are all priced at £1.00 including postage. All are available from the Administrator (see page 2).

PATH DESCRIPTIONS

(Please note that as each Path Description is revised, we shall be using the new accurate distances accordingly)

Minehead to Lynmouth (22 miles / 35 km)
Lynmouth to Ilfracombe (18 miles / 30 km)
Ilfracombe to Croyde Bay (13 miles / 20 km)
Croyde Bay to Barnstaple (16 miles / 25 km)
Barnstaple to Westward Ho! (17 miles / 28 km)
Westward Ho! To Clovelly (11 miles / 18 km)
Clovelly to Hartland Quay (10 miles / 16 km)
Hartland Quay to Bude (14 miles / 22 km)
Bude to Crackington Haven (9 miles / 15 km)
Crackington Haven to Tintagel (12 miles / 20 km)
Tintagel to Port Isaac (8 miles / 13 km)
Port Isaac to Padstow (12 miles / 19 km)
Padstow to Porthcothan (12 miles / 20 km)
Porthcothan to Newquay (10 miles / 15 km)
Newquay to Perranporth (11 miles / 18 km)
Perranporth to Portreath (13 miles / 20 km)
Portreath to Hayle (12 miles / 19 km)
Hayle to Pendeen Watch (19 miles / 32 km)
Pendeen Watch to Porthcurno (15 miles / 24 km)
Porthcurno to Penzance (11 miles / 18 km)
Penzance to Porthleven (13 miles / 21 km)
Porthleven to The Lizard (13 miles / 22 km)
The Lizard to Helford (24 miles / 38 km)

Helford to Falmouth (10 miles / 15 km)
Falmouth to Portloe (13 miles / 22 km)
Portloe to Mevagissey (12 miles / 19 km)
Mevagissey to Fowey (17 miles / 27 km)
Fowey to Looe (12 miles / 19 km)
Looe to Plymouth (21 miles / 33 km)
Plymouth (River Tamar) to Wembury (River Yealm) (14 miles / 22 km)
Warren Point (Wembury) to Bigbury-on-Sea (14 miles / 22 km)
Bigbury-on-Sea to Salcombe (13 miles / 21 km)
Salcombe to Torcross (13 miles / 20 km)
Torcross to Dartmouth (10 miles / 16 km)
Dartmouth to Brixham (11 miles / 18 km)
Brixham to Shaldon (19 miles / 30 km)
Shaldon to Sidmouth (21 miles / 32 km)
Sidmouth to Lyme Regis (17 miles / 27 km)
Lyme Regis to Abbotsbury (18 miles / 30 km)
Abbotsbury to Weymouth (14 miles / 23 km)
Isle of Portland Circuit (14 miles / 22 km)
Weymouth to Lulworth Cove (11 miles / 18 km)
Lulworth to Kimmeridge, Lulworth Range (7 miles / 11 km)
Kimmeridge to South Haven Point, Poole Harbour (20 miles / 31 km)
Alternative Inland Route, West Bexington to Osmington Mills (18 miles / 28 km)

A History of the South West Coast Path

The Association has written a history of the origins of the Coast Path. This book also includes an account of walking the Coast Path in 1854, and an account of a protracted legal case involving access to the Coast Path on the Devon / Dorset border in the mid 19th century.

Price £2.50 including postage.

The Reverse Guide

The Association has written a description of the Trail in the Poole - Land's End - Minehead direction. It deals only with the path, so this Annual Guide will be necessary for all the other information.

Price £3.50 including postage.

THE ASSOCIATION'S SHOP

Log Book

Why not keep a day by day record of your walk in an easy to carry, pocket size booklet, with a page per section in which to record your daily journey round the coast path (all 613 miles / 982 km!). Whether you do it all in one go or over a period of time, you will have a permanent record of your walks round some of the most beautiful country in the British Isles.

Price £2.75 including postage

Polo Shirt

In an attractive jade green, with the Association logo embroidered on the shirt, with 'SOUTH WEST COAST PATH' embroidered around the logo.

A good quality garment, easy to wash (65% polyester / 35% cotton), in Small, Medium, Large, Extra Large and Extra Extra Large.

Price £18.25 including postage

Sweat Shirt

In bottle green embroidered with the Association logo on the left side, and 'SOUTH WEST COAST PATH' around the logo (70% polyester / 30% cotton). It comes in five sizes, Small, Medium, Large, Extra Large and Extra Extra Large.

Price £25.00 including postage

Cloth Badge

Good quality cloth badge, showing the Association logo, with 'SOUTH WEST COAST PATH' embroidered below, approximate size 4" x 3" (10 x 8 cm). Suitable for sewing onto shirt or rucksack, coloured logo in green and yellow on a blue background.

Price £2.70 including postage

Coast Path Embroidery

We have designed this unique counted cross stitch embroidery to celebrate the South West Coast Path. The embroidery kit contains everything you need to complete the project, and a leaflet containing full details can be obtained from the Administrator. Guidance is also given on how to personalise your embroidery to include your own completion date of the coast path.

Price £25.00 including postage

Notelets

The Coast Path Embroidery has been used as the cover design for notelets, which come in packs of 10.

Price £7.50 including postage

Whisky Tumblers

Cut glass whisky tumblers with the Association logo sand-blasted on the glass. In a presentation box.

Price £16.00, £28.00 for a pair, prices including postage. PLEASE ALLOW 28 DAYS FOR DELIVERY

Glass Beer Tankards

Glass beer tankards, plain glass with the Association logo sand-blasted onto the glass. Suitably packaged.

Price £11.50 including postage. PLEASE ALLOW 28 DAYS FOR DELIVERY

TO ORDER:- Please send details of the sizes of garments and / or quantity required, together with a cheque made payable to: **The South West Coast Path Association** to:- Sarah Vincent, The Administrator, 25 Clobells, South Brent, Devon TQ10 9JW. Tel/Fax: 01364 73859

Certificates

These are now available to persons who have walked the whole path. To members - £1.50 and to non-members - £2.50 including postage. Contact the Administrator.

BOOKS

This list is not exhaustive; there are a number of other books available but we have tried hard to list all those which are really useful and even those not really useful that you might think would be. These publications are available from most good bookshops.

South West Way - Minehead to Penzance

South West Way - Penzance to Poole.

Both these excellent pocket sized books are by Martin Collins. We can recommend them as most useful. Available from Cicerone Press, 2 Police Square, Milnthorpe, Cumbria, LA7 7PY at £8.99 each.

National Trail Guides - published by Aurum Press in association with the Countryside Agency. They are available from bookshops, or in case of difficulty, from Aurum Press, 25 Bedford Avenue, London WC1B 3AT. These are good guide books with good maps. An excellent venture by those involved.

Minehead to Padstow by Roland Tarr (3rd Edition 1996)

Padstow to Falmouth by John Macadam (2nd Edition 1996)

Falmouth to Exmouth by Brian Le Messurier (3rd Edition 1999)

Exmouth to Poole by Roland Tarr (3rd Edition 1996)

LANDFALL WALKS BOOKS - Bob Acton of Devoran has written twelve splendid books that contain well over 100 circular walks in Cornwall. These feature sections of the coast path throughout the county. They will enable walkers to progress along the coast path by basing themselves at one location. Write to Landfall Publications, Landfall, Penpol, Devoran, Truro, TR3 6NW for full list, or (Tel: 01872 862581).

Footpath Touring with Ken Ward. Land's End and The Lizard. Price £3.75 including postage. Available direct from 'Sea Chimney', South Down, Beer, EX12 3AE. An excellent guide to this section of the path by one of the co-authors of the well-known Letts Guides.

Two Moors Way (now illustrated) - by Devon Area Ramblers' Association - Price £3.00. This is not our path: one is enough! This describes the path from Lynmouth in North Devon to Ivybridge near Plymouth - and very well done it is too.

Two Moors Way by John Macadam. This is a new recreational guide published by Aurum Press and Ordnance Survey. £12.99.

Classic Walks Cornwall - 56 half day circular walks involving the coast path. From Cornish Publications Ltd, PO Box 12, Perranporth. £4.99 plus 75p P&P.

Classic Walks Devon - 60 Half-day Circular Walks - Many involving the coast path (as for Classic Walks Cornwall).

Most Tourist Information Centres (see our Accommodation section) have good supplies of leaflets and books relating to their local areas. We suggest you telephone or write to them and ask what is available.

THE NATIONAL TRUST 'COAST OF DEVON' LEAFLETS

At long last a new series of detailed leaflets with maps is becoming available. These each include four walks covering the coastline owned by the National Trust in Devon. Each leaflet contains good maps and information on the history, flora and fauna and general information of the areas.

They are available from National Trust shops in Devon or from the Devon Regional Office, Killerton House, Broadclyst, Exeter, EX5 3LE, at 75p each plus post and packing:

The West Exmoor Coast   Wembury
Watersmeet and Countisbury   Walks around the Salcombe Estuary
Woolacombe to Baggy Point   Walks around Dartmouth
Bideford Bay to Welcombe Mouth

THE NATIONAL TRUST 'COAST OF CORNWALL' LEAFLETS

A series of detailed leaflets with maps, covering the coastline owned by the National Trust in Cornwall. Each leaflet contains information of the history, flora and fauna of the area as well as general information on points of interest. Available from National Trust shops in Cornwall or from the Cornwall Regional Office, Lanhydrock, Bodmin, Cornwall PL30 4DE.

Please make cheques payable to The National Trust and include postage & packing (see guidelines below).

No 1	Bude to Morwenstow	80p
No 2	Crackington Haven	60p
No 3	Boscastle	80p
No 4	Tintagel	80p
No 5	Polzeath to Port Quin	70p
No 6	Trevose to Watergate Bay, including Bedruthan Steps (not NT)	70p
No 7	Crantock to Holywell Bay	70p
No 8	St. Agnes and Chapel Porth	70p
No 9	Godrevy to Portreath	70p
No 10	West Penwith: St. Ives to Pendeen	90p
No 11	West Penwith: Levant to Penberth	90p
No 12	Loe Pool and Mount's Bay	80p
No 13	Lizard, West Coast	80p
No 14	Lizard, Kynance, Lizard Point & Bass Point	80p
No 15	Lizard, East Coast, Landewednack to St. Keverne	80p
No 16	Helford River	80p
No 17	Trelissick	80p
No 18/19	The Roseland and St Anthony Head	80p
No 19	St Anthony Battery	70p
No 20	Nare Head and the Dodman	80p
No 21	Fowey	90p
No 22	East Cornwall	80p

Country Walks Leaflet : Cotehele Estate   90p
Country Walks Leaflet : Lanhydrock   80p

Focus on Wildlife   £1.99

When ordering, please add the following rates for postage and packaging:

Quantity	1st Class	2nd	Quantity	1st Class	2nd	Quantity	1st Class	2nd
1	27p	19p	7	70p	55p	13-14	£1.17	93p
2	39p	31p	8-9	80p	64p	15-16	£1.30	£1.05
3-4	49p	38p	10-11	92p	73p	17-19	£1.60	£1.25
5-6	60p	45p	12	£1.04	83p	20-22	£2.00	£1.45

Tel: 01208 74281 Fax: 01208 77887

THE NATIONAL TRUST WESSEX REGION

The following illustrated guided walks leaflets are available from the Wessex Regional Office. To order copies, please write to: The Box Office, The National Trust, Wessex Regional Office, Eastleigh Court, Bishopstrow, Warminster, Wiltshire, BA12 9HW enclosing a cheque or postal order to include 50p towards postage and packing. Cheques should be made payable to 'the National Trust (Enterprises) Ltd.'

Isle of Purbeck (5 walks)	£2.75
Holnicote (Horner Wood)	
- Valley Walk	£0.60
- Hill Walk	£0.60
Golden Cap - Walks from Stonebarrow	£0.50
Golden Cap - Walks from Langdon Hill Wood	£0.50
Explore Holnicote	£1.00
Holnicote - Bossington and Coastline Walk	£0.60
Holnicote - Allerford and Selworthy woods walk	£0.60
Cerne Abbas Giant and Dorset Hill Forts	£1.50
Exploring Corfe Common	£0.50
Holnicote - Dunkery and Horner Wood	£0.60
Holnicote - Luccombe and Woodland	£0.60
Holnicote - Selworthy and Bury Castle	£0.60
Holnicote - Upland Archaeology	£0.60

NATIONAL TRUST REGIONAL MARKETING AND COMMUNICATIONS MANAGERS

Devon Regional Office, Killerton House, Broadclyst, Exeter, Devon EX5 3LE (Tel: 01392 881691).

Wessex Regional Office, (for Dorset and Somerset) Eastleigh Court, Bishopstrow, Warminster, Wilts. BA12 9HW (Tel: 01985 843600).

Cornwall Regional Office, Lanhydrock, Bodmin, Cornwall PL30 4DE (Tel: 01208 74281)

All Long Distance Paths

We recommend the Long Distance Walker's Handbook: 6th Edition: Completely revised and updated. Contact - Brian Smith, 10 Temple Park Close, Leeds, West Yorkshire LS15 0JJ (Tel: 0113 264 2205). (£11.99 inc postage).

Information on Long Distance Routes can also be obtained from the Ramblers' Association, 1/5 Wandsworth Road, London SW8 2XX. (Tel: 020 7339 8500)

RAILWAYS

Throughout the year there is a regular service of direct First Great Western Trains linking London Paddington with Taunton, Exeter St. David's, Newton Abbot, Plymouth and Cornwall. There are also regular Virgin Cross Country Trains' services linking Birmingham, the North West, North East and Scotland with Taunton, Exeter St. David's, Plymouth, Cornwall, Bournemouth and Poole. All these services offer a range of on-train facilities including catering and on most First Great Western services during the school holidays, coach E is dedicated for the use of families. During the high season (May to September), demand for seats is high so it is recommended that seats are reserved in advance to ensure a comfortable journey. On Saturdays, additional services run to and from the West Country to the Midlands, North of England and London with a direct service operated between London and Newquay during the summer only.

There is a regular South West Trains' service linking London Waterloo with Bournemouth, Poole, Wareham (for Swanage), and Weymouth for those who intend to walk the Dorset end of The South West Coast Path. East Devon is served by an approximate two hourly service from London Waterloo to Axminster (for Lyme Regis and Seaton) and Honiton (for Sidmouth). In addition to these services South West Trains also offer a service of trains linking London Waterloo, Basingstoke, Salisbury, Exeter Central and Paignton.

The South West Coast Path

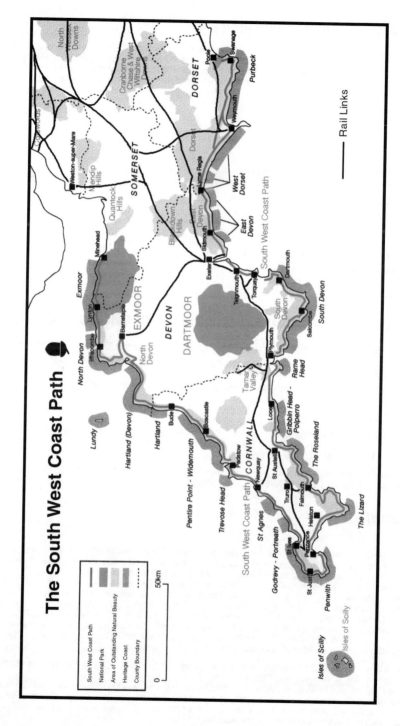

Rail Links

South West Coast Path
National Park
Area of Outstanding Natural Beauty
Heritage Coast
County Boundary

0   50km

Wales & West Passenger Trains Ltd offers a regular service of long distance and local trains in the South West. The long distance trains link Cardiff, Manchester, Bristol and Swindon with Penzance, Plymouth, Paignton and Exeter. The local services on the branch lines of Devon and Cornwall offer reasonable connections into and out of First Great Western and Virgin Cross Country services. Most of Wales & West Passenger Trains' local services operate on a Sunday during the summer months with the first four with asterisks, below also operating a limited Sunday service during the winter months.

* Westbury - Yeovil - Weymouth
* Exeter - Barnstaple
* Exeter - Exmouth
* Newton Abbot -Torquay - Paignton
  Plymouth - Gunnislake

Liskeard - Looe
Par - Newquay
Truro - Falmouth
St Erth - St Ives

A wide variety of attractive reduced-rate fares is often available during the summer months, details of which can be obtained from enquiry at stations and Travel Centres. The method of obtaining train information, to reserve seats or make general rail enquiries has been simplified with the setting up of a National Rail Enquiries bureau. The telephone number for all rail matters is 08457 484950 and contact can be made 24 hours a day. This number can be busy, but do persist and await a reply.

Private Branch Line Railways

Bishops Lydeard to Minehead - The West Somerset Railway PLC runs steam trains through 20 scenic miles (32 km) to Minehead. Bishops Lydeard is 4 miles (6 km) outside Taunton and easily accessible by bus. The service operates between March and October. For details contact the company at 'The Station', Minehead TA24 5BG (Tel: 01643 704996).

Paignton to Kingswear (Dartmouth) - For the rambler who is also a railway enthusiast, the Paignton and Dartmouth Railway is a `must'. This most attractive line runs from Paignton to Goodrington, Churston and Kingswear and operates preserved Great Western steam locomotives and rolling-stock. The line passes through some delightful coastal and river scenery, and a trip on the railway could easily be combined with a walk to make a very pleasant day out. It operates from March to December. For details contact - Queens Park Station, Torbay Road, Paignton TQ4 6AF (Tel: 01803 555872).

Bodmin Parkway to Bodmin Town is a service that could prove useful for those requiring bus transport to the coast. (Tel: 01208 73666).

BUS SERVICES

A new National Transport Enquiry Service has been established. For all timetable enquiries in South West England, call Traveline on 0870 6082608

Tourist Information Centres can help with bus enquiries. For details of all coastal TICs see our Accommodation section of the back of this book.

ACCESS TO THE START OF THE PATH:
Access to the start of the path can be made locally and from outside the region, with Southern National's bus service 28 linking Minehead to the Great Western Rail Line at Taunton.

Service 28 Taunton-Minehead currently operates on an hourly frequency up to the early evenings from Monday to Saturdays. On Sundays service 28 operates less frequently. For service 28 timetable enquiries telephone Southern National - Taunton. (Tel: 01823 272033).

National Express operates direct services to Minehead. For more information about national coach services to the South West, telephone National Express (Tel: 0990 808080) (this is charged at local call rates).

BUS INFORMATION:
Listed below, in path order, are details of services and information available from County Councils and local bus operators; it is intended for guidance use only. All information provided is correct at the time of going to print; responsibility for any inaccuracies or changes cannot be

accepted by County Councils or bus operators. For up to date bus service information, telephone the relevant numbers given in the following paragraphs.

SOMERSET:

For service 28 from Taunton to Minehead and services 31, X31, and 31C from Taunton to Lyme Regis and Weymouth contact Southern National Ltd, The Bus Station, Tower Street, Taunton, TA1 4AF (Tel: 01823 272033).

ATMOS Ltd Transport Services (part of the W S Atkins Group) on behalf of Somerset County Council produces timetable booklets twice a year in Spring and Autumn. The 5 booklets are based on the District Council areas and are available from Libraries and TIC offices. A countywide bus map is also produced annually listing all the services in the county. In addition a leaflet showing the network of Sunday services is now available. All literature can be obtained from ATMOS Ltd Transport Services, The Crescent, Taunton TA1 4XE, telephone (01823) 358299.

NORTH DEVON:

The North Devon coast has a range of bus services which may be of use to coastal walkers. The greatest choice of coastal destinations is provided from Barnstaple. The principal services are: 309/310 Barnstaple to Lynton; Services 1, 2 & 30 Barnstaple to Ilfracombe; 308 Barnstaple to Georgeham (and Woolacombe in the summer); 1, Barnstaple to Bideford and Westward Ho!; 2 Barnstaple to Appledore and 319 Barnstaple to Bideford, Clovelly, Hartland to Bude 119 - two trips on Tuesdays and Fridays. Note that the number prefix refers to the bus route number. During the summer, service 300 operates daily from Barnstaple to Ilfracombe, Lynton and Minehead, with glorious coastal views along much of the route.

From Bideford there are frequent services to the coast. The principal services are 2, Bideford to Appledore; 1 Bideford to Westward Ho! and 319 Bideford to Clovelly, Hartland to Bude 119 - two trips on Tuesdays and Fridays.

Those who are not walking the entire path in one go may find the Western National X9 service from Exeter to Bude a useful link to or from the coast.

The above services are operated by First Red Bus North Devon Ltd., First Western National for timetable enquiries telephone Devon County Council's DEVONBUS ENQUIRY LINE - Barnstaple (Tel: 01271 382800) or Exeter (Tel: 01392 382800), Monday to Friday 0830 - 1700hrs.

Devon County Council produces timetable guides summer and winter entitled 'North Devon Public Transport Guide'. They are available from Tourist Information Centres, Libraries, bus operators or by telephoning the DevonBus enquiry line (number given above). Email: devonbus@devon.gov.uk Website: www.devon.gov.uk/devonbus

CORNWALL:

Cornwall County Council, in conjunction with First Western National, produces a series of 5 area public transport timetables. The booklets, published twice yearly in May and September, cover: 1 Penzance, St Ives, Camborne and Redruth; 2 Truro, Falmouth and Helston; 3 Newquay and St Austell; 4 North Cornwall; 5 South East Cornwall. Complete sets are available from the Passenger Transport Unit, Cornwall County Council, County Hall, Truro, TR1 3AY (Tel: 01872 322142) price £1.50, with cheques made payable to Cornwall County Council. The timetables can also be obtained free locally from bus stations, Tourist Information Centres and libraries, as can a county public transport map showing all bus and rail routes, with a summary of frequencies.

There is no comprehensive county bus enquiry number in Cornwall. First Western National bus information is available from Western House, 38 Lemon Street, Truro, TR1 2LS. Their enquiry lines are West Cornwall (Tel: 01209 719988), East Cornwall (Tel: 01208 79898). Details on Truronian Services can be obtained from 24 Lemon Street, Truro, TR1 2LS (Tel: 01872 273453) for services between Perranporth, Truro, Helston, Falmouth and The Lizard. Information on other operators can be obtained from Cornwall County Council's Passenger Transport Unit.

The principal routes serving coastal areas are:

First Western National Services: 1 Penzance to Land's End, 2 Penzance to Helston to Falmouth, 15 (summer only) St Ives to Land's End, 16/17 Penzance to St Ives, 86/87 Truro to Perranporth to Newquay, 88/89 Truro to Falmouth, 24 St Austell to Fowey, 26 St Austell to Mevagissey, 55 Bodmin Parkway Station to Bodmin to Wadebridge to Padstow, 124 Wadebridge to Port Isaac,

122 Wadebridge to Tintagel to Bude, X9 Exeter to Bude, X10 Exeter to Boscastle and Tintagel, 56 (summer only) Newquay to Padstow, 57 (summer only) Newquay to Padstow to St Ives.

Truronian Service T1 Perranporth to St Agnes to Truro to Helston to The Lizard, T34 Redruth to Helston. Liskeard and District Omnibus Co Liskeard to Looe and Polperro, Hambleys Coaches Polperro to Looe to Plymouth, Polruan Bus (summer only) Polruan to Polperro to Looe. Western Greyhound Service 592 Truro to Newquay, 594 Truro to Wadebridge.

SOUTH DEVON:
The coastline between Plymouth and Exeter is accessible by bus from many inland towns. The principal services are:

80 Plymouth to Torpoint; 33/B and 34/B Plymouth City Centre and Admirals Hard for Cremyll Ferry (buses meet ferry and through ticket available); 74 Union Street (short walk from Cremyll Ferry) to Mountbatten (and Bovisand in the summer); 49 Plymouth to Heybrook Bay; 48 Plymouth to Wembury; 94 Plymouth to Noss Mayo; 92 Plymouth to Salcombe; 93 Plymouth to Kingsbridge & Dartmouth; X80 Plymouth to Paignton & Torquay; X38 Plymouth to Exeter; 87 Ivybridge to Bigbury-on-Sea; 164 Totnes to Kingsbridge; 89 Totnes to Dartmouth; 162 Kingsbridge to Hope Cove; 606 Kingsbridge to Salcombe; 200 Kingswear to Torquay; 22 Kingswear to Brixham; 12 Brixham & Paignton to Torquay and Newton Abbot; 85 Torquay to Teignmouth, Dawlish and Exeter; 85A Newton Abbot to Teignmouth, Dawlish and Exeter.

The above services are operated by First Western National, Tallo Ho!, Plymouth Citybus and Stagecoach. For timetable enquiries telephone Devon County Council's Devon Bus enquiry line: 01392 382800, Monday to Friday 0830 - 1700.

Western National produces timetable guides summer and winter for the South Devon area. They are available from the Travel Office at Plymouth Bus Station or by telephoning the Devon bus enquiry line, or Western National enquiries 01752 595204.

Plymouth Citybus map and services are available from the Public Transport Department, Plymouth City Council, Civic Centre, Plymouth, PL1 2EW.

EAST DEVON:
The East Devon coastline is accessible by bus from Exeter, Ottery St. Mary, Honiton and Axminster. The principal services are:

X53 Exeter to Beer, Seaton, Lyme Regis, Bridport, Weymouth; 20 Taunton to Seaton; 57 Exeter to Exmouth, Budleigh Salterton and Sidmouth; 52 Exeter to Sidmouth; 382 Ottery St. Mary to Sidmouth; 340 Honiton to Sidmouth; 885 Axminster to Seaton; 31 Taunton to Axminster & Lyme Regis (and continues to Bridport, Dorchester and Weymouth); 899 Sidmouth to Lyme Regis. On Sundays (all year round) service 378 operates along the East Devon coast from Sidmouth to Seaton, Axminster and Lyme Regis.

The above services are operated by Stagecoach, First Red Bus Services, Axe Valley Mini-Travel and First Southern National. For timetable enquiries telephone Devon County Council's **DevonBus enquiry line** - Exeter (Tel: 01392 382800) or Torquay (Tel: 01803 382800) or Plymouth (Tel: 01752 382800) or Barnstaple (Tel: 01271 382800), Monday.to Friday 0830-1700.

Devon County Council produces timetable guides summer and winter, entitled `East Devon Public Transport Guide'- they are available from Tourist Information Centres, libraries, bus operators or by telephoning the DevonBus enquiry line.

Bus Map - Other useful information provided by Devon County Council includes the public transport map. This depicts all bus routes and railway lines throughout the county and gives a summary of service frequency. It is available from Tourist Information Centres, libraries and bus stations or by telephoning the DevonBus enquiry line.

DORSET:
The Dorset Coast is accessible by bus from various inland points with train connections for the distant traveller. The principal routes are listed below.

Service 29 between Swanage - Wareham - Wool - Lulworth Cove and service 30 between Weymouth - Lulworth Cove operate as 'Dorset Linkrider' on Monday to Saturday and Sunday in summer. In winter a reduced service is operated. (Please note service 29 does not operate on Saturday and only runs some journeys on Monday, Thursday & Friday in winter.) For full details please contact Swanage Taxis for Swanage to Lulworth Tel: 01929 553528 or Weaverbus for Weymouth - Lulworth Tel: 01305 834730.

Service 31 provides hourly journeys on Mondays to Saturdays from Weymouth Dorchester - Bridport - Lyme Regis - Axminster. This service also operates until late evening with a two hourly Sunday service. Most buses will connect with trains at Axminster and Dorchester South. Passengers will also benefit from Low Floor buses that provide easy access and greater comfort. Please contact First Southern National, 80 The Esplanade, Weymouth DT4 7AA Tel: 01305 783645.

Service 210 operates between Bridport - Weymouth along the coastal route serving many picturesque villages including Burton Bradstock, Puncknowle, Litton Cheney, Long Bredy, Little Bredy, Portesham, Abbotsbury. This service provides three return journeys on Mondays to Saturdays and is operated by First Southern National Ltd Tel: 01305 783645.

Service X53 operates between Weymouth - Lyme Regis - Exeter travelling along the coast between Weymouth and Bridport. Operates Monday to Saturday and provides four return journeys. This service is operated by First Southern National Tel: 01305 783645.

Service 150 operates from Bournemouth - Swanage via Sandbanks Ferry with Service 142/3/4 operating from Poole - Swanage via Wareham and Corfe Castle. Both services run Monday - Saturday and Sundays. Please contact Wilts & Dorset Ltd, Travel Office, Bus Station, Poole BH15 1SN. Tel: 01202 673555.

Service 152 operates from Sandbanks Ferry to Poole Bus Station (5 minutes walk to railway station). No Sunday service from October to April. Please contact Wilts & Dorset Ltd, as above.

Dorset County Council annually produces a series of local public transport timetables listing bus and rail services and companies by area. A county-wide Bus and Rail Map listing all services in rural Dorset with frequency guide is also produced together with two Heritage Coast maps providing enhanced map details and timetables. These are available from Tourist Information Centres or The Passenger Transport Section, Dorset County Council, County Hall, Dorchester DT1 1XJ. (Tel: 01305 225165)

SEA TRANSPORT AND COASTAL CRUISES

The famous pleasure steamers Waverley and Balmoral provide both cruises and transport, to and from the Exmoor Coast.

From May until late September these big, and fast, sea-going ships provide transport between South Wales, Bristol, North Somerset, and the Exmoor Coast.

Sailings are to and from Ilfracombe, Lynmouth & Minehead. The timetable is subject to the Bristol Channel tides which have the second highest rise and fall in the world. Free copies of the full programme are available from Waverley Excursions Ltd., Gwalia Buildings, Barry Docks, CF62 5QR - telephone 01412 432224 or from Tourist Information Centres in West Somerset and North Devon.

USEFUL ADDRESSES

Countryside Agency, South West Region, Bridge House, Sion Place, Bristol, BS8 4AS. (Tel: 0117 973 9966).
Countrywide Holidays Association, Miry Lane, Wigan, Lancs. WN3 4AG.
Exmoor National Park Authority, Exmoor House, Dulverton, Somerset TA22 9HI (Tel: 01398 323665).
HF Holidays Ltd, Imperial House, Edgware Road, Colindale, London NW9 5AL (Tel: 020 8905 9558).
Ramblers' Association, Second Floor, Camelford House, 87-90 Albert Embankment, London, SE1 7TW

COUNTY COUNCILS

Somerset County Council, County Hall, Taunton, TA1 4DY (Tel: 01823 355455).
Devon County Council, County Hall, Exeter, EX2 4QW (Tel: 01392 382000).
Cornwall County Council, County Hall, Truro, TR1 3BE (Tel: 01872 322000).

Dorset County Council, County Hall, Dorchester, DT1 1XJ (Tel: 01305 251000).

Addresses of Ramblers' Association contacts in the West Country

All path obstructions or other problems not on the Coast Path itself should be addressed to the relevant County address.

Devon - Mrs E. M. Linfoot, 14 Bladen Cottages, Blackborough, Cullompton, EX15 2HJ.
Cornwall - Mrs C. James, Chy-vean, Tresillian, Truro, TR2 4BN.
Dorset - Mr A. Brown, 2 Walkford Way, Walkford, Christchurch. BH23 5LR.
Somerset - Mr A. Harding, 21 Hollam Drive, Dulverton, TA22 9EL.

MAPS

1:50,000 Map. Ordnance Survey

The Metric 1:50,000 Landranger Series needed to cover the coast from Minehead in Somerset to Studland in Dorset are as follows, working round the coast from Minehead.

181	Minehead & Brendon Hills	200	Newquay & Bodmin
180	Barnstaple & Ilfracombe	201	Plymouth & Launceston
190	Bude & Clovelly	202	Torbay & South Dartmoor
200	Newquay & Bodmin	192	Exeter & Sidmouth
204	Truro & Falmouth	193	Taunton & Lyme Regis
203	Land's End & The Lizard	194	Dorchester & Weymouth
204	Truro & Falmouth	195	Bournemouth & Purbeck

The two tourist 1" maps of Dartmoor and Exmoor available are of no advantage except that Exmoor could be used instead of Map 181 and nearly all 180.

1:25,000 Maps. Ordnance Survey

In path order, from Minehead the coast path on $2^1/_2$" maps.

Outdoor Leisure 9	- Exmoor
Explorer 139	- Bideford, Ilfracombe and Barnstaple
Explorer 126	- Clovelly, Hartland and Bideford
Explorer 111	- Bude, Boscastle and Tintagel
Explorer 109	- Bodmin Moor (depicts coast path from Boscastle to Portgaverne)
Explorer 106	- Newquay, Padstow, Wadebridge and Port Isaac
Explorer 104	- Redruth, St Agnes, Camborne and Perranporth
Explorer 102	- Land's End, Penzance, St Ives
Explorer 103	- The Lizard
Explorer 105	- Falmouth and Mevagissey
Explorer 107	- St Austell, Fowey and Looe
Explorer 108	- Looe, Rame Head
Outdoor Leisure 20	- Plymouth and South Devon
Explorer 110	- Torquay and Dawlish
Explorer 115	- Exmouth and Sidmouth
Explorer 116	- Lyme Regis and Bridport
Outdoor Leisure 15	- Purbeck and South Dorset

All these maps may be obtained from bookshops. They may also be obtained from KenRoy Thompson Limited, 25 Cobourg Street, Plymouth, PL1 1SR (Tel: 01752 227693) POST FREE TO UK MEMBERS OF THE SOUTH WEST COAST PATH ASSOCIATION (Credit cards accepted).

TAXIS

Coast Path walking can be arduous in places but some of the hard work can be eliminated. We have been informed that the use of local taxis can ease the muscles. Transport is not for the walker, naturally, but for rucksack transfer from B&B to B&B. Local taxi firms will be pleased to give a price for the service. Consult yellow pages or ask the locals for details of taxi operators.

NATIONAL TAXI HOTLINE
Many taxi operators subscribe to the 'National Taxi Hotline' which works on a Freephone number - 0800 654321. When you dial that number your call will be automatically routed through to the subscribing taxi operator nearest to your location and you have your taxi.

We think it a grand scheme. It is free so no worries about having the appropriate coins when you are tired, wet through and fed up.

BANKS

We suggest you contact your own bank for a list of where their branches along the trail are located. Probably a Girobank account or Post Office National Savings account would prove to be the most convenient as there are small Post Offices in most villages.

TELEPHONES

We urge you to consider buying BT Phonecards or BT Chargecards. Life is easier when you do not have to seek change for a call box.

MOBILE PHONES

These are always useful to have whilst on the Coast Path. However, do not rely on them as coverage is not always good in the South West. You may also have difficulty in obtaining top-up cards in some areas.

ORGANISED WALKING HOLIDAYS

We have compiled a list of organisations that run either self-guided or guided coast path holidays. Some also provide baggage transfer services. For a copy of this list please write to the Administrator and enclose £1.50 to cover printing, postage and administration time.

DOGS

For many years most district councils and unitary authorities have implemented dog bans on beaches generally from 1st May to 31st October. Our Association and most of the general public regard this as a sensible measure.

There are several sections of the South West Coast Path that cross beaches and are officially marked as such. These beaches are Croyde Bay in Devon, Harlyn Bay, Constantine, Treyarnon and Perranporth in Cornwall, and Studland in Dorset.

The routing of the Coast Path (with its designation as a National Trail) across these beaches means that they are public rights of way. Our enquiries now reveal that a public right of way DOES carry precedence over seasonal regulations banning dogs, and ultimately any walker in the process of walking along, but not stopping on, these sections of the path may be accompanied by a dog under TOTAL control.

However we strongly recommend the following:-

a) If an alternative route is provided and signposted, that you use it.

b) That residents near to dog ban beaches use other walks and do not use the beach path during the ban period.

c) Total control means that the dog should be on a short (not extendable) lead.

MARCH 2001
LOW WATER
From 25th, add 1 hour for BST

Days	Morning Time	Afternoon Time
1 Th	0253	1514
2 Fri	0329	1554
3 Sa	0417	1650
4 Su	0531	1819
5 Mo	0715	1959
6 Tu	0846	2121
7 We	0958	2226
8 Th	1057	2320
9 Fri	1148	-
10 Sa	0008	1235
11 Su	0053	1318
12 Mo	0134	1358
13 Tu	0212	1434
14 We	0247	1507
15 Th	0320	1540
16 Fri	0356	1616
17 Sa	0439	1704
18 Su	0539	1811
19 Mo	0700	1941
20 Tu	0850	2119
21 We	0952	2212
22 Th	1037	2253
23 Fri	1115	2330
24 Sa	1151	-
25 Su	0004	1224
26 Mo	0036	1255
27 Tu	0106	1324
28 We	0135	1353
29 Th	0204	1423
30 Fri	0235	1455
31 Sa	0313	1535

APRIL 2001
LOW WATER
add 1 hour for BST

Days	Morning Time	Afternoon Time
1 Su	0402	1632
2 Mo	0517	1802
3 Tu	0701	1945
4 We	0834	2108
5 Th	0944	2210
6 Fr	1039	2302
7 Sa	1128	2348
8 Su	1212	-
9 Mo	0030	1254
10 Tu	0110	1332
11 We	0146	1406
12 Th	0220	1438
13 Fr	0252	1508
14 Sa	0325	1542
15 Su	0405	1626
16 Mo	0503	1733
17 Tu	0619	1853
18 We	0747	2020
19 Th	0905	2126
20 Fr	0954	2213
21 Sa	1036	2253
22 Su	1114	2331
23 Mo	1150	-
24 Tu	0006	1226
25 We	0041	1300
26 Th	0115	1334
27 Fr	0150	1408
28 Sa	0226	1446
29 Su	0308	1531
30 Mo	0402	1631

MAY 2001
LOW WATER
add 1 hour for BST

Days	Morning Time	Afternoon Time
1 Tu	0517	1756
2 We	0650	1928
3 Th	0815	2045
4 Fr	0921	2146
5 Sa	1015	2238
6 Su	1103	2323
7 Mo	1147	-
8 Tu	0006	1228
9 We	0045	1305
10 Th	0121	1339
11 Fr	0155	1411
12 Sa	0227	1442
13 Su	0300	1514
14 Mo	0338	1556
15 Tu	0430	1656
16 We	0538	1809
17 Th	0650	1920
18 Fr	0758	2025
19 Sa	0857	2121
20 Su	0947	2210
21 Mo	1033	2254
22 Tu	1116	2337
23 We	1158	-
24 Th	0018	1239
25 Fr	0100	1320
26 Sa	0141	1401
27 Su	0224	1445
28 Mo	0312	1534
29 Tu	0407	1633
30 We	0513	1743
31 Th	0629	1901

JUNE 2001
LOW WATER
add 1 hour for BST

Days	Morning Time	Afternoon Time	Days	Morning Time	Afternoon Time
1 Fr	0744	2013	16 Sa	0702	1930
2 Sa	0850	2116	17 Su	0803	2031
3 Su	0947	2210	18 Mo	0901	2128
4 Mo	1037	2258	19 Tu	0955	2221
5 Tu	1122	2341	20 We	1046	2311
6 We	1203	-	21 Th	1135	-
7 Th	0022	1242	22 Fr	0000	1223
8 Fr	0100	1317	23 Sa	0048	1310
9 Sa	0135	1350	24 Su	0136	1357
10 Su	0208	1421	25 Mo	0224	1444
11 Mo	0241	1453	26 Tu	0312	1532
12 Tu	0316	1529	27 We	0402	1623
13 We	0358	1615	28 Th	0456	1719
14 Th	0452	1717	29 Fr	0558	1823
15 Fr	0557	1825	30 Sa	0705	1933

JULY 2001
LOW WATER
add 1 hour for BST

Days	Morning Time	Afternoon Time	Days	Morning Time	Afternoon Time
1 Su	0814	2042	16 Mo	0714	1947
2 Mo	0917	2142	17 Tu	0821	2053
3 Tu	1011	2235	18 We	0924	2155
4 We	1059	2321	19 Th	1023	2252
5 Th	1143	-	20 Fr	1118	2346
6 Fr	0004	1223	21 Sa	1211	-
7 Sa	0044	1300	22 Su	0038	1301
8 Su	0119	1333	23 Mo	0128	1349
9 Mo	0152	1404	24 Tu	0215	1435
10 Tu	0223	1433	25 We	0301	1518
11 We	0253	1502	26 Th	0345	1602
12 Th	0325	1535	27 Fr	0429	1648
13 Fr	0403	1617	28 Sa	0519	1742
14 Sa	0454	1718	29 Su	0617	1847
15 Su	0602	1834	30 Mo	0730	2005
			31 Tu	0847	2119

AUGUST 2001
LOW WATER
add 1 hour for BST

Days	Morning Time	Afternoon Time
1 We	0950	2217
2 Th	1042	2306
3 Fr	1126	2349
4 Sa	1206	-
5 Su	0028	1243
6 Mo	0103	1315
7 Tu	0133	1344
8 We	0200	1409
9 Th	0226	1434
10 Fr	0252	1501
11 Sa	0322	1535
12 Su	0401	1621
13 Mo	0456	1731
14 Tu	0622	1908
15 We	0749	2028
16 Th	0902	2138
17 Fr	1007	2239
18 Sa	1106	2335
19 Su	1158	-
20 Mo	0026	1248
21 Tu	0114	1333
22 We	0158	1416
23 Th	0239	1455
24 Fr	0318	1534
25 Sa	0356	1614
26 Su	0438	1700
27 Mo	0529	1802
28 Tu	0639	1929
29 We	0820	2103
30 Th	0934	2203
31 Fr	1025	2249

SEPTEMBER 2001
LOW WATER
add 1 hour for BST

Days	Morning Time	Afternoon Time
1 Sa	1107	2330
2 Su	1146	-
3 Mo	0006	1221
4 Tu	0039	1252
5 We	0108	1318
6 Th	0133	1343
7 Fr	0157	1406
8 Sa	0222	1433
9 Su	0250	1504
10 Mo	0325	1546
11 Tu	0414	1650
12 We	0537	1839
13 Th	0726	2012
14 Fr	0849	2126
15 Sa	0956	2227
16 Su	1052	2319
17 Mo	1142	-
18 Tu	0007	1228
19 We	0052	1311
20 Th	0134	1351
21 Fr	0212	1428
22 Sa	0248	1504
23 Su	0322	1540
24 Mo	0359	1623
25 Tu	0446	1722
26 We	0555	1849
27 Th	0745	2043
28 Fr	0911	2140
29 Sa	0959	2223
30 Su	1040	2301

OCTOBER 2001
LOW WATER
until 27th, add 1 hour for BST

Days	Morning Time	Afternoon Time
1 Mo	1117	2336
2 Tu	1151	-
3 We	0007	1222
4 Th	0036	1250
5 Fr	0104	1316
6 Sa	0131	1343
7 Su	0158	1411
8 Mo	0227	1445
9 Tu	0303	1528
10 We	0352	1633
11 Th	0517	1824
12 Fr	0710	1959
13 Sa	0835	2112
14 Su	0940	2209
15 Mo	1033	2259
16 Tu	1121	2345
17 We	1205	-
18 Th	0027	1247
19 Fr	0108	1325
20 Sa	0144	1402
21 Su	0218	1436
22 Mo	0250	1511
23 Tu	0325	1551
24 We	0409	1647
25 Th	0515	1805
26 Fr	0643	1951
27 Sa	0824	2059
28 Su	0919	2144
29 Mo	1002	2222
30 Tu	1040	2258
31 We	1115	2331

NOVEMBER 2001
LOW WATER

Days	Morning Time	Afternoon Time	Days	Morning Time	Afternoon Time
1 Th	1149	-	16 Fr	0003	1223
2 Fr	0004	1222	17 Sa	0043	1302
3 Sa	0037	1254	18 Su	0119	1339
4 Su	0108	1326	19 Mo	0153	1413
5 Mo	0140	1400	20 Tu	0225	1448
6 Tu	0215	1438	21 We	0259	1527
7 We	0255	1526	22 Th	0339	1615
8 Th	0349	1635	23 Fr	0434	1719
9 Fr	0510	1809	24 Sa	0547	1833
10 Sa	0649	1938	25 Su	0704	1945
11 Su	0812	2048	26 Mo	0814	2044
12 Mo	0916	2145	27 Tu	0909	2132
13 Tu	1009	2235	28 We	0955	2215
14 We	1057	2321	29 Th	1037	2256
15 Th	1141	-	30 Fr	1118	2335

DECEMBER 2001
LOW WATER

Days	Morning Time	Afternoon Time	Days	Morning Time	Afternoon Time
1 Sa	1157	-	16 Su	0022	1244
2 Su	0014	1237	17 Mo	0100	1322
3 Mo	0154	1317	18 Tu	0135	1358
4 Tu	0133	1358	19 We	0208	1432
5 We	0214	1443	20 Th	0240	1506
6 Th	0300	1533	21 Fr	0314	1543
7 Fr	0353	1633	22 Sa	0354	1629
8 Sa	0459	1745	23 Su	0447	1728
9 Su	0617	1904	24 Mo	0555	1834
10 Mo	0736	2016	25 Tu	0705	1939
11 Tu	0844	2117	26 We	0810	2039
12 We	0943	2210	27 Th	0909	2134
13 Th	1034	2258	28 Fr	1002	2224
14 Fr	1120	2342	29 Sa	1051	2312
15 Sa	1203	-	30 Su	1139	2359
			31 Mo	1225	-

d) That your progress should be as unobtrusive as possible to other beach users. To aid this, close attention should be paid to the actual route marked on the map.

e) Lastly, but most importantly that, should the worst happen, any dog mess MUST be removed from the beach.

RIVER CROSSINGS

The walker tends to view that feet are the only certain method of progress - and why not? Unfortunately, the absolute purist would need to be an olympic-class swimmer not to have to use ferries on the South West Coast Path. However, a certain amount of scepticism is helpful, absolute reliance on ferries is not advised.

There are other ferries available on the Path which walkers may wish to use for diversions or shortcuts. We have attempted to list those directly necessary.

Tide Tables (see pages 19 and 20)

The tide tables included in this edition refer to the times of low water at Devonport. These tables will act as a guide for those wishing to wade across the Gannel (Newquay), Gillan Creek, and the Erme and Avon (Bigbury-on-Sea). Please be sure to read the warnings given under each section. We have been criticised for being too cautious over the times we suggest for wading the rivers, and know that some walkers cross at other times. We believe our attitude is correct as there certainly are dangers, but you may wish to try at low tide on other occasions to see if conditions will permit a safe crossing. Variations in barometric pressure can affect tide levels. Remember there are different levels daily of low water; if in doubt seek local knowledge.

Newquay (The Gannel)	Deduct 30 minutes	Gillan Harbour	Deduct 15 minutes
R. Erme	As at Devonport	Bigbury/Bantham (R.Avon)	As at Devonport

*The Tide Tables on pages 19 and 20 are Crown Copyright. Produced from Admiralty Tide Tables with the permission of the Controller of Her Majesty's Stationery Office.

SUGGESTED ITINERARY

For some the fun of planning their own itinerary is a major part of the enjoyment of their holiday. If you are one of these, DO NOT READ THIS SECTION.

On the other hand there are some who have been put off tackling our path because they just could not see how to pack over 600 miles' (965 km) walking into a normal holiday. The answer is, of course, you cannot. Our Path, we reckon, needs about seven weeks to accomplish. That being so, we have tried to divide it up sensibly into seven roughly equal sections. Obviously, if we are going to suggest weekly stages, the beginning and end of each one must have reasonable accommodation and public transport. That presents a problem in itself, so after some thought we have broken it down into six 7-day, one 6-day and one 8-day week. As usual, we would be very glad to hear from anyone who has tried one of our weeks and to hear their comments on it.

If you are a seasoned walker then there is a lot to be said for walking the whole path, albeit at different times, in our usual anticlockwise order. However, if you are not experienced, then obviously we should point out that the South Cornwall week, the fourth one in our schedule, is much the easiest if you want to start with something less demanding.

To keep the weeks set out below in a simple format the information is only an outline. IT IS ESSENTIAL TO CONSULT THE DETAIL IN THE REST OF THE GUIDE TO EFFECTIVELY PLAN YOUR HOLIDAY. Distances can vary depending on where you actually stay. Furthermore, our distances are only approximate because they are all 'rounded'.

After some of the place names we have added 'River Crossing'. You are advised to consult the appropriate section in this book for ferry and low tide suggestions.

Kilometres	Miles	Week 1 (Seven days)
		MINEHEAD Rail Services to Taunton & S. National to Minehead
		Direct Nat. Express coach services.
15	10	PORLOCK WEIR
20	12	LYNMOUTH/LYNTON
21	13	COMBE MARTIN
20	13	WOOLACOMBE
27	16	BRAUNTON
20	12	INSTOW (River Crossing)
18	11	WESTWARD HO! Filers/Red Bus to Barnstaple & Rail services
		to Exeter. Direct Nat. Express coach services.
141	87	

Week 2 (Seven days)

		WESTWARD HO! Rail services to Barnstaple & Filers/Red Bus to
		Westward Ho! Direct Nat. Express coach services
18	11	CLOVELLY
16	10	HARTLAND QUAY
25	15	BUDE
27	17	BOSCASTLE
22	14	PORT ISAAC
28	18	TREVONE
31	19	NEWQUAY Rail services to Par (the Great Western main line)
		Direct Nat. Express coach services
167	104	

Week 3 (Six days)

		NEWQUAY Rail services to Newquay (from Par)
		Direct Nat. Express coach services (River Crossing)
18	11	PERRANPORTH
20	12	PORTREATH
29	18	ST IVES
22	14	PENDEEN WATCH
25	16	PORTHCURNO
18	11	PENZANCE Rail services (Great Western main line)
		Direct Nat. Express coach services
132	82	

Week 4 (Seven days)

		PENZANCE Rail services to Penzance
		Direct Nat. Express coach services
23	14	PORTHLEVEN
22	13	THE LIZARD
17	11	COVERACK
21	13	HELFORD (River Crossing)
16	10	FALMOUTH (River Crossing)
22	14	PORTLOE
20	12	MEVAGISSEY W. National to St. Austell & Rail services from
		St Austell (Great Western main line)
141	87	

Week 5 (Seven days)

		MEVAGISSEY Rail services to St. Austell & W. National to
		Mevagissey
19	12	PAR
21	13	POLPERRO
20	12	PORTWRINKLE
21	13	PLYMOUTH (Cremyll Ferry)
24	15	WEMBURY POINT (River Crossing)
22	14	BIGBURY-ON-SEA (River Crossing)
22	14	SALCOMBE Tally Ho! to Kingsbridge & W. National to Totnes
		& Rail services from Totnes (Great Western main line)
149	93	

Week 6 (Six days)

		SALCOMBE Rail services to Totnes & W. National to Kingsbridge & Tally Ho! to Salcombe
21	13	TORCROSS
16	10	DARTMOUTH (River Crossing)
17	11	BRIXHAM
17	11	BABBACOMBE
27	16	EXMOUTH (via Starcross/Exmouth Ferry)
21	13	SIDMOUTH Stagecoach to Exeter & Rail services from Exeter (Great Western main line and Waterloo line)
119	74	

Week 7 (Eight days)

		SIDMOUTH Rail services to Exeter & Stagecoach to Sidmouth
17	11	SEATON
23	14	SEATOWN (Dorset)
19	12	ABBOTSBURY
17	11	FERRY BRIDGE (Wyke Regis)
21	13	ISLE OF PORTLAND
23	14	LULWORTH
23	14	WORTH MATRAVERS*
22	14	SOUTH HAVEN POINT Ferry-Sandbanks, Wilts & Dorset to Poole or Bournemouth & Rail services Nat. Express coach services from Bournemouth to London.
165	103	

* See pages 84 & 85 for opening times of Army Ranges and alternative routes.

THE SOUTH WEST COAST PATH

General

This is a series of notes on the state of the path which we hope will help you in your walking. Obviously it is very difficult to keep something as extensive as this both up-to-date and concise. Suggestions for improvement or amendments will always be welcome. We can only keep you right up-to-date with the state of the path if YOU will keep us posted about conditions as you find them on any stretch of the path. Your fellow members will be grateful, and so will we.

If you have any complaints about ordinary maintenance or signposting on the path, please write either to the Exmoor National Park Authority or the relevant County Council, Devon, Cornwall or Dorset. They should see this is done, and what is generally not realised is that any work carried out is 75% grant aided from the Countryside Agency for official National Trails such as the South West Coast Path. If you have any major problems or difficulties we would always be glad to be advised as well.

Each section has a reference to the Ordnance Survey map relevant to it - Outdoor Leisure (OS OL) and Explorer (OS E).

Towns and villages are now marked T or V respectively but the places at the end of each section appear as the first entry in the next one. We obviously stick our necks out to try and classify towns and villages. To us a town should have a reasonable range of shops, maybe even something as exotic as a laundrette. Villages should at least have a pub and a village store open all the year round, and a bus service. There are, of course, numerous other places you can get refreshment in season, but precious few out of it. Please note that all sections end at reasonable access points, usually having parking facilities.

Places which can be reached by rail are marked.

Distances

As a result of the 1999/2000 survey of the Coast Path end to end using a Global Positioning System, we now have access to very precise distances. The survey, carried out by the South West Coast Path Team, included the Isle of Portland - having done so we have become optimistic about our lobbying for the inclusion of The Isle into the official route. We have, therefore, jumped the gun and adjusted our book to include it.

We now know the Coast Path to be 630 miles (1014 km) long. This includes the Isle of Portland. When one considers we estimated the Coast Path to be 613 miles end to end, without including The Isle, we were not far out.

The section distances are shown in four columns.

The first - distance of the section in kilometres
The second - cumulative distance in kilometres
The third - distance of the section in miles
The fourth - cumulative distance in miles

The distances are measured along the officially designated route of the Coast Path, not along any diversions we suggest offering more scenic experiences than the route installed by the authorities.

Grading

Each section is graded as Easy, Moderate, Strenuous or Severe. Please note we no longer take into consideration lack of escape routes, distances from public transport, etc; it is purely a question of physical difficulty. We will try to highlight in the sections other considerations when they apply.
We would like to underline one point; the whole of our path is certainly not easy. Some parts of it are but other parts are not. We have had a number of letters from people who have walked The Pennine Way and who have been literally amazed at the severity of some of our tougher sections. Perhaps as a further comment we may add that recently we walked two 6 mile (10 km) adjacent sections. The time taken for one was 50% more than the time taken for the other. This may give additional emphasis to the importance of studying terrain if you wish to compute time.

THE REVERSE GUIDE - POOLE TO MINEHEAD

The Association has written a description of the Trail for those walking in the Poole to Minehead direction. It deals only with the path so this annual guide will be necessary for all the other information. The Reverse Guide supplement is available from the Administrator at £3.50 including postage.

THE TRAIL DESCRIPTION - Minehead to Poole
FOLLOW THE NATIONAL TRAIL WAYMARK (THE ACORN SYMBOL)
CAUTION

This guide book describes the *official* route of the National Trail known as the South West Coast Path. Along its whole length it is maintained by the county councils of Devon, Cornwall and Dorset; the National Trust and Exmoor National Park.

Where you find we have little to say about the route we consider that it is highly unlikely that the walker will run the risk of going astray.

We are sometimes asked if you require a map as well as a guide book and our advice is certainly yes. One does not get as badly lost on the Coast Path as you can on inland paths, but a map is an asset nonetheless. Furthermore many walkers derive much interest from looking at their route in relation to the rest of the countryside on ordinary walks, and the same applies just as much, if not more so, on our Coast Path. The National Trail Guides offer a partial solution with their maps, but even these are not as useful as a map sheet.

Those who set forth upon this beautiful trail must remember it is mainly a cliff top path - in places it can be a very high cliff top. We stress it is unwise to leave the path on the seaward side of any of it. These paths are safe but if you leave them you can put yourself in danger.

Now and again we suggest an alternative path away from the officially designated route. This will be for a more scenic and enjoyable experience. The above authorities have failed to create them as the designated route despite our representations over many years.

These alternative, recommended paths follow rights of way and in a few instances 'permissive routes' which are maintained by the landowner.

THIS ASSOCIATION STRESSES THAT WALKERS SHOULD NOT WANDER OFF THESE PATHS, ESPECIALLY SEAWARD OF THEM.

YOU CAN FALL A LONG WAY IF YOU DO. IF YOU FALL A LONG WAY - YOU CAN DIE.

LIABILITY DISCLAIMER

Information included or available through the South West Coast Path Association (SWCPA) is given in good faith and is believed to be accurate and correct at the time of going to print - however it cannot be guaranteed not to include inaccuracies or typographical errors.

Advice received via the SWCPA should not be relied upon for personal decisions and you should take into account the weather and your own capabilities before following the walks set out in this Guide. It is for the individual concerned to weigh up the risks of each of the walks described in this book.

The SWCPA makes no representations about the suitability of walks to any one person and will accept no liability for any loss or damage suffered as a result of relying on this book: it should be used for guidance only.

In no event shall the SWCPA be liable for any personal injury or any loss suffered as a result of using this publication.

FOOTNOTES

In certain sections we have added footnotes commenting on two books where you may be led astray. These are as follows:

'CP' - Martin Collins' two South West Way books by Cicerone Press.
'NTG' - Four National Trail Guides - published by Aurum Press in association with the Countryside Agency.

1	Minehead to Porlock Weir (Car Park)	OS OL9 (T) Minehead

Grading: Official Route - Moderate Alternative - Strenuous	Distance -	15.3	15.3	9.5	9.5

See also our Minehead to Lynmouth Path Description.

We hope that, by the time you read this, the celebratory marker on Minehead sea front, a little to the east of the harbour, will be in place. The Coast Path will start (or finish) from this marker, which, representing a pair of hands holding a map, was designed by local art student Sarah Ward, and sculptured by Owen Cunningham.

You cross the road and walk between two cottages on the sea front.

The official route, although a good moorland walk, does not follow the traditional coastal route. Strong walkers looking for something better can start at the westerly end of the sea front road, proceed via Greenaleigh Farm to Burgundy Chapel and then make a steep ascent up North Hill. An easier alternative to this first piece is at Greenaleigh Farm, immediately before the house and the signpost 'To Burgundy Chapel and Beach' to fork left and then turn back, signposted 'North Hill'. This path zigzags back to pick up the official route, so avoiding the steep climb after Burgundy Chapel.

When taking the steep ascent from Burgundy Chapel at the T-junction go left - the path to the right goes only to a view point - and at the next junction go forward.

When you have gained the summit of North Hill, there is an acorn sign pointing to Selworthy and Bossington. Follow the line of this until you come to the next coast path sign, where there is a right fork marked 'Rugged Cliff Top Path'. Ordinary walkers should proceed forward on the official route but the more adventurous can fork right and proceed, walking seaward by what is a well-defined path.

Alternative - Rugged Coast Path

The 'Rugged Cliff Top Path' is a splendid alternative to the official path, with good views to seaward. It is well marked, but there are signs prohibiting dogs. At the stile take the left fork and soon you follow the rough track down by a boggy stream to the bottom of Grexy Combe at 937 481. From here take the well-defined diagonal path leading up the hill to the wall which is the National Trust boundary. This wall can be followed towards the sea at first and then along parallel to the sea all the way to Western Brockholes. After Western Brockholes the path bears inland, but is well signposted and rejoins the official path behind Hurlstone Point.

Coast Path continues

Those who have taken the official route, when reaching Bossington Hill should take the definitive right of way which goes down Hurlstone Combe. There is a much more spectacular route around Hurlstone Point which can be used apart from gale force conditions. If you stay on the official path, take care to descend the path to the left of Hurlstone Point and do not be tempted to take the more obvious path to the left (no signpost) contouring round Bossington Hill.

The official path goes inland from Hurlstone Point via Bossington and then out to the sea again. However, because of high storms the pebble ridge has been pushed back over the path and a deep impassable gully has been formed. You can take the path that has been signposted to Porlock from the road to Bossington Beach, missing the pebble ridge. An alternative is to walk on the first part of the Coast Path at the back of the pebble ridge past the lime kilns and then turn left at the signpost marked 'Footpath to Porlock Avoiding Flooded Marsh'. This will bring you to Sparkhayes Lane and into Porlock.

At Porlock the Visitor Centre and the Doverhay Museum are both worth a visit. The Ship Inn is an historic old pub. St Dubricius' Church is famous for its effigy monuments.

If you do not want to go to Porlock, follow the route of a new permissive path that is shortly to be opened up at the edge of the flooded lagoon to Porlock Weir, enabling you to see the wildlife around the lagoon. We hope that this will be opened by the time you read this.

To get to Porlock Weir from Porlock you take the road on the right - NOT the one that turns right past the Visitor Centre and is signposted to Porlock Weir - (unless you want to walk along the road) but the next turning on the right past the village hall and there is a footpath on the right that takes you through the woods at the back of West Porlock.

| 2 | Porlock Weir to Lynmouth (Visitor Centre) | OS OL9 |

Grading: Moderate   Distance -   19.8   35.1   12.3   21.8

See also our Minehead to Lynmouth Path Description

The path leaves Porlock Weir in front of the Anchor Hotel; turn left at the sign for Culbone.

This path is well marked. At Culbone turn right if you want to visit the small church. There is also a refreshment hut where you help yourself and leave your payment. From the church, retrace your steps up the path and turn right onto the Coast Path; in about 300 yards (275 m) turn right into Culbone and Embelle Woods and on into Yenworthy Woods.

The path nearest the sea has a sign 'Alternative permitted coast path to Lynmouth'. This is the shortest route and the route we recommend. (The official coast path route takes you on an inland route through Silcombe and Broomstreet Farms and down the permissive path at Wheatham Combe, but this route is not clear in poor conditions.)

When you get to Yenworthy Combe there is a sign to the Pinetum. This is a pleasant diversion through the Pinetum past an Ice House to Glenthorne Beach. You will have to return and proceed to Sister's Fountain, where there is a legend that Jesus drank here with Joseph of Arimathea on his way to Glastonbury. Continue uphill through a pair of wild boar head gateposts, which was the entrance to the Victorian Woodland Lodge, which usually has barking Jack Russell dogs in its garden.

At Caddow Combe, the official route is again signposted inland 'Countisbury 1.5 miles'. The surefooted might prefer the right of way signposted 'Lighthouse' which proceeds out to the Foreland Point Lighthouse. Just before the entrance to the lighthouse where the wall commences on the right, the path takes off up the bank to the left. The beginning is clearly marked because the authorities tell you they no longer maintain the path. This path is more exposed than the official route and careful walking is advised. It has magnificent views if you are surefooted and the weather is calm.

The National Trust has a good path which can be taken down the seaward side of the main A39 coastal road so avoiding the upper reaches of Countisbury Hill. Lower down the hill the path joins the road but a new path on the seaward side ensures that you will not get run down.

You come out on the foreshore. Walk along into Lynmouth crossing the footbridge, and there turn right down to the sea front turning left up the steps before the cliff railway, that is assuming you are a purist and are not actually going to use the railway which you can well do if you wish! If you use the railway you do suffer slightly at the top in that you will have to walk nearly into Lynton and then out again to regain the North Walk. After all, it serves you right for not having walked the whole way!

3   Lynmouth to Combe Martin (Car Park)   OS OL9 (T) Lynton/Lynmouth

Grading: Strenuous   Distance -   21.4   56.5   13.3   35.1

See also our Lynmouth to Ilfracombe Path Description.

Please note there is a long, lonely section onward from Heddon's Mouth to Combe Martin without any chance of refreshment.

The path itself out from Lynton is a Victorian idea for a coastal footpath called the North Walk and although to our modern ideas, tarmac might not be the ideal footpath medium, it is a very fine high level walk indeed. This takes you very happily out to Castle Rock. Unfortunately, the official route is then on the road all the way through to Woody Bay.

However, there are diversions which will save you some road walking. The first takes off to the right after the turning circle (roundabout) at the end of the Valley of Rocks and then goes in a loop back, to come out by the Lodge at the beginning of Lee Abbey. The second alternative is a left turn immediately opposite Lee Abbey which is labelled 'Woodland Walk' (each end) and rejoins the road about 0.75 mile (1200 m) further along.

If you do not follow the 'Woodland Walk' but follow the road past the toll house and refreshment stop (seasonal), you will climb up a hill and come across a new footpath on your right, that goes along the field edge to Crock Point and through the woods at Crock Pits. This is an excellent addition to the Coast Path, taking you off a busy road, with some stunning coastal walks, and we thank the Exmoor Park Authority for making this possible.

This is one of the finest pieces of Coast Path in North Devon and should not be missed by anyone who is reasonably surefooted, or unless weather conditions are very bad. The path takes off just before the Woody Bay Hotel opposite the Red House and the beginning of the path is marked by a signpost on the right which says 'Public Footpath to Woody Bay Beach 0.75 mile'. This path comes out on another road where you turn up left. There will be another sign 'Footpath Hunter's Inn 2.25 miles'. You will cross a stile with a sign 'Heddon Valley Hunter's Inn'. This is a superb path which is now the new official route. It is much nearer the coast giving splendid views. As the path reaches the river you turn left (upstream) and cross the first bridge you come to. On the other side you turn right and within a few yards the path angles sharply to the left. Take the steep zigzag path; halfway up is a wooden bar across the path. Here you turn right towards the sea and wonderful views at Peter Rock. (In strong winds you could step over that wooden bar, continue up the zigzag then turn seaward at the top.) From Peter Rock the route takes a seaward path to East Cleave. Whilst in the valley of Heddon's Mouth, those requiring refreshment have easy access to the Hunter's Inn and the National Trust shop selling very good ice cream.

Just west of East Cleave you will regain the old official route passing along High Cliff and North Cleave. At map reference 628 482 take the short walk across open heathland to avoid the walk up to the old Trentishoe Down Road.

27

As there are many sheep tracks by Sherrycombe, we suggest you follow the grass track along the top of the combe to the inland end of it to pick up the path down.

When ascending Great Hangman from Sherrycombe you reach a seat. Keep alongside the wall on your left. There is a number of well-walked paths going out to the right but they are all wrong! From Great Hangman the path is clear to Little Hangman where more stunning views are available.

When you come to the shelter above Combe Martin, turn right on the unmarked path; this has the better views.

CP - The official route no longer goes to Hunter's Inn and Trentishoe. See fourth paragraph above.

---

4 | Combe Martin to Ilfracombe (Harbour)   OS OL9 (T) Combe Martin

Grading: Moderate, Strenuous in parts   Distance-   8.6   65.1   5.3   40.4

See also our Lynmouth to Ilfracombe Path Description.

The path leaves the lime kiln car park, passing the Exmoor National Park Visitor centre; fork right and join the A399 road. Turn right (Seaside Hill Road) above the beach. Turn right onto a narrow tarmac lane, which climbs steeply to rejoin the A399 road.

Walk on the slightly raised path along the road side through two gates. Having gone along a path beside a field to the flight of steps, you should turn left up the newish slip road back to the main road and to the brow, passing the bus shelter. You then turn right to follow the road down to the old main road with a bus shelter over to the right, which is now used as an information point for the Heritage Coast. Here you turn left beside the entrance to the Sandy Cove Hotel to follow a track towards Watermouth Cove.

Watermouth Castle, built 1825, comes into view. At Watermouth it is possible to cross the foreshore at low tide to a flight of steps; take care as the rocks can be slippery. This is not possible at high tide when one has to continue along the road with no pavement for approximately 200 yards (185 m) and there is then a stile off right into the woods. Take care whilst walking this road section.

The next section of the path is very pleasant on the western side of Watermouth and continues out and around Widmouth Head. This section provides some very spectacular walking; we particularly commend the view back from Widmouth Head over Watermouth, whatever the state of the tide or sea. This will be your last good viewpoint of the dramatic setting of the Great Hangman and the Little Hangman eastwards above Combe Martin. After Widmouth Head the path continues in front of the coastguard cottages going to Rillage Point.

This fine section ends with a road walk down into Hele. Turn right and look out for some steps on the far left of the beach. The path then zigzags passing Beacon Point with a fine view of Ilfracombe, until it reaches the top of Hillsborough. There are several paths to choose from here but they all end up in Ilfracombe. We have asked for an additional waymark to route you onto the harbour road.

---

5 | Ilfracombe to Lee Bay   OS E139 (T) Ilfracombe

Grading: Easy to moderate   Distance-   5.3   70.4   3.3   43.7

See also our Ilfracombe to Croyde Bay Path Description.

Walk along the edge of the harbour, bear left at the slip and then right into Broad Street. At a T-junction, turn left into Capstone Road next to the Sandpiper Inn. After about 170 yards (150 m), turn right and walk around Capstone Point. Follow the path from Capstone Point down to Wilder beach and now take the flight of steps that goes up the back of the Landmark Theatre. Follow this path up to the top of the gardens and the gate by a shelter. Pass through this gate and bear right to walk along Granville road, before bearing right onto an unmetalled road which takes you to the Torrs Walk: it is well waymarked.

At the top of the Torrs Walk bear right and follow the path down the field to the stile in the corner. Continue ahead around the hill and beware of the steep drop on your right, to the stile. Now cross the field to the old coach road ahead, bearing right onto it and follow it all the way to Flat Point. Along Flat Point the Coast Path follows the route of the old coach road. (Flat Point is National Trust land with its open access policy, and it can be roamed at your own risk and offers good sites for picnic stops.) Passing through a field gate your route is along a narrow, pleasant road down into Lee.

Refreshments are available all year round at the Grampus Inn in Lee village, which is only a minor diversion from the coast.

6 | Lee Bay to Woolacombe   OS E139 (V) Lee Bay

Grading: Strenuous, becoming easy	Distance -	6.4	76.8	4.0	47.7

See also our Ilfracombe to Croyde Bay Path Description.

This section will take you longer to walk than you think as it includes some up and down work but is a lovely piece of path to walk.

Proceed up the road from Lee, turn right onto a path by the National Trust sign 'Damage Cliff'. To the left of the path are the remains of a pre war golf course. Before Bull Point the path crosses two steep valleys, Hilly Mouth and Bennets Water. The lighthouse is one of the few manned stations left in the country. Rockham has a fine stretch of sand that is very popular in the summer. Morte Point is a spectacular jagged slate ridge rather like a dinosaur's back emerging from the sea. Offshore is the often submerged Morte Stone and this 'Rock of Death' was aptly named in the last century. At certain states of the tide an awesome tidal race can be seen; many ships have been wrecked off here.

7 | Woolacombe to Croyde Bay (Beach)   OS E139 (T) Woolacombe

Grading: Moderate	Distance -	10.2	87.0	6.3	54.0

See also our Ilfracombe to Croyde Bay Path Description.

This section starts at the Waterfall Hotel and runs parallel to the Esplanade road, then turns up Chalacombe road. This is now waymarked but a vital waymark has been removed to indicate where the route turns off the road into the warren. This path is about where the National Trust sign has been placed. The official route stays in the Warren; the alignment shown on 139 OS Explorer map is incorrect.

This section starts rather poorly along the road south from Woolacombe and tries hard to lose itself in the enormous dunes. Waymarking, however, has been improved and you should not go astray. A possible alternative is to walk the Marine Drive which gives fine views. If the tide is out it is easier to walk Woolacombe Beach but it should not be attempted on a flood tide as you may not be able to get off the beach at Vention.

If you have used the official path, it leaves the Warren by a set of steep steps. At the top turn right and after 500 yards (460 m) a path leaves the official route; this takes you down to a car park (refreshments and toilets). Pass to the left of the caravan site, over a stile and up the cliff slope to rejoin the official route to Baggy Point.

The high level path out to Baggy Point is pleasant. If the visibility is good you will get a good chance as you turn the corner to look at the path for a number of miles ahead across Bideford Bay. At Baggy Point itself, when you have turned the corner, do bear right on to the lower path; it is no further and provides much better sea views.

Passing the National Trust car park, there is a road walk of about 545 yards (500 m) before the turn off to the beach. Do not be tempted to use the first slipway as it would be very difficult walking over the rocks.

8 | Croyde Bay to Barnstaple (Long Bridge)

Grading: Easy   Distance -   **23.1   110.1   14.4   68.4**

See also our Croyde Bay to Barnstaple Path Description.

Distances are measured walking via Crow Point, and around Horsey Island, through Velator to join the disused railway track all the way to Barnstaple.

The path crosses the top of Croyde beach, and on to the low cliffs at Down End, turns left and after reaching the old coastguard lookout, one has to cross the main B3231 road. This is a very busy road so take great care as you cross over the road which has to be done at this point. Walkers are advised NOT to take dogs onto this beach between May and September.

Turn left and walk downhill a short way to reach some stone steps. After a short climb, the path contours round Saunton Down, parallel to and above the road.

From this path there are some spectacular views down the length of Saunton Sands, and if clear, across the estuary to Appledore. On the hillside to the left some ancient cultivation terraces can be seen.

The large flat-roofed building is the five-star Saunton Sands Hotel owned by the Brend family. Wonderful food; they welcome all, including walkers.

At this point you are confronted with three routes from which to choose:-

1. *The official route* crosses the B3231 road and passes around the hotel and descends to the large Saunton Sands car park. (The refreshment hut is open from Easter to the end of September.)

    Continue in an easterly direction across the car park and pick up a sandy lane near some holiday chalets. At the end of this lane you return to the B3231 road.

    Take care now as there is 400 yards (365 m) of that road to walk along until just past the Saunton Golf Club driveway. Turn right here. The path then wanders around the landward side of the golf course. It is well marked.

2. This route does not involve crossing the B3231. At the bottom of the slope before the road, turn left onto a public footpath. You climb steeply with the path bearing right. It passes near to Saunton Court and continues on to the B3231 road opposite the red brick house. You then follow the official route as described in Option 1 above.

    This diversion eliminates 400 yards (365 m) of very dangerous road walking. The Heritage Coast Service suggests this route and we have asked for signs to be installed.

3. This third choice is probably the one preferred by most walkers. Cross over the B3231. Pass around the Saunton Sands Hotel and descend to the large car park. Walk south along the beach via Airy Point to Crow Point. After 3.5 miles (5.5 km) along the beach, just after the groyne watch out for a slatted wooden catwalk on your left. This is your beach exit so walk along this to Broad Sands. As you do so you will have regained the official route.

The official route after options 1 and 2 now enters the Braunton Burrows nature reserve.

These burrows are renowned for their great wealth and diversity of their plant life, and over 400 species of flowering plants have been recorded here.

When the Burrows car park is reached the path uses the so-called American road to Broad Sands. It should be noted that the American road is often flooded across making this section of the walk sometimes difficult.

Arriving at Broad Sands, either by the Burrows walk or the beach walk (Option 3), the path becomes a little vague, but keep the estuary on your right hand side and you cannot go wrong. Head for the white cottage on the estuary side.

The route now follows the estuary side on top of the Great Sea Bank. The path keeps to the top of this sea wall all the way to Velator. If you wish to visit Braunton turn left at Velator and walk along the old railway track into the village.

From Velator the route now follows the old Barnstaple to Ilfracombe railway track into Barnstaple: the railway was closed in 1970.

In the summer months, the walker will have a problem on this section of the path, as not only is it the South West Coast Path, but it is also a cycle track used by many hundreds of cyclists. Few bikes seem to have any audible means of warning you of their approach, so walking can become very hazardous. After leaving Velator you will pass the old railway station at Wrafton and after about 1 mile (1500 m) the path suddenly emerges onto the estuary side. When the tide is high it presents a very fine picture and in the winter months there are many ducks and waders to observe.

After Heanton Court, a possible stop for refreshments, continue following the old railway track which follows the banks of the estuary to Barnstaple. By the time this Guide is published the new bridge over the River Yeo should be in place. Cross the new bridge and continue along beside the wharf towards the old Long Bridge over the river in Barnstaple.

9 | Barnstaple to Westward Ho! (Amusement Arcade)
OS E139 & OS E126 (T) Barnstaple (Trains); (T) Bideford

| Grading: Easy | Distance - | 30.7 | 140.8 | 19.1 | 87.5 |

See also our Barnstaple to Westward Ho! Path Description.

Distances are measured walking through to Bideford: approximately 6 miles (10 km) can be avoided by using the Instow to Appledore Ferry, but this is seasonal and subject to the tide.

Having passed the old Barnstaple railway station, you soon pass a new recreation area with seating, a good spot for a break. Continue along beside the river to the Long Bridge and take the steps up to the left which bring you onto the bridge. Cross the bridge - there is no need to cross the road. On the other side of the bridge pass the Leaderflush/Shapland works on your right and then turn right by the roundabout. Follow this road and when it bears right, cross over to pick up the path ahead behind the houses. Follow this to where it joins the Tarka Trail by the old railway bridge, bearing right along the old railway track. Again be aware of cyclists as you follow this all the way to Instow where there is the option of using the ferry, tides permitting. However, remember the official route of the South West Coast Path is in to Bideford.

Contact Mr Ommanney   Easter to October 7 days per week - every 15 mins
The Sea Chest   Tidal - Approximately two hours each side of high water
Market Street
Appledore EX39 1PW
Tel: 01237 476191

Please note, however, that absolute reliance on ferries is not advised, so if the ferry is not running, rejoin the old railway track by the old level crossing and signal box.

Continue on to Bideford under the new Bideford bridge. The old Bideford railway station is the base of the Hartland Coast Heritage Service. Refreshments are available in season in the reconditioned railway carriage.

Cross the Bideford Long Bridge, turn right and walk along the quay. Continue walking by the riverside path now named Landivisau Walk (Bideford's twin town in France) keeping the car park on your left. At the end of the car park there is a waymarked lane passing the Bideford RFC stadium. Continue walking on a road to pass under the new high level road bridge, then up a rough track, turn right by the waymark, and walk down a narrow track. This rejoins the riverside by a small beach at Lower Cleave. There is some more road walking passing the Yeoldon House Hotel. Be sure to keep to the waymarked lane; do not stray up any of the many private drives. After the second war tank traps, fork right and the route enters the National Trust property of Borrough Farm. This is a very pleasant section through some riverside woods with fine views back up the river to Bideford.

There is now a steep descent to another small beach with stepping stones over a marshy area. After the second National Trust sign turn right. There are now two options here. A high tide inland diversion has been installed due to a breach in the sea wall but at low tide, continue on along the sea wall. These routes are both well waymarked. With the steps now provided it is not difficult to negotiate the breach in the sea wall. Having done that the path turns inland to meet up with the high tide route. Follow the waymarked route around the Appledore shipyard to reach the road, turn right and into Appledore via Myrtle Street.

At Appledore plenty of accommodation and refreshment places are available. Along the Quay you meet the ferry slipway from Instow. The route now continues into old Appledore, passing the homes of the old sailing captains to near the lifeboat house. Walk along the side of the road past the DCC recycling centre and out towards the mouth of the Taw/Torridge estuary.

Here for some distance you are walking on the seaward side of the dunes turning to the golf links side to pass Sandy Mere, then it is a straight walk into Westward Ho!. At most states of the tide it is possible to walk the beach, but be warned, the sand can be rather soft in places. Westward Ho! has plenty of accommodation but refreshment places are limited out of season.

10 Westward Ho! to Clovelly (Mount Pleasant) OS E126 (T) Westward Ho!

Grading: Strenuous   Distance -   18   158.8   11.2   98.7

See also our Westward Ho! to Clovelly Path Description.

After passing the last of the holiday chalets, the path follows the track of the old Bideford to Westward Ho! railway. This is a fine stretch of the Coast Path over Cornborough and Abbotsham cliffs. At Greencliff a very poor coal was once mined. The path now climbs steeply over Cockington cliffs only to drop again to sea level to cross a pebble beach before climbing again via a wooden staircase, to cross Babbacombe cliffs. At Peppercombe turn inland to cross the stream and then the path meanders through Sloo Woods to join the new section through Worthygate Wood.

NOTE: The route shown on OS Explorer map 126 at Gauter Pool is wrong. The path does not turn to the south but goes on through the woods dropping to Buck's Mills.

At Buck's Mills refreshments are available and a walk down to the old Quay is worthwhile. On leaving Barton Wood, keep to the bottom edge of the field until you cross a bridge into Hobby Drive. The walk along the Hobby Drive is nearly 3 miles (5 km) long, and takes longer than you think. There is a path which takes you off the Hobby Drive down to the harbour; by walking down it and then up to the village street again, you can rejoin the Coast Path.

11 Clovelly to Hartland Quay (Hotel) OS E126 (V) Clovelly

Grading: Moderate to strenuous   Distance -   16.6   175.4   10.3   109.0

See also our Clovelly to Hartland Quay Path Description.

This is a very fine section indeed, what coastal walking is all about! Allow yourself plenty of time to really enjoy it. You leave Clovelly by following the coast path sign through the large gate in the wall/fence on the left of the road going down the hill - do not go down the hill. Follow the track round to the right, to the coast path signpost, where you follow the path down to the right (yellow waymark). After a while you pass through the kissing-gate and follow the fence on your right until reaching the small kissing-gate in the shrubbery. Follow this path and soon a covered seat appears on the right. Carry on through the shrubbery and through the next two kissing-gates. After a while turn right at the T-junction, following the coast path sign, and right again at the next fork. Soon you come to an original seat called the 'Angels Wings', with nice woodcarvings. On reaching the track, take the coast path hard to the right - do not go along the track. Follow this path to a wonderful viewpoint before it descends steeply into a valley to a track. Go right and before going immediately left and immediately right again there is an easy detour that is very worthwhile. Having turned right off the steep descent, go ahead instead of sharp left up the track beside the cliff edge. When this track levels out, look out for some indistinct steps up to the right and follow these to a cutting in the rock which take you through to a marvellous lookout platform with lovely views.

Returning back through the rock cutting, turn right and go down to the old shelter, passing through the pointed-arch doorway. Further excellent views along the coast to the waterfall open up before you. There is a further viewpoint past the shelter but the views are quite restricted. We now recommend that you return back to the coast path sign bearing right down to the main track where you turn hard right to follow this track down the valley to the shore. Go down the narrow path, crossing the stream by the stepping stones. Pause at the shore and notice the rock formations and the waterfall along the coast to your left (at low tide). Also note the old lime kiln. Now follow the grass track inland past the lime kiln and old building. Shortly take the Coast Path up to your right. Half way up follow the steps to the right ignoring the path going on ahead. On reaching the top, cross the stile by the NT sign for Brownsham.

The path proceeds through one field and over another stile which is multistepped on the eastern side, then across another field to the stile in the right hand fence, and then proceed down the steps, across the bridge at the bottom, turning left, and then take the first turning on the right. This is the more seaward route and is now the official path. We asked for this path and are grateful to the National Trust for having provided it. At Becklands there is a small memorial plaque in memory of the crew of a Wellington bomber that crashed into these cliffs in April 1942.

The route now continues practically on the coast all the way to Eldern Point and then on to Shipload Bay. The true coastal path from Shipload Bay to Barley Bay seaward of the radar station is now open and freely available. (Seasonal refreshment hut - Hartland Point car park.)

The path down into the Smoothlands Valley and out to Damehole Point is a wonderful part of the coast path. Those requiring further exercise may like to walk over the cliff top on the north of the Smoothlands Valley and it does give wonderful views, but it is not the official path. We confidently recommend Damehole Point itself to the sure-footed as not only being one of the most dramatic pieces of definitive Right of Way in the whole country but also as an ideal picnic spot.

To cross Abbey River the path goes inland behind the cottage to a stone bridge.

After crossing Abbey River, those who want the most scenic route should not turn left as directed at the next coastal path sign. Continue right out to the coast at Dyer's Lookout and then turn left up the cliff edge. It is a little further but scenically much better. On reaching the old Rocket House by the road inland to Stoke, bear right to follow the path downhill to Hartland Quay, soon picking up the small road down to the seasonal refreshments, museum, toilets and hotel.

12 | Hartland Quay to Bude (Canal Bridge)   OS E126 & E111

Grading: Severe   Distance -   24.8   200.2   15.4   124.4

See also our Hartland Quay to Bude Path Description.

This is a most rewarding but very tough section. It will almost surely take you longer than you think although the beginning is comparatively mild. Before reaching Bude you will have crossed ten river valleys.

The path from Hartland Quay is largely track and becomes a grassy footpath behind St Catherine's Tor. There is then a climb up and down to the waterfall at Speke Mill's Mouth. In our opinion this is the most dramatic waterfall on the whole of the path and we do not forget Pentargon ahead.

The path keeps to the eastern side of the stream for about 150 yards (135 m) then crosses it by a new wooden footbridge. Follow the signs up the valley to the east of Swansford Hill. The path over Swansford Hill is still walkable but should not be attempted in strong wind conditions.

Take care at Sandhole Cliff after joining the metalled road to watch for the signpost after about a 0.33 mile (500 m) directing you to turn right to rejoin the Coast Path. If you miss this you may find yourself doing about a 2 mile (3 km) walk down the road to Welcombe Mouth. Our Association has been urging the North Devon Coast and Countryside Service to install a true coast path along Sandhole Cliff; those who have been this way before will notice that they have installed half of what we requested.

On the descent into Marsland Mouth, look out for a little stone building, once the seaside lookout of the author, Ronald Duncan. It will provide a shelter from the elements.

As you come across the Cornish Border you will start to find a series of extremely helpful and well-thought-out posts. You might smile at the first which says 'Cornwall' but thereafter not only do they point the way in each direction, but they also tell you where you are down the shank of the post. Our thanks and appreciation to whoever had this idea - surely the best yet!

The diversion to visit Morwenstow Church is worth consideration. In season refreshments are available at the old rectory. The eccentric Parson Hawker was vicar here in 1830; look out for his hut which he constructed out of driftwood on Vicarage Cliff, when you regain the Coast Path.

At Steeple Point there is a tendency to keep too far inland. The official path keeps well to seaward. To cross the stream in Coombe Valley (where there are refreshments and toilets), there is a footbridge.

At Sandy Mouth there is a National Trust cafe. In season it is a welcome refreshment point, but watch the daylight as there is no electricity and the cafe surely closes at darkness at the latest.

The walking now becomes easier. Soon after Northcott Mouth, Crooklets Beach is reached. Keep to the cliffs passing the cricket pitch. This is the official route and the best way into Bude.

13 | Bude to Crackington Haven (Beach)   OS E111 (T) Bude

Grading: Strenuous   Distance -   16.4   216.6   10.2   134.6

See also our Bude to Crackington Haven Path Description.

A colourful free guide to the coast is available at the Bude Tourist Information Centre.

Bude has good shops and accommodation, being a fair-sized town. Before you leave do try a short beach walk to the north on the falling tide and look at those cliffs - alternating bands of sandstone and shale in beautiful curving waves and with eroding continuations of the strata extending out across the beach. This pattern has been with you since Hartland, but as you go south there will soon be a series of changes - from tightly compressed folds to violent crumplings and igneous intrusions of a much more complex nature.

The southbound path starts from the sea lock on the historic Bude Canal, climbs to the cliff top at Compass Point and on to Efford Beacon. Looking back if the tide is out, the magnificent beach stretches before you for several miles going absolutely due north, with the dish aerials of the satellite tracking station visible beyond. To the south east if the weather is clear the high tors of Dartmoor can be seen, and to the south west the prominent outline of Cambeak on the south side of the Crackington Haven inlet.

The path over Efford Down and on to Upton is easy enough to follow, and then it is sandwiched between the cliff edge and the road to Widemouth. The beach at Widemouth is popular for swimming and surfing. Toilets, cafes and accommodation are available, but apart from the fine beach with its prominent Black Rock, an unusual stack of slump breccia, Widemouth is not attractive; but be prepared, there will be no more facilities until you reach Crackington Haven.

South of Widemouth the path follows the low cliff for a short distance and then diverts inland slightly at Wanson Mouth to join the coast road by the stream valley. Turn west and climb up to Penhalt Cliff. Major subsidence is occurring and the coast path has long gone, but don't blame the County Council, you will see that the road is going as well! At the southern end of the cliff top car park the Coast Path proper recommences through a field and then descends steeply into Millook Haven.

Those with a geological interest should go on to the stony beach to view the remarkable chevron folded rock strata in the cliff on the north side - a classic textbook photograph and in sharp contrast to the curving folds to the north beyond Widemouth.

Follow the steep road beyond the stream crossing in Millook for a short distance, then branch right on to the cliff top path at Raven's Beak. From here the path climbs steadily but is fairly easy going all the way to Chipman Point. Note the ancient stunted oak wood in the area of Dizzard Point. The stream valley at Chipman Point is steep and deep, one of a series ahead, some with spectacular waterfalls cascading over into the rocky beach below. A tough ascent, then a further drop into the valley at Cleave Strand followed by a ridge walk at Castle Point giving tremendous views. The descent to the Coxford Water stream is severe and the climb onwards to Pencannow Point will certainly exercise the heart/lung system. Pause to recover and enjoy the views before the descent into Crackington Haven.

CP - Dizzard Point - The path is nearer the coast than the map suggests.

14 | Crackington Haven to Boscastle (Footbridge) OS E111 (V) Crackington Haven

Grading: Strenuous   Distance -   10.9   227.5   6.8   141.4

See also our Crackington Haven to Tintagel Path Description.

At Crackington Haven it is usually safe for a swim, but never go out of your depth on Cornwall's north coast. There are toilets and a seasonal shop, pub and cafe, and a long, tough, remote stretch ahead. The folds in the rock strata are remarkable, with interesting patterns down on the beach at Tremoutha Haven. Take particular care to the west of the Cambeak headland - keep away from the cliff edges and just admire the views - Hartland and Lundy Island to the north; Tintagel and Rumps Point to the south.

The path is now relatively level and generally stays above the massive landslip zone at Strangles Beach. There is a good path down through the landslip to the beach, which is interesting and pleasant at low tide, but it is an arduous climb back. At the northern end of the beach is the conspicuous Northern Door rock arch. There is access to the road and car parking at the National Trust Trevigue Farm (Coast Information Centre).

Ahead looms High Cliff, the highest point on the Coast Path in Cornwall and best avoided when a gale is blowing. Just before High Cliff the path goes round the back of a small stream valley where there is a diversity of minor paths, but then just aim for the top. The southbound descent from High Cliff is precipitously steep so take it slowly, then the path up through the massive landfall at Rusey Cliff twists and turns through the brambles and gorse. This is a major geological fault zone. The path is easier to follow than it used to be, but the ground here is soily and the vegetation grows rampantly in summer which presents a continuing problem to the County Council which has difficulty keeping it cleared back.

Once at the top of Rusey Cliff there follows an easier stretch through grassy sheep fields, with the approach to Buckator now being more coastal than shown in earlier guides.

The sheer black cliff of Buckator hangs over the sea inlet, with impressive white bands of quartz running through, quite different from the brown and grey cliffs of predominantly sandstone to the north. The path dips slightly to cross a marshy stream where stepping stones provide firm footing, then continues on at high level to Fire Beacon Point. Here the descent is steep but there are attractive slate steps on the most precipitous part. The path then keeps close to the cliff edge and into the Pentargon inlet where an impressive waterfall cascades down to the sea. The best view of this is now from the southern side, cliff falls having caused the path on the north side to be diverted and the old viewpoint has been lost. You are advised NOT to leave the official Coast Path to attempt a better view of this Waterfall. It is a long way down.

Further cliff falls seem imminent on the south side of Pentargon, but from here on it is easy going into Boscastle. Aim for the white mast atop Penally Hill, then follow the path to the beautiful harbour inlet and past the Youth Hostel into the village of Boscastle. Penally Point is well worth the detour, an exciting viewpoint, but the slate rock is dangerously slippery when wet. Note the extraordinary small scale distortions in the strata alongside the path.

15 | Boscastle to Tintagel (Haven)   OS E109 (V) Boscastle

Grading: Moderate	Distance -	7.4	234.9	4.6	146.0

See also our Crackington Haven to Tintagel Path Description.

There are shops, pubs, toilets, accommodation and an excellent Heritage Coast Centre in Boscastle, and the old village up the lane by the Wellington Hotel is well worth exploring.

The next section on to Tintagel is shorter and easier then the two previous sections. The path leaves from the south side of the harbour and climbs steeply past the gully to Eastern Blackapit to the Willapark headland with its prominent white watch tower. Go up to the watch tower, or take the short cut across the back of the headland past the ancient Forrabury strip field system now preserved by the National Trust. The path soon descends into the stream valley of Grower Gut - there are some granite stepping stones to help you if the water is in flood. Further on the path turns sharp right to keep to the seaward side of the Manor House and onto a prominent headland which overlooks Short Island. If you are a birdwatcher, here is a good place to stop, picnic and observe through binoculars. Both Short Island and its neighbour Long Island are densely populated with breeding seabirds during the early summer, including guillemots, razorbills and a few puffins. Always look down on the water; they tend to float around in groups when off duty.

As you go on past Firebeacon Hill look for the Ladies Window rock arch in the gully to the right - walking west it is easy to miss this attractive photo opportunity. From here to Rocky Valley the going is level, but do look back to the dramatic pinnacles below Trevalga Cliff. On your left you are soon confronted by a conspicuous cliff top caravan/camp site - the path runs seaward of it. Trewethet Gut is a dangerous and eroding inlet that has necessitated a slight diversion of the path, and then you descend into the exquisite Rocky Valley. Look for seals in the surging sea as you cross the footbridge, and for the dippers in the water of the stream. There is a path through Rocky Valley to the coast road, where cars may be parked.

From the footbridge a steep climb to high level again, and you find yourself overlooking Bossiney Haven. There is a crossroad of paths giving access to the beach from Bossinney village, and indeed this is an excellent place for a swim just after low tide. But the Coast Path goes on straight ahead and bears right to another prominent headland called Willapark, the second in just 2 miles. Again birdwatchers should go to the end and scan The Sisters and the ocean through binoculars. There are often terns, gannets and even shearwaters further out, but beware the precipitous cliff edge as you return to the path. Then on to Barras Nose headland, dominated by that awful hotel eyesore, and down to Tintagel Haven below the Castle ruins. Here there are toilets and a cafe.

16 | Tintagel to Port Isaac (Beach)   OS E9 & E106 (T) Tintagel

Grading: Severe   Distance -   14.7   249.6   9.1   155.1

See also our Tintagel to Port Isaac Path Description.

Tintagel has many shops, cafes and guest houses. The Old Post Office, owned and restored by the National Trust, dates back to the fourteenth century when it was no doubt a house of some importance.

Around The Island and down in Tintagel Haven there is some interesting and complex geology with older rocks (Devonian) overthrust on top of more recent rocks (carboniferous), and bands of lava and tuff. The severe erosion, which is no doubt compounded by these faults and thrusts, is making access to The Island increasingly difficult to maintain. In the shelter of Tintagel Haven sailing ships used to be loaded with the high quality slate that is still extracted from several quarries inland away from this highly disturbed coastal zone.

The path to Trebarwith Strand climbs up from Tintagel Haven below and to the left of the Castle entrance and gives an excellent view of the rocks on the south face of The Island. From here on and past St Materiana's Church it is easy going. The Youth Hostel at Dunderhole Point was once a quarry office building. The best route, for glorious views, is the National Trust path out around the headlands of Penhallic Point, rather than the boring official route across three fields. There are further old quarries ahead as you approach Hole Beach and Trebarwith Strand, and surprisingly sailing ships were loaded under the cliffs at Penhallic Point, where the remains of the wharf can still be seen. The path drops down by the toilets in Trebarwith Strand, and opposite is a welcome pub serving hot food. The beach is worth exploring at low tide, but watch that you don't get cut off, and do be warned that swimming can be dangerous here.

From here to Port Isaac the path is long and very tough in parts. The descents to the valley streams and up again on the other side are about the steepest on the whole of the Coast Path. Do not leave Trebarwith Strand unless you have food, energy and plenty of time in hand. The climb up out of Trebarwith Strand, which is stepped almost all the way, will give you a foretaste of what lies ahead. And having reached the top, you must go all the way down again into Backways Cove, then up again to a more restful level stretch for about 1 mile (1500 m) to the stream valley behind Tregardock Beach, where you are confronted by a detached and eroding piece of the cliff known as The Mountain. As you descend on the inland side of The Mountain you will meet a crossroad of paths from Tregardock village to the beach. The beach is worth a visit at low tide but your route lies straight ahead and you have quite a long way to go.

From here the stretch marked on the maps as Tregardock Cliff is easy enough, but at Jacket's Point the deepest and steepest valley of all lies before you - the commencement of The National Trust Dannonchapel property. An excellent job has been done on the path, the stream crossing and the staircase of steps on the ascent on the south side. However having reached the top, you drop down again into yet another deep valley. There are more steps up on the south side of the valley, then you go over to the Barrett's Zawn stream valley where another mineworking adit faces you. This gave donkeys burdened with slate access to Barrett's Zawn beach - don't even think about it as this tunnel is collapsing.

On the climb up round the Barrett's Zawn cliffs you will certainly see that there have been massive rock falls and that another will occur any time. You then descend very steeply on the south side into the next stream valley at Ranie Point, and as you slide down the stony slope you may well feel that the path here could be improved. Some walkers evidently complain about the staircases of steps on these valley sides, but they are so exceptionally steep we believe that steps are the best option and we have been urging the hard-pressed County Council to put some here.

Now at last the path levels out through the sheep meadows with just a small valley to cross at St Illickswell Gug where a boardwalk takes you across the marsh. When you reach the road at Cartway Cove the official path is directly opposite and drops down by the side of the hotel at Portgaverne. But, for the best views, take the path to the right and go round the headland and if the tide is out walk along the old harbour quay, where sailing ships were once loaded with slate. Either way there is then a short road walk up to the cliff car park at Port Isaac. Go through this past the public toilets and follow the well-signed path round to overlook the attractive inlet and thence the village street.

17 | Port Isaac to Polzeath (Beach)   OS E106 (V) Port Isaac

Grading: Strenuous   Distance -   14.2   263.8   8.8   163.9

See also our Port Isaac to Padstow Path Description.

Port Isaac is a gem, with narrow streets and tiny cottages which are no doubt easier to look at than to live in. There are two excellent pubs and one of the cafes is in an extremely old and crooked little building. Do take time to explore the back streets and the small fish market, and see if you can find Squeeze-ee-belly Alley!

Another tough walk lies ahead and there are no facilities until you reach Polzeath, but the scenery is superb. Take the road to the right behind the fish market and past more toilets. The path bears right along the cliff in front of two prominent guest houses and takes you on past Lobber Point then down into Pine Haven. From here on the path is relatively new and apart from an unpleasant fenced corridor cutting off Varley Head, it really is magnificent, and keeps close to the cliff edge all the way to Port Quin. The fence stays on your left for over a mile of steep ups and downs, but it does protect you from the enormous herd of beef cattle that generally roams the meadows during the summer. Watch out for the peregrines that hunt along this stretch, the occasional adder basking in the sun, and seals on the rocks below.

At Kellan Head The Rumps promontory faces you at the far end of Portquin Bay. Then as you turn the corner the path overlooks the beautiful Port Quin inlet and descends to the village, once a busy little pilchard port, but there are no facilities here now although there is a tap marked drinking water on the wall in front of you as you descend the steps into the harbour. Follow the road westbound until half way up the steep hill where a new slate stile gives access to the south side of the inlet. You are on National Trust land and free to explore Doyden Point, formed from rocks of greenstone. The path follows the stream valley some distance in front of the old Prison Governor's House, and soon passes two fenced mineshafts where you might still find interesting mineral samples amongst the loose spoil material nearby - but keep away from the dangerous cliff edge.

At Trevan Point there is a sharp descent to Epphaven Cove which, with its neighbour Lundy Bay, has a beautiful beach at low tide. You then enter a surprisingly wooded valley where in late spring you will hear the delightful call of the willow warbler. As you climb up out of the bay look out for the startling Lundy Hole behind a protective fence on your right. On the cliff top again as you approach The Rumps you will see the earth ramparts of an Iron Age Fort in the lower ground in front of the headland. When you get there the detour through the entrance and on round the rocks overlooking The Mouls island is well worthwhile and can give good seabird watching; puffins nest on The Mouls most years.

It is then quite easy going on to Pentire Point, another headland formed from pillow lava. A perfect cross-section can be seen in the small vertical rock face on your left as you leave The Rumps headland, the rounded hollow shapes having been formed of molten lava under the sea. The walling stone alongside the path reveals the structure of small holes in the rock caused by gases and steam, but do not remove pieces as samples; the National Trust spends much time and money maintaining these walls and they provide wind shelter for the sheep.

There are many good viewpoints on the Coast Path, but that from Pentire Point is one of the best. In clear conditions south to Trevose Head and beyond, and north to Bude, the satellite tracking station and even Hartland Quay and Lundy Island are visible, but you will need binoculars! Then follows an easy descent into Polzeath with the Camel Estuary before you and Stepper Point with its Daymark Tower on the opposite side. In contrast to the last 20 miles of perfection, the cliff top housing and car parking in New and Old Polzeath are unfortunate, but the sea, the sand and the surf are magnificent. There are toilets on the left as you reach the road beyond Pentireglaze Haven. The path continues along the cliff edge to the village centre and gives access to the beach on the way.

Grading: Easy   Distance -   **4.7**   **268.5**   **2.9**   **166.8**

See also our Port Isaac to Padstow Path Description.

Polzeath is a surfers' paradise with several shops, cafes, accommodation and campsites. On the left by the park is a small Tourist Information Centre and there are toilets opposite.

Follow the road past the beach car park and take the path right by the cottages where the road bends sharp left on the steep hill. The path follows the edge of Tristram Cliff where you can watch the expertise of the surfers. From here to Daymer Bay the path along The Greenaway is intensively walked throughout the year, and measures have had to be taken to discourage people from wandering off the route and scarring the fragile turf with alternative tracks. In fact this path is so good it is now classed as suitable for wheelchair users, which is almost unique on the Coast Path. There are houses on your left, but the coastal scene is beautiful with a rocky sea-washed platform below - the haunt of curlews, redshanks, grey plover and oystercatchers, with the headlands of Stepper Point and Pentire Point in the background. Many fishing and pleasure boats can be observed entering and leaving from Padstow, some 2 miles (3 km) up the Camel Estuary.

Just off Trebetherick Point is the Doom Bar, noticeable only at low tide when the waves are breaking over the sand; there were many wrecks here during the days of sail when ships were largely at the mercy of wind and tide. There are toilets and a cafe in Daymer Bay car park and the beach is one of the safest for a swim - but keep out of the estuary channel at low tide.

The Coast Path goes down the steps on to the beach and then through the dunes and over a footbridge just below Brea Hill. To visit little St Enodoc Church, which was once buried beneath the blown sand, turn left midway along the dunes and follow the white markers across the golf course. You must then retrace your route back to the dunes, or you can go on through the golf course to rejoin the Coast Path in the dunes on the far side of Brea Hill, but this is a busy golf course and you may wish you had a protective helmet and visor. Your route through the golf course is marked by large white painted rocks. From the footbridge you can go either way round Brea Hill, or straight over the top! Alternatively, if the tide is out you can walk along the beach to Rock and the Padstow ferry. All routes are pleasant and the sheltered estuary surroundings make quite a change from the exposed cliffs that you have been used to. The official path goes through a hollow just behind the dunes on the south side of Brea Hill, a Site of Special Scientific Interest for the rare plant life that thrives on the calcium-rich sand. At the southern end the path branches left to a higher level and on to Rock car park, but you can continue on along the beach, except at very high tide. There are toilets in the car park and the ferry landing is on the shore below. Be warned however that at exceptionally low tides the ferry may sail from quite some distance downstream in front of the dunes, so keep a lookout as you walk.

Rock/Padstow (River Camel)
Black Tor Ferry
Padstow Harbour Commissioners,
Harbour Office, West Quay,
Padstow, Cornwall PL28 8AQ.
Tel: Padstow (01841) 532239
Fax: (01841) 533346

Ferry operates all year at 20 min intervals
No Sunday service from last
Sunday in October to
1st Sunday in April
(or Easter if earlier)

We understand that this ferry company is no longer keen to issue single fares, but we have been told that they will do so for genuine walkers on request and accordingly you should ask for a single fare if that is what you require.

The Saints' Way long-distance path, which links the north coast with the south at Fowey, starts at Padstow.

19 | Padstow to Trevone (Car Park)

OS E106 (T) Padstow

Grading: Easy   Distance -   **9.1   277.6   5.7   172.5**

See also our Padstow to Porthcothan Path Description.

Normally the Padstow ferry will take you into the harbour, but at low tide it will deposit you a short distance downstream at St Saviour's Point, just below the path to Stepper Point. Do not take this as an opportunity to cut out Padstow; you should go into the town and explore. The harbour area, the narrow lanes in the old town and up to St Petroc's Church are attractive and fairly traffic free. A glass of beer and a genuine Cornish steak pasty make an excellent traditional lunch. A visit to the Tourist Information Centre on the harbour is recommended, and on your way it is interesting to look at the places of origin of the many fishing boats - all ports from the Hebrides to the Channel Islands!

The Coast Path starts on your left at the north end of the harbour and is wide and well trodden. In the early summer blackcaps and warblers sing in the wooded stream valley at St George's Cove. From Gun Point you can, if the tide is out, take a short cut across the beach to Hawker's Cove by the prominent old Lifeboat House. If the tide is in you can enjoy a quiet swim; this is a very pleasant and usually wind sheltered beach. Go round the back of the old pilots' houses from Hawker's Cove and then climb up to Stepper Point, with its disused coastguard lookout and the stone-built Daymark Tower. From this high ground there is a remarkable panorama behind you and on a clear day you will see the granite tors of Bodmin Moor in the distance.

So now you are back on the exposed Atlantic Coast. Approaching the precipitous inlet of Butter Hole Cove, look out for the small Pepper Hole a few yards to the right of the path. There follows a long easy stretch to Gunver Head, followed by a steep descent to the small stream valley. The rocky pinnacles of the Merope Islands just behind you are spectacular. After a short climb up again you will see the Marble Cliff and Porthmissen Bridge ahead. The cliff comprises many bands of hard limestone and softer shale on which razorbills, guillemots and kittiwakes nest in the summer. At Roundhole Point the path skirts the impressive Round Hole collapsed cave which should be approached with caution, and then descends to the car park at Trevone.

20 | Trevone to Porthcothan (Footbridge)

OS E106

Grading: Easy   Distance -   **12.7   290.3   7.9   180.4**

See also our Padstow to Porthcothan Path Description.

There are toilets, a cafe and a good beach in Trevone, but little else of interest to the walker, except perhaps some bed and breakfast accommodation. The path passes behind the little headland on the south side of the bay and follows the cliff edge round rocky Newtrain Bay. There are refreshments, toilets and a beautiful beach at Harlyn.

The stream generally has to be crossed via the road bridge, and then the path follows the beach for about 330 yards (300 m) before climbing slightly into the dunes and so on past the end of the bay to Cataclews Point. The hard erosion-resistant dolerite rock here was used to make the polished font in Padstow Church. In Mother Ivey's Bay there are some unpleasant man-made features which mar the coastal scene, including an often foul smelling sewage discharge which frequently contaminates the nearby beaches. There is a huge and conspicuous caravan site near Trevose Farm, and access to the headland by the new Padstow Lifeboat Station is barred by an ugly concrete and mesh fence, reminiscent of prison camps which is in sharp contrast to the old tamarisk hedges nearby. How sadly all this compares with the painstaking remedial and conservation work that has been carried out by the National Trust on long stretches of the coast to the north of the Camel Estuary.

At Trevose Head you can generally visit the immaculately kept lighthouse, but keep away when the fog horn is blowing. On a clear day you will see the granite hills of West Penwith behind St Ives to the south and the satellite tracking dish aerials beyond Bude to the north. Turning south, the path passes yet another large Round Hole as it descends to Booby's Bay. There is something of a rocky scramble to get through to Constantine Bay, but it is beautiful here with a particularly attractive beach at low tide - not really safe for swimming unfortunately. Beyond the dunes the path leaves the beach to go round Treyarnon Point, revealing another attractive beach at

Treyarnon Bay. The Youth Hostel is on the left, and in the car park area there are toilets and refreshments. If you are intent on swimming, observe the safety notices which will certainly tell you not to do so at low tide.

An unusually indented coastline follows beyond Trethias Island, but the path cuts across the narrower headlands. Between Pepper Cove and Warren Cove are the ramparts of an Iron Age Fort, and in Fox Cove you may see the remains of a ship which ran aground in 1969. Minnows Islands and the cove beyond are quite spectacular. The path turns into Porthcothan Bay, descending through the protected National Trust strip which contrasts with the housing development on the opposite side. To reach Porthcothan's pub, the Tredrea Inn, take the road before the bridge and go uphill for approximately 500 yards (458 m).

21 | Porthcothan to Newquay (Harbour)   OS E106

Grading: Moderate   Distance -   17.9   308.2   11.1   191.5

See also our Porthcothan to Newquay Path Description.

Porthcothan has toilets, a shop, limited accommodation and a pub. The path leaves past the shop and keeps in front of the houses and on round the headland overlooking Trescore Islands. There is a steep descent into Porth Mear valley, a popular spot for birdwatchers, and an equally steep climb up again, then it is an easy walk to Park Head, another spectacular viewpoint. Ahead lies the famous Carnewas property of the National Trust, with a beautiful beach at low tide. As you leave Park Head you will see that the cliff is slowly sliding down, although it has been like this for many years. Bedruthan beach itself has a recurring accessibility problem due to the dangerous condition of the cliffs, but a great deal of money is being spent on the long flight of steps down. If the tide is on its way out, it is worth going down to explore the rock stacks, Bedruthan Steps, but don't get cut off and don't even think about swimming. The National Trust cafe and Information Centre in the car park are open throughout the summer.

Bedruthan Steps can be a busy place, but few people stray far from their cars and you will soon find yourself on a quieter stretch of path to Trenance Point. A steady descent into Mawgan Porth follows, where the road must be used for a short distance in order to cross the stream; there are toilets and shops here. The southbound path leaves to the right on the sharp road bend on the hill out of Mawgan Porth. Then follows a long high level stretch to Watergate Bay, with minor descents at Beacon Cove and Stem Cove, between which across Griffin's Point headland are the ramparts of another Iron Age Fort. Just inland is the airport and RAF station at St Mawgan, and you may find yourself being targeted by high-powered military jet aircraft as they come in to land. Ahead lies the magnificent Watergate Beach, but the path remains at high level until it crosses to the road behind the Watergate Bay Hotel.

After crossing the stream bridge by the car park, where there are toilets, the path leaves to the right from the road to Newquay and again climbs to the high cliff top where it remains all the way to Whipsiderry. Here some ugly cliff top development has been permitted, but the coastal scene is great, with Newquay and Towan Head in the background. The cliffs at Whipsiderry are high and precipitous, but there are steps down to the beach and some caves to explore. The path just manages to squeeze between a guesthouse and the cliff edge, and then takes you on to Trevelgue Head.

We recommend that you cross the footbridge on to the island, where a rough sea can be most spectacular. Then you must return to the road at Porth Beach where there are toilets and cafes. You may then walk out along the southern edge of the beach rather than taking the official road route, joining the path by more toilets. From here it crosses the headland between Porth and Lusty Glaze. This short cut avoids the road and takes you round the cliff edge at Lusty Glaze Cove and into the Barrowfields Park. Then you are on the road into Newquay town centre, but if the tide is out you can walk along the magnificent beach from Lusty Glaze or from Barrowfields all the way to the harbour.

Grading: Moderate   **Distance -**   **10.2   318.4   6.3   197.8**

See also our Newquay to Perranporth Path Description.

Newquay is the biggest town on the north coast and the pedestrianised shopping centre is quite attractive. There is no shortage of restaurants, pubs and accommodation here, and there is even a railway station! But do explore the beaches and the harbour before you leave, and if the tide is out you can gain access to the coast path by the steps at the back of the harbour.

The Coast Path leaves just above the harbour and climbs past the old Huer's Hut to Towan Head. In the cliffs below the Hut is a noisy kittiwake colony and this is a very good spot to observe the differences between kittiwakes, fulmars, black-headed gulls and the rest. Towan Head is particularly good for seabird watching; with binoculars you may spot gannets, petrels and shearwaters further out.

From Towan Head the path follows along the back of Fistral Beach. This is probably the most popular surfing beach in the British Isles and international competitions are held here. The path climbs to the cliffs at the southern end, passing in front of the housing development at Pentire, then across the headland at The Warren over to The Gannel river estuary.

There are four ways that you can cross the River Gannel, three of which are available, tide permitting, throughout the year. The distances via the Penpol crossing assume that you have walked via Fern Pit; the same applies to the other two crossings of Trenance Footbridge and the A3075 main road route. However, it is possible to reach the Trenance and Trevemper crossings from the town itself.

1. Newquay to Crantock via Penpool

This is now the official crossing of the River Gannel. Up river there is ferry and a tidal footbridge off Trevean Lane which crosses over to Penpol Creek. If you are at Fern Pit and need to go upstream, go east (inland) along Riverside Crescent, Riverside Avenue, Fistral Crescent, turn right into Pentire Crescent, continue along Penmere Drive and turn right into Trevean Way, then turn right at the coast path sign. Be warned; there is an earlier footpath sign to Crantock - DO NOT take it because you may find it is under water. Having crossed the Gannel, turn right to follow an estuary side path. Presently it becomes a track and you pass a house on the right, then some bungalows and can soon turn right down into the National Trust car park at Rushey Green. Take the exit practically opposite where you came in. There is a seasonal cafe close to the car park. (Note that the NTG refers to this crossing as being at the bottom of Trethellan Hill.)

2. Newquay to Crantock via Fern Pit Ferry Crossing (summer only); (deduct approx. 2 miles / 3 km)

Newquay/Crantock (River Gannel)   Spring Bank Holiday
Fern Pit Cafe and Ferry   End of May to mid-September
Proprietor - G A Northey   continuous 7 days a week
Fern Pit, Riverside Crescent, Newquay. TR7 1PJ.
Tel: 01637 873181

You have to pass Fern Pit to reach the official crossing of the Gannel. If the ferry is running, it is a comfortable and scenic way to cross; there is even a cafe on the Newquay side so that you can while away your waiting time with refreshment. However, neither the ferry nor the footbridge, which is used at low tide instead of the ferry, is available when the cafe is closed.

3. Newquay to Crantock via Trenance Footbridge (add approx. 3 miles / 4.8 km)

Further up stream again, just before the estuary becomes a river, there is another footbridge which we call 'Trenance'. It is beside the new A3075 Gannel Road just before the boating lake on the left and its junction with Trevemper Road. If you are in Newquay and know the tides are against you, the quickest way to get here is to walk down the new Gannel Road (A3075). On the other side of the footbridge, walk forward for about 165 yards (150 m) keeping the hawthorn hedge on your left, until you come to a clearing on your left, offering various routes for you to choose. You can either turn right through the pedestrian gate that is a permissive path (this path is dependent on the tide, and should be navigable for two hours either side of low tide) or, if you have any doubts about the tide, you are advised to take the old bridleway through the big gate going towards Trevemper. Proceed forwards uphill and having gone over the brow, turn right before you get to the tarmac. You walk via Treringey coming to Penpol Creek and so on, to Rushey Green as described above.

41

4. Newquay to Crantock via the A3075 (add approx. 4.5 miles / 7.2 km)

However if all these crossings fail there is the A3075 main road itself, which is the only all-states-of- the-tide and all-seasons route. Those taking the A3075 should proceed along it until just after the roundabout where the A392 branches off. In about 100 yards (90 m) take the little unsigned lane on the right. You immediately pass a partly ruined barn on your right and soon you pass a house on the outskirts of Trevemper. Then as the road bears left, go forward and right. Pass through a gate and turn left to go via Treringey to Penpol Creek and so on to Rushey Green. Needless to say the A3075, although the one route that is always certain is quite the longest and certainly the most uninteresting.

Coast Path continues

Crantock Beach is attractive at low tide and can give good views of terns fishing in the Gannel below the cliffs of Pentire Point East. The path passes behind the dunes to the National Trust car park at Rushey Green, then westwards through the dunes to the cliffs of Pentire Point West. Alternatively you may walk along the beach to gain access to the path by scrambling up at the western end of the dunes.

Porth Joke is a sheltered sandy inlet, then follows a climb to Kelsey Head, another Iron Age site. From here in the distance can be seen St Agnes Head with Bawden Rocks offshore. Holywell Beach lies before you and the path descends to the dunes and then into Holywell. Those continuing onwards can take advantage of the splendid new National Trust footbridge across the river seaward of the village.

NTG Page 35 (Map) The official path goes out onto Towan Head and back.

---

23   Holywell to Perranporth (Beach car park)   OS E104

Grading: Moderate, sand dune route - Strenuous.   Distances -   7.3   325.7   4.5   202.3

See also our Newquay to Perranporth Path Description.

The path cuts across Penhale Point headland and then skirts the seaward edge of the rather ugly Penhale Camp, where there is a short fenced section. The army presence here has however served to preserve the beautiful wild dunes area inland from being overrun by campsites and chalets, and it now deserves to be protected as a nature reserve. The path goes out to Ligger Point and you get the first good view of the long Perran Beach.

The easiest path, if the tide permits, is now along the great stretch of firm beach to Perranporth rather than over the dunes. Even if, as is sometimes the case, you can only walk part-way along the beach it is worth going down to do this, there being a number of 'escape routes' up from the beach going south. The important point to watch if you want an easy descent to the beach is to fork left along the sandy path after the old wooden stile; the right fork is quicker but much steeper. It is essential that you stay on the marked route through the dunes as there is recent news of collapsing mine shafts.

The official path takes you towards the dunes where you will see the rusty coloured Perran Iron Lode in the cliff quarry. The path descends behind this and follows the back of the beach for almost a mile then climbs up through the dunes behind the rock cliff at Cotty's Point. The incoming tide will reach the foot of the cliff here but there are escape steps to the dunes at each side, and if the tide is out you can continue on along the beach rather than going over the top. The path descends to the back of the beach just south of Cotty's Point, crosses the stream by a footbridge and so takes you into the town or the car park where there are toilets.

---

24   Perranporth to St Agnes (Trevaunance Cove)   OS E104 (T) Perranporth

Grading: Moderate   Distance -   6.0   331.7   3.7   206.0

See also our Perranporth to Portreath Path Description.

Perranporth is a busy holiday centre during the summer and has good shops and accommodation. The eroding rock stacks at the southern end of the beach are interesting, and may be explored using the beach access at the far end of the car park in front of the hotel terrace.

Round the corner you will find a staircase from the beach up to the cliff car park at Droskyn Point. The official route leaves west from the town car park and follows the hill up Cliff Road, but just to the left of the Atlantic House Hotel there are some steps up and a footpath which takes you past the Droskyn Point car park. Whichever way you have chosen, keep inland of the prominent castellated building and on along Tregundy Lane to the end of the houses. The southbound Coast Path is signposted half left at the entrance drive to the Youth Hostel and the South West Water sewage pumping station. It then descends slightly to the right before climbing to the cliffs overlooking Shag Rock.

From here on you will see increasing evidence of mining activity. The path is fairly level going, passing the small outcrop of granite at Cligga Head which has been quarried and displays conspicuous stripes of greisen (for the chemistry of which you must consult the textbooks!). The mineralisation along the coast here and to the south is attributable to the intrusion of the granite which extends over a considerable area below the surface. Walking southbound through the quarry and mineworkings, you are unlikely to lose the path. Hanover Cove is named after a shipwreck. The Hanover was lost in a storm in December 1763 on route from Lisbon to Falmouth: all hands were lost plus a cargo of gold. It is rumoured that there is £50m of gold still onboard. The rock formations around the cove are dramatic and green copper stains the cliffs. There are many mineshafts in this area capped with conical steel mesh which allows access for bats.

The long stretch to Trevellas Porth is level easy going alongside the airfield perimeter; you will progress much faster here than you did further north. There is a sharp descent into Trevellas Coombe where there are many mine workings with their decaying buildings. Go upstream to the bridge which crosses the stream in front of the Blue Hills engine house and then right over the top to Trevaunance Cove. The southern path is the recommended route here, as the current official path passes close to the cliff edge. Cross over the road and turn right behind the four storey grey rendered housing block and the official path takes you past the toilets. If you go down into the cove, where there is a seasonal cafe, there is a footpath behind the Jubilee Terrace and steps back up to the path near the Trevaunance Point Hotel. This has a pleasant garden where you can enjoy the view and a glass of beer.

It is possible to cross the beach from Trevellas Porth to Trevaunance Cove at low tide, but be warned that the boulders are dangerously slippery. Surprisingly there was once a harbour under the cliff on the west side of Trevaunance Cove, but all you will find now is a tumbled mass of granite blocks.

25 | St Agnes to Porthtowan (Commodore Inn)   OS E104 (V) St Agnes

Grading: Moderate   Distance -   7.4   339.1   4.6   210.6

See also our Perranporth to Portreath Path Description.

Beyond the Trevaunance Point Hotel, the path climbs left past some unusual mine workings. From the top it stays at high level out to St Agnes Head, passing many mineshafts and waste tips on the way. Here you are circumnavigating St Agnes Beacon, a small outcrop of granite 0.5 mile (800 m) back from the coast. As the path turns south, you will see Godrevy Lighthouse across the bay, with St Ives and the massive granite of Penwith beyond. The going is relatively easy and soon you will pass the much-photographed Towanroath Engine House, part of the Wheal Coates tin and copper mine and now preserved by the National Trust. The path then descends into Chapel Porth where there is a car park, toilets and a seasonal cafe. At low tide, if you walk some distance north along the beach, you will see a streak of copper ore in the cliff beneath the Towanroath shaft.

The southbound path leaves The National Trust car park, travelling inland for 200 yards (185 m) on the right of the small stream, before joining the wide rough track to Mulgram Hill, then there is a good cliff top walk to Porthtowan. The path descends to the back of the beach and on past the car park where there are toilets. The transition from mining to tourism here has produced some unattractive features, but the beach is beautiful and extensive at low tide, from Tobban Horse in the south to Chapel Porth in the north.

Porthtowan to Portreath (Harbour)   **OS E104 (V) Porthtowan**

Grading: Strenuous   Distance -   6.3   345.4   3.9   214.5

See also our Perranporth to Portreath Path Description.

Porthtowan is popular for surfing and has accommodation, a pub, a few shops and seasonal cafes. To find the southbound path turn right along West Beach Road then left up the narrow road to the cliff top. On the headland the path turns south, passing many mineworkings, and keeps some distance back from the crumbling and dangerous cliff edge. At the steep valley drop to Sally's Bottom, where steps have been installed on either side, then on reaching high level again you find yourself walking alongside the unattractive Nancekuke fence which encloses the large military establishment just inland. It stays with us for over a mile and almost to Portreath, where the Daymark above the harbour entrance can be seen ahead. The path turns south just before you reach the Daymark, avoiding another dangerous cliff edge, and joins the road down to the harbour. The long narrow inlet is unusual, but the protective pier which extends over the rocks on the south side is now out of bounds; too many people have been swept off by waves breaking over.

---

27 **Portreath to Hayle (White Hart Hotel)**   **OS E104 & E102 (V) Portreath**

Grading: Strenuous in parts   Distance -   19.9   365.3   12.4   226.9

See also our Portreath to Hayle Path Description.

There are shops, cafes and bed and breakfast accommodation in Portreath, but the beach is small in comparison with most on this coast. To gain the southbound path go round the harbour to the beach car park, then to the right up Battery Hill. Where this road drops to the beach again at the western end, the Coast Path branches left up the valley. In approximately 5 yards (5 m) there is a low National Trust sign marking Western Hill. The official Coast Path begins with well made steps and leads round Western Hill; you have views from here after your initial effort to gain the cliff top.

At Bassett's Cove you go through a big car park and start several miles of easy cliff top walking. There are practically no signs, but there are only two points at which you are likely to go astray: for 1.5 miles (2.5 km) you get closer to the road and then start to get away from it again; after a further 0.5 mile (800 m) you should observe a small field ahead and to your left; here you have to fork right and then turn right.

You pass Hell's Mouth which has a seasonal cafe just across the road, then when you are approaching another field you come out onto a track where you turn right, but this time do not take the next right as it is a beach path only.

There is then a very pleasant walk around Navax and Godrevy Points; there are good views out to sea, ahead to St Ives and what to many is a surprise southwards. You then have to negotiate a big car park but by keeping well to seaward you can miss most of it and the road that leads to it.

You will find Godrevy Cafe, which is open from 10am till sunset during November to February and from 10am till 6pm the rest of the year. It also closes every Monday, except for bank holiday Mondays, and on Christmas Day and Boxing Day. To find the Red River footbridge leave the car park's southwestern corner along a board walk. You will see the bridge to your left. After crossing it walk seaward along the bank of the river.

The walking is easy along the shingle bank which takes you towards a lifeguard hut. You then begin a stretch following way-posts which are well sited and lead you accurately, provided you follow the arrows carefully. As the waymarks sometimes become firewood for barbecues and as the path zigzags, you may find yourself heading too far inland, in which case you just head for the sea.

Once Black Cliff is behind you, avoid taking the route to the beach and walk towards a chalet called Silver Spray. Leave this house to your right and walk along a line of chalets on your left. Keep straight on. You soon go through a car park and take the track which follows the old quay. You then cross a swing bridge and turn right into Hayle and continue on to the White Hart Hotel.

28 | Hayle to St Ives (Western Pier) OS E102 (T) Hayle (Trains); (V) Lelant (Trains)

Grading: Moderate   Distance -   9.0   374.3   5.6   232.5

See also our Hayle to Pendeen Watch Path Description.

Distance is measured from the railway viaduct / the White Hart Hotel at Hayle, around the estuary to Lelant then along the coast to St Ives.

Note that between Lelant and Marazion there is a cross peninsula path, St Michael's Way. This could be used to make a circular trip around Penwith by walking round the coast and then coming back inland from Penzance or Marazion to Carbis Bay.

From the viaduct, the quickest but dreariest route is straight along the main road, Carnsew Road. There is a longer but somewhat more attractive alternative not to be missed by bird watchers. Go along the road passing the 30 decontrol sign and at the end of the long building on the right is a footpath signposted 'The Weir half a mile'. At the end of a tall hedge bear right, then bear left by a bridge. Then as the ground widens bear left again to walk along a lagoon embankment. Presently you come out again on the main road and have to turn right. Whichever way you did that first stretch from Hayle, turn right on the A3074 signposted St Ives, passing the Old Quay House.

Here again is decision time as for some incredible reason the official path continues along the A3074 road through Lelant. At the end of the main street, where the main road bears left, you go ahead on a minor road to the church. If you wish to do this, fair enough, but we recommend a quieter alternative of the same length below.

After the Old Quay House go along the road passing under the railway bridge. Then turn right, signposted 'St Ives Park and Ride'. When you come to a toilet block cut through to the road on your left in front of the price board for the car park. Follow the road to your right which eventually comes out at Lelant Church.

At the church continue on the same line, go ahead across the golf course and under the railway again. Here turn left to proceed along the seaward side of the railway. Eventually you come onto a pedestrian level crossing and then bear right; on the descent avoid two beach paths on your right.

About 200 yards (185 m) before Carbis Bay there is an opportunity to go down to the beach and save yourself one last hill. If you stay with the path you go up to join a road and turn right down this. Circle round on the inland side of the cafe complex to leave Carbis Bay on a tarmac path above the beach but to seaward of the hotel.

Ascend, crossing a railway footbridge, then keep ahead avoiding the path on the left. Continue along ignoring 'Private road pedestrians only' on the right. The path becomes a minor road where the road bears left and there is another private road on your right; go ahead. Cross the railway again on a more substantial old fashioned bridge to bear right and downhill. You come down to Porthminster Cafe and then you can walk either side of the little park, continuing along below the railway station.

29 | St Ives to Pendeen Watch (Lighthouse)   OS E102 (T) St Ives (Trains)

Grading: Severe   Distance -   22.3   396.6   13.9   246.4

See also our Hayle to Pendeen Watch Path Description.

You are now starting on the longest and most deserted stretch of coast on the whole South West Coast Path, so think about accommodation. Out of season you will have to walk three whole sections, 22 miles (35 km), even in season two sections, 17 miles (27 km), before you find refreshment on the path. You can divert as listed below inland but this will increase the distance and all suggestions are subject to some seasonal closing and opening hours. There is not even a telephone box on the path. It is magnificent walking, but do not start out unprepared.

Refreshment possibilities are Zennor, Bosigran Farm, Pendeen/Botallack and St Just. There is sometimes a mobile snack wagon in Cape Cornwall car park (on the path).

One other warning, the path is often rough and rocky, the terrain is severe and in places after rain surprisingly boggy; few will average 2 miles (3 km) an hour; in other words it will take you longer than you expect.

Many use St Ives as a staging post; if however you should just wish to walk through, continue along the path below the railway station by which you enter. This becomes a tarmac lane which proves to be called The Warren at its end. Keep as close as you can to the harbour until you reach its north west corner. Here you have a choice; the purists will stay with the harbour and walk out round what is called The Island or St Ives Head; it is a pleasant walk. The less pure or perhaps those with still a lot of miles to cover can cut the corner by following signs to the Tate Gallery - this will bring you out behind Porthmeor Beach. Those going out to The Island can walk right round the harbour to turn left signposted 'The Museum'.

You can walk round The Island but the interesting little St Nicholas Chapel is on the high point in the middle. When you have completed your circuit you turn right to pass along in front of the Tate Gallery.

Go along behind the beach passing the Tate Gallery ignoring the ramp going down to the beach. The road starts to rise; there is a car park on your right and the path you want starts to bear off right by some public conveniences. You pass a bowling green and continue along the deteriorating tarmac path out into the country.

One place where it is easy to go wrong because of inadequate signposting is shortly after Clodgy Point on Burthallan Cliff; a path goes inland here and currently it is better marked than the main Coast Path.

The Coast Path cuts behind the National Trust property of Pen Enys Point; if you should have time on your hands, it is a pleasant extension.

If the weather is clear, Carn Naun Point is the place to look back and gloat at what you have done. A little later, be careful just before the stream, where you should avoid a path down to the beach. You should also ignore a path running inland just after the stream. Look for seals out on the Carracks - they are often there.

You pass the old mine building at Treen Cove and come out behind Gurnard's Head. Here again if you have time it is a splendid diversion out to the Head but so often walkers are pressed for time and cut across the neck.

The area around Porthmeor Cove is particularly spectacular if you can take your eyes briefly off where you are putting your feet!

As you drop off Carn Veslan, look ahead to the ridge of Bosigran Cliff and aim for the high point (not the big hill inland with the tower). The path drops then starts to bear left uphill, crosses through a ruined wall then bears right. Shortly you do go left up another clear path but in only a few yards turn right up a more indistinct path heading for the high point. As you get nearer you pass round to the left of it to drop into the valley. Here you go across a main track used by climbers and on across a little stone bridge. You go straight up the other side, only bearing right again as you approach the top wall.

On Rosemergy cliff there is a currently unmarked four way junction; go straight ahead.

30 | Pendeen Watch to Cape Cornwall (Car Park)   OS E102 Inland (V) Pendeen; Inland (V) St Just

Grading: Moderate   Distance -   6.5   403.1   4.0   250.4

See also our Pendeen Watch to Porthcurno Path Description.

Remember what was said about refreshment in section 29.

The official path from Pendeen Watch goes along the road to the far end of the row of coastguard cottages and turns right.

There is a better unofficial coastal route from Pendeen Watch which you can find by walking along to the right of the road and going down along the cliffs as the road bears away from the coast. Naturally avoid the marked and fenced-off mine shaft. Presently you come opposite a close inshore islet, The Enys, with a broken-down cairn on the top. Follow the path over the shoulder to join the official route by turning right over the stream.

The route is well-defined and brings you to the old Levant Mine dressing floors. A minor inland diversion is recommended to Geevor Mine, where you will find a museum, refreshments and toilets.

Refreshments may also be obtained a pleasant 0.75 mile (1200 m) walk away by turning left at the Levant Beam Engine up a track that becomes Levant Road, into Trewellard where there is a pub, and, a few steps on the left, a seasonal tea room.

After the Levant Mine the path bears right along tracks which are not coastal and what few signs there are you may trip over but are unlikely to see! Watch for the turning out to Kenidjack Castle- it is now properly signed.

Out on Kenidjack Castle, the path goes down to a stile and reaches a track where you are signed left. You leave this track at a sign directing you right, into the valley. Continue into the valley to a cottage to bear right and cross a footbridge. The path then bears right to a junction by a ditch. The official path bears left, zigzagging uphill to turn right at the top. An easy alternative, although somewhat overgrown in places, continues right. If you take this, proceed along the path; just before a small piece of ruined wall on your left, scramble up a few yards to turn right on a similar path above, which leads to the road.

When you reach the road whichever way you came you must turn down it. The official path goes down towards Cape Cornwall but does not go out onto it. Therefore those in a hurry may prefer to turn left just before the car park, but be careful if you want refreshment as the snack wagon, if it is there, will be down in the car park. Alternatively if you have the time, go out on the Cape; it is a wonderful spot owned by the National Trust for 57 good reasons and open to all. It was once considered to be 'Land's End' so maybe it has had a lucky escape!

31   Cape Cornwall to Sennen Cove (Beach Car Park)   OS E102

| Grading: Moderate | Distance - | 8.1 | 411.2 | 5.0 | 255.4 |

See also our Pendeen Watch to Porthcurno Path Description.

After Cape Cornwall you climb up the track to Ballowall Barrow; the road bears off left but the Coast Path goes ahead. This is probably one of the grandest sections of the whole coast path.

In the Cot Valley, turn right onto the road and follow it to the car park at the bottom where a National Trust granite sign points you across the stream.

At Carn Barges the path takes a little inland loop to avoid the worst of the sand dunes. If the tide is out a quicker option is to walk along the firm sand to Sennen Cove (all year round refreshments available).

32   Sennen Cove to Porthcurno (Beach)   OS E102 (V) Sennen Cove

| Grading: Moderate | Distance - | 10.6 | 421.8 | 6.6 | 262.0 |

See also our Pendeen Watch to Porthcurno Path Description.

Leaving Sennen Cove you pass the Round House; go on into the car park area and turn left at the public toilets. Proceed ahead shortly to turn right and then head for the battlemented look-out.

Paths from Sennen to Land's End and for several miles beyond are so ubiquitous that it is impossible usually to give precise directions, you just follow the coast and your fancy and are unlikely to go seriously astray. There has in time past been publicity in the national press about footpath access to Land's End. This in no way concerns the Coast Path which is as freely available as it has been for years.

Regarding the Land's End complex itself, you have two options. If you want to use the cafes or other facilities head straight for it. If you wish to pretend it is not there, though that may be difficult, keep right out on the coast and only look out to sea! For what it is worth the official route goes via Gleeb Cottage with its collection of animals rather than using the path nearer the sea.

The short length just before Nanjizal Cove is perhaps the best bit of a very fine section; if you are lucky enough to pass that way in early spring you will see that it was once a bulb growing area. After you have crossed the stream do not turn right at once but proceed ahead for 30 to 40 yards (28 - 36 m) then turn right.

After a climb you are heading out to Gwennap Head and Tol-Pedn-Penwith. Tol-Pedn means the holed headland and it is spectacular. To find the hole, proceed up to the Coastwatch hut and walk on a bearing of 140 degrees for 153 yards (140 m), then walk along a path which bears 190 degrees. UNLESS YOU INTEND TO BE VERY CAUTIOUS, DO NOT GO TO LOOK FOR THE HOLE: GREAT CARE IS REQUIRED. You drop down over a natural bridge with the hole on your left - walk round it, do not fall down it and then leave again on the obvious path which soon climbs back on the cliff top; you do not have to go back the way you came.

At Porthgwarra, if you turn down the slipway it is possible to make a short diversion by way of a tunnel through which boats were once hauled. The only snag with this innocent entertainment is that you will have bypassed the seasonal cafe above. If you use the cafe turn first right afterwards.

Although the path from Porthgwarra leaves by an inland route, you can walk out round Carn Scathe if you wish. To do this, when you have turned down from the cafe bear right just before granite gate posts between the cliff top and a garden. The first few yards are overgrown but you will soon be glad you went that way. When you get back to the main path turn right.

After climbing out of Porthgwarra the path levels off and stays with the cliff tops. As you descend towards Porth Chapel Beach take a short excursion out onto a granite point for glorious views of the beach. Returning to the path it descends to the back of the beach passing by St Levan's Holy Well. Do not continue down to the beach, unless you want a swim, but turn off left above it. Another rewarding diversion from the official path is out and around the headland of Pedn-mên-an-mere.

You come out into the car park behind the Minack Theatre through an unusual kissing gate. Go through the car park to leave at the other end on a path parallel to and behind the Theatre entrance. There are various warning notices but you would need to be very infirm or suffer from vertigo not to be able to go down the steps. At the bottom turn left and do not, unless you want a swim, go down to the beach but keep along the path contouring above the beach.

In Porthcurno there is a good cafe usually open from Easter to the end of the season, but you will have to make a short detour left up the valley to reach it. Also, further up the valley, is an excellent museum to celebrate that Porthcurno was once the world centre of communications.

33 Porthcurno to Lamorna Cove (Harbour)   OS E102

| Grading: Strenuous | Distance - | 8.8 | 430.6 | 5.5 | 267.5 |

See also our Porthcurno to Penzance Path Description.

There is again fine walking in this section and some of it easy going; however parts of it are not easy and it may well take longer than you expect.

If you have visited the cafe you can take the old path and miss out Percella Point but the views from it over Porthcurno are spectacular. After Percella Point the official path is way inland with fields between it and the cliff top. How it can be named 'the coast path' is anybody's guess. However, you will not be cheated out of a more seaward path because the National Trust has a splendid coastal route. So before you get to those fields, watch out for a path on your right leading seaward of the official route. That is the one this Association calls 'a coast path'. You can even divert from that to drop down to Pendvounder Beach for a swim. Further east along Treen Cliff this path rejoins the official one.

The next chance of a diversion is at Treryn Dinas, which is an extra not to be missed by anyone who likes a scramble, to go up and onto the famous Logan Rock.

Unfortunately you have to go back inland again to continue on your way to Penberth, a scenic gem. Cross the slipway, passing the old capstan and go up the other side outside the house to climb a cove-side path. You come up to a headland which is worth another ten minute stop.

Around St Loy the authorities have so far failed to make the good path they should, so you therefore get shunted inland then have to use what in wet weather can be a very mucky path to get to the beach. There is no path at all for a few yards, but in response to representations by this Association, a path of sorts has been formed by the authorities along the bouldery beach, but watch out for the turn inland again after about 55 yards (50 m); we have had reports of a walker missing this in misty weather and getting cut off by the tide.

Be careful on Carn Barges not to be diverted onto the inland path to Lamorna; the official and better route is round the coast. Look for the cross just before Lamorna unless you are in too much of a rush to get to the seasonal cafe.

34 | Lamorna Cove to Penzance (Railway Station)   OS E102 (V) Mousehole; (V) Newlyn

| Grading: Strenuous and then easy | Distance - | 9.7 | 440.3 | 6.0 | 273.5 |

See also our Porthcurno to Penzance Path Description.

After the cafe you bear right behind the harbour and cross the bridge. You go up past a most complicated waymark which, unless you look at it carefully, almost sends you the wrong way. However keep right but with only one house still on your right.

Few find the right route into Mousehole because it is never signed properly. We will describe it here in case you would like to join that exclusive bunch. Descend the hill passing the Wild Bird Hospital on your left. There is a post box on your right with a coast path sign pointing the way you have come but not the way you are going! After 33 yards (30 m) turn right opposite 'Lowena', and at the sign for Merlin Place, head towards the rocks, St Clement's Isle, which you can see out to sea. Just before the foreshore bear left along a terrace and fork right into a car park. Go to the bottom right end of the car park to continue briefly along the harbour side. You then have to turn in again left and then first right. However those with an interest in history before turning right should go forward past the house with pillars to read the plaque on the other side. The turn right brings you out on to a busier street; bear right along it to come behind the harbour again.

The official route leaving Mousehole goes up a narrow road without pavements but we suggest you do not. At the other end of the harbour, go into and pass through the car park there, down a ramp and along a concrete path. Go round the corner and up steps past a lifebuoy. At the top turn right along the pavement.

On approaching Newlyn, as you are a pedestrian you can use the NO ENTRY road or, even better, follow the right hand pavement as it slopes down, looking as though it is a private entrance, and continue just below the road.

Go round the back of Newlyn Harbour passing the War Memorial then bear right over the little bridge, with the Seaman's Mission on the right. A diversion a few yards upstream takes you to the award winning Pilchard Works, a working museum. Over the bridge bear right to come out once again behind the beach. After you have passed the tennis courts or remains of them, the path comes back to the road; here you go across the corner of the beach to go up steps and walk along the promenade.

At the end of the promenade pass the swimming pool and continue round to pass Penzance Harbour and on to the railway station.

35 | Penzance to Marazion (Market Place)   OS E102 (T) Penzance (Trains)

| Grading: Easy | Distance - | 5.4 | 445.7 | 3.4 | 276.9 |

See also our Penzance to Porthleven Path Description

Note that between Lelant and Marazion there is a cross-peninsula path, St Michael's Way. This could be used to make a circular trip around Penwith by walking round the coast and then coming back inland from Penzance or Marazion to Carbis Bay.

Currently under construction is a much improved route which leaves the station car park and follows the top of the sea wall to join the official route near the heliport. If this new path has not been installed when you get there your route is from the bottom of Market Jew Street going out onto the main road alongside the railway station, but the pavement runs out on the seaward side, so it is better to keep landward for a while. When you get to the B3311, cross over and later you join the A30 at the end of the Penzance ring road. Just before the heliport is a footbridge on your right, which you cross, and the Coast Path now goes along the top of the sea wall towards Marazion.

An alternative to this boring road walk is available. If you are fortunate enough to be leaving Penzance when the tide is low enough (low water neaps are not low enough), you will find a walkway behind the bus station. To find the start, having crossed the swing bridge by the harbour, head for the red navigation buoy at the far side of the car park on your right. Just beyond this buoy is the start of the walkway. At the far end drop down to the beach for about 0.5 mile (800 m) till a ramp takes you up to join the official route near the heliport.

As you pass the cafe known as 'The Station', you emerge onto the road and head for Marazion. Just before the large white Marazion sign, cut through to the right and after a few yards you will cross a pedestrian bridge just seaward of the road bridge. You now go just seaward of the fields/car parks and then up a side road to join the main road.

36 | Marazion to Prussia Cove (Bessy's Cove)   OS E102 (V) Marazion

Grading: Moderate   Distance -   6.8   452.5   4.2   281.1

See also our Penzance to Porthleven Path Description.

Walkers are treated badly at the beginning of this section, as there is no path at all for a while and then the first coastal length is on a beach.

You go up the road in Marazion, zigzagging if you wish to use a pavement, and pass the 40 sign. When just ahead is the sign which thanks you for driving carefully, turn right into a driveway. As the driveway bears right into a private house, you go left down a little concrete staircase and then follow the path down to the shoreline. At the bottom you are on a beach, walk along to ascend some hideous metal steps.

There is a short temporary diversion for a cliff fall which starts at Trenow Cove. Follow the track indicated on the notice for 274 yards (250 m) and look out for a low yellow arrow pointing you back to the coast.

After that you should have no trouble getting to Perranuthnoe where there are refreshments in season. The path turns inland here behind some houses, comes out onto the road to go up the lane opposite. Go right at the fork passing Blue Burrow Cottage and bear right.

When you get back to the coast do not go down the track to the beach but turn left into the next field. At Cudden Point the path cuts slightly inland but then the true Coast Path goes seaward again before Little Cudden.

At Bessy's Cove the path goes up to join a track by a letter box. Continue ahead bearing right to turn right over a stone stile beside a massive gate. The official route is down the path but the parallel track to its left is easier.

37 | Prussia Cove to Porthleven (Harbour)   OS E102 & E103

Grading: Strenuous   Distance -   10.3   462.8   6.4   287.5

See also our Penzance to Porthleven Path Description.

The path at Prussia Cove is quite a surprise, a sunken lane between two large stone buildings. You continue along a lane with the old coastguard row up on your left to pass through a gate, after which the track becomes a path and you should fork right at the first junction.

The path later becomes a green track down to Praa Sands where there are plenty of opportunities for refreshment in season.

The presently poorly marked route takes you down on the beach to leave it again as soon as you have passed the beach cafes up wooden steps. At the top turn right and proceed along to turn left to the well marked path through the sand dunes, shortly to turn right along the road through the estate.

If you do not wish to go down on the beach there is nothing to stop you turning left after the first cafe you come to; go inland past the public conveniences and then turn back right through the car park to reach the coast. Then proceed as above from the top of the wooden steps. If you like beach walking and the tide is out you can walk the length of the beach.

Assuming you have gone through the estate, bear right at the other end to pick up the path just inland of the big stones in the road.

At Rinsey Head the path bears inland cutting off the point. You pass an old railway coach and at the top turn left and then immediately right, going through the National Trust car park. As you drop down you should see two paths ahead, one going uphill which you do not want, the other going down, which you do. Pass the restored engine house to pick up the path below it on the other side.

At Trewavas Head the path bears inland of the old mine ruins; this used to be difficult to follow but recently waymarking has been improved.

As you approach Porthleven the path becomes semi-tarmac. You pass a cross erected in memory of those buried on the cliffs in unconsecrated ground. You go through a gate, or round the gatepost to join a lane, and bear right as you reach the main road to go down to the harbour.

38 | Porthleven to Mullion Cove (Harbour)   OS E103 (V) Porthleven

Grading: Moderate   Distance -   11.4   474.2   7.1   294.6

See also our Porthleven to The Lizard Path Description.

At Porthleven as so often you have to walk right round the back of the harbour and out the other side. You go beyond the battlemented tower-like building to keep up the coastal road, using Mounts Road although it says it is a cul-de-sac.

Shortly after the last building on the right, a hotel, turn left off the track into the National Trust property Parc-an-als Cliff to avoid a landfall. Over the top you pick up the track again to proceed on and down to the beach.

If you have plenty of time there is a walking route right around Loe Pool, the biggest natural lake in Cornwall.

As you cross Loe Bar look for the path going up just to the right of the field but divert to see the white cross on your right. You pick up the path you want on 126 degrees from the cross. After the path levels out you pass a wooden seat and about 100 yards (90 m) after this, fork right to pick up the old route.

At Gunwalloe Fishing Cove you come out onto a gravelly road; do not take the first right which goes down to the beach but bear right on the second turning to pass inland of a house. At the top of the hill there is a stile where walking gardeners should look left.

Above Halzephron Cove you bear round to join the old road. Turn right shortly before you come to a barrier. You enter National Trust Halzephron Cliff - do not turn right immediately but continue ahead to turn right just before the next field gate.

At Gunwalloe Church Cove there is an alternative. If you want to see the church, and it is interesting, when you join the road go right and after you have seen the church you can usually cross the beach and its stream.

If a church visit is not for you, the correct route bears left aiming for buildings which prove to be public conveniences and a very seasonal cafe. There is a sign where you join the road but it is badly sited so is not obvious. Proceed down the road with the National Trust Gunwalloe Towans sign on your right. Bear left off the road just before a turning space. Cross a bridge over a stream and turn right round the back of the beach. The path is narrow until you come to a track where you turn left uphill.

At the top there is a small car park; as soon as you have gone through this you can bear right to walk along the cliff tops and so miss a length of tarmac road.

There is a seasonal cafe at Poldhu Cove. You walk round the back of the beach on the road and go up the drive of the residential care home. Turn right off the driveway shortly before you get to the big house.

Skirt around the back of Polurrian Cove to go up the steps, then take a track to turn right on a road. Where the road bears left proceed ahead on a path. If you are a purist the coast path goes in front of the old coastguard lookout, but this bit of path is seldom cleared.

Just past the Mullion Cove Hotel the path veers right, through the car parking spaces opposite starting by an old cannon. At the bottom turn left.

39 | Mullion Cove to The Lizard (Lighthouse)   OS E103

Grading: Moderate   Distance -   10.9   485.1   6.3   300.9

See also our Porthleven to The Lizard Path Description.

This is a wonderful, spectacular section with lots of interest, and it can be accomplished without great effort. Unless the weather is inclement you will certainly enjoy this stretch. If you can arrange the transport it makes a spectacular long half day excursion.

You go up the road; a very little way turn right and then right again.

After Mullion Cove in several places there are alternative paths but usually it makes little difference which you take, except as mentioned below.

After Parc Bean Cove going up Lower Predannock Cliff you want the higher path not the lower and at the top bear right.

After Vellan Cliff just before Gew-Graze, the path veers slightly inland for a stile.

Taking the path down to Kynance Cove, as you go down aim for the further headland you can see which is Lizard Point. Later you will see a sign close to the sea where you have to turn left; go down further to cross a wide concrete bridge by a house.

There is a good, long season cafe at Kynance Cove. Unless the tide is right in, the quickest route is to cross the few yards at the back of the beach and go up the steps the other side. If the tide is right in you have to go up the drive before the cafe and bear right at the top.

Leave the car park just to the right of the public toilets.

Lizard Town is exceptionally well footpathed so if you are lodging there you have a great many options.

Turn left above the Most Southerly Cafe and go along in front of the lighthouse.

40 | The Lizard to Coverack (Dolor Point)   OS E103 1 mile to (V) Lizard Town

Grading: Moderate but strenuous in parts   Distance -   17.1   502.2   10.6   311.5

See also our The Lizard to Helford Path Description.

A word of warning; old stone stiles are made of the local serpentine which can prove very slippery when wet, so take care on wet polished rock.

Unless you suffer from vertigo, do not miss diverting right shortly after the lighthouse to see the spectacular Lion's Den, which although is only about 20 yards (18 m) off the path, is still missed by many.

You pass Housel Bay Hotel and later go through a kissing gate. The path is odd in that it keeps to the top edge of the field until the next gate, where it turns to the seaward edge again.

You pass the old Lloyd's Signal Station and come out on a drive by a house. You go along this only a short way and the Coast Path then takes off right.

At Kilcobben Cove you come just inland of the top building of the lifeboat station, walk round it and go down the first little flight of steps but then go forward and not down the long flight of steps to the lifeboat.

At Church Cove where refreshment is available, go across diagonally behind one building to go through beside a big gate. Avoid the next four right turns to go uphill and over a stile.

After Polgwidden watch for a sharp right turn going along in front of an isolated house; the wrong path goes forward and looks more impressive.

Those with a taste for adventure and a resilience to scratches may like to divert down the cliff on the southern end of The Devil's Frying Pan before Cadgwith. It is possible to go over the top of the natural arch and so down to the bottom of the pit. This is the way to really appreciate the size of this natural feature but we stress it is only for the adventurous with nerves of steel.

You pass the National Trust Devil's Frying Pan sign and the true Coast Path is diagonally ahead, down steps into the car park and out the other end to turn right. In fact it has lately been signposted avoiding the car park; the choice is yours. Whichever way you went you drop down a lovely path through a garden. Watch for the right turn just after you have gone over a stone stile next to a metal gate.

You drop into Cadgwith behind the beach where there is a chance of refreshment, and then start up the hill staying with the road to turn first right just past Veneth Cottage.

After Enys Head there is a poorly marked section: you come to a fork where you go left, soon there is another right turn which you ignore, then you come down to a gate where you turn right. Go down until you see the National Trust Poltesco sign on the left. Here turn right going down steps and over a bridge. Avoid both the next right turns unless you wish to see the old Poltesco serpentine works. At the next junction, as you go up, bear right and again at the next junction. Later you go through a golf course area at the end of which you bear right. You come out on a road where you turn right. If the road is busy you can presently go across and take a permissive path to the beach, but it is not as rewarding as you might hope.

At Kennack Sands (refreshments in season) the path is behind the beach towards the toilets and then is well marked behind the two beaches. If the tide is well out you can walk along both beaches to the far end but as the proper path, at the time of writing, is well maintained there is little gained. What you do need to watch for at the far end of the second beach is that you take the Coast Path which looks fairly insignificant starting up nearly on the cliff edge; there is a bigger, wide path going inland but do not take it. There is another minor junction shortly where you keep right again.

Care should be taken in front of Borgwitha and behind the cliff castle Carrick Luz, because you cut across the neck of the peninsula and do not go inland or seaward. Improved waymarking should mean that you do not now go astray.

There is a very steep if scenic drop to Downas Cove and up the other side. After Beagles Point there is another smaller drop; cross a bridge and go up what is almost a stone chute the other side. At the top turn right.

After Black Head there is a very fine viewpoint for looking ahead along the South Cornish Coast. The path has been much improved and for a long way goes along the top of the cliffs. After you pass a piggery the route gets complicated. You come to a track, bear left but after about 30 yards (28 m) go ahead on a path where the track bears left.

You cross an old stone stile, pass an old fashioned pump and come to a grassy area with caravans. Here turn sharp right and turn right again when you get to the tarmac drive. There is a shorter, alternative route if needed: when you get to the drive, turn left along it, and very soon divert off right on a field path to Coverack. Go along the left side of this until just before a sign forbidding access. Here turn sharp left and go down steps; there is a junction here left which is a quick but incorrect route, right is correct and more scenic. Go down to the next junction where ahead is Chynall's Point, a cul-de-sac but part of the Coast Path. Left is your route towards Coverack.

As you enter Coverack you reach a tarmac path; turn right and go down to join a road. If you wish to do all the Coast Path, there is then a little loop that many miss. 20 yards (18 m) down the road the path goes away right above a children's playground. The path then looks as though it is going to end, but press on over a slight rise to go down steps and turn left in front of a house.

Keep right of the back of a pub into the car park, turn left and left again to pass the front of the same pub.

41 | Coverack to Helford (Ferry)   OS E103 (V) Coverack

Grading: Moderate   Distance -   21.1   523.3   13.1   324.6

See also our The Lizard to Helford Path Description.

This distance includes the walk around Gillan Creek. If you arrive there at low tide and paddle across, deduct 2 miles (3.2 km).

Note: Evening meals can present a problem in Helford. At busy periods the Shipwright's Arms (01326 231235) will only serve pre-booked meals. The Riverside Restaurant (01326 231443) is an alternative. There is also the Rose Tea Gardens which serves meals but shuts earlier. Think about this before leaving Coverack or you may go to bed hungry.

In Coverack the Coast Path continues behind the harbour and the beach and where the main road bears inland, go ahead up the small tarmac road. The tarmac ends just before a small rise; go over this and start to drop down and look for a path turning off right just before a gate across the road.

The path out to Lowland Point is improved, but the further you go the less evidence of path there is. However the basic ploy is to keep close to the shore, going east until you have to turn north at the point.

After Lowland Point the Coast Path goes through Dean Quarry. This Association fought hard to get the path on the coast here rather than a long diversion inland. Heed the notice for times of blasting; at these times the path will be closed but you can use the diversion if travelling north.

Most of the quarry area is well signposted, but it is important that when you come up level with the first building, you start down the steep ramp to the beach - the footpath goes left off this. Towards the end of the quarry area, signs are more scarce but keep with the track close above the sea to go down on to the beach at Godrevy Cove.

Walk just over half way along the beach, crossing the stream bed which sometimes has water but is often dry, then turn half left to circumvent a marshy area and pick up the path at the back of the beach. Here turn left until you can turn inland through fields. At present the correct path is a sunken, usually muddy, lane on your right, so that most stay in the fields to join the track up to Rosenithon.

At the T-junction in Rosenithon turn right and go up the hill. The road bears right and just after this the footpath takes off left into a field. Cross one field and a traditional Cornish stile, surely the forerunner of the modern cattle grid. Cross two more fields in the same direction and surprisingly, the stile is just below the gate you come to.

Turn left on the road then first right down into Porthoustock. From Porthoustock to Porthallow the official route again goes inland to avoid the now unused quarries around Pencra Head and Porthkerris Point. However, there is a coast path.

Coastal Route
In Porthoustock, keep right of the telephone box and pass the entrance to the beach, forking left up a bank passing in front of a thatched cottage. You soon come to a big metal gate; the pedestrian access is just to the right round the wall.

Continue along the track and take the left fork approximately 150 yards (137 m) beyond the northern end of a disused quarry, which leads to a steep uphill slope. 20 yards (18 m) beyond the top of the slope, fork right for the shorter route to Porthkerris beach, except around high water spring tides. The simpler route for any state of the tide is to proceed up along the track for a further 450 yards (410 m), and turn right onto another track through a field which leads down to behind Porthkerris beach.

Walk straight up the hill opposite, passing the way up to a restaurant on the left. Where the road bears left, carry straight on through two fields parallel to the coast to a kissing gate. Proceed ahead up the path and then steeply down to the beach at Porthallow.

Official Route
You leave Porthoustock going up the hill, but soon, where the road bears right, go ahead on a track. You pass houses on your right, the track ends and you keep ahead into a field. Here turn steeply up the field 302 degrees joining the right hand field bank at the top. Keep close to the bank to a sunken stile in the corner then slightly more right 338 degrees to another sunken stile just left of the gate.

Bear left on the road which later bears left to Trenance; here turn right. At the next T junction look for the footpath ahead and a few yards to your right. Go down alongside a vineyard to join the road where you turn right down to Porthallow. There are seasonal refreshments available here.

You leave Porthallow by taking the second turning on to the beach and immediately turning left to go along the back of the foreshore and up steps, bearing right at the first junction.

As you approach Nare Point, ignore a metal kissing gate which you pass on the right to shortly turn left along a one-time track which served the lookout. You go through a gateway and when the track bears uphill, proceed ahead across a footbridge.

After the second National Trust property `The Herra', you come to a small beach where you go across the back. You come to a second beach, Flushing Cove, where you turn right on a path behind the beach.

A very short distance beyond the beach, a footpath takes off left and it is decision time. If you know the tide is in and you want to walk round, turn left.

Gillan Creek - Walking Round
It is about 2.25 miles (3.5 km), say an hour, easy walking but nearly all road. This distance is extra to the mileage shown for the section. If time is of the essence, you can go via Manaccan and be in Helford in 3 miles (5 km), but that is of course not walking the Coast Path.

Go up the grass-centred concrete track to and along a made-up road. At a left bend the Coast Path is signed to the right of a pebbledashed house. Proceed along a short stretch of a narrow, possibly overgrown, path into a field. Keep to the hedge on the left to a six bar gate, then go diagonally across the next field over a stile just left of another gate. Turn sharp left and make for the gate just in front of a white bungalow. Go through to the farm road, then right up to the main road. Turn right here down to Carne and right again beyond the creek head to St Anthony.

Gillan Creek Crossing
No ferry but it can usually be forded from one hour before Low Tide to one hour after. Predicted low water is 15 minutes earlier than shown in the Tide Tables. But do proceed with care.

There are two possible crossing places. Proceed until you can go no further along the path by the river, descend steps to the beach and wade across towards two caravans on the far shore.

A little further upstream you can cross part way on stepping stones in two sections: however this is not the easy option it sounds because they are extremely slippery and do not go across the whole river. It is advisable to carry handfuls of sand to scatter onto the stepping stones and even then be careful. If you do not use the stepping stones, it is possible to paddle across.

Once across turn right to pass in front of the church. Turn left up the hill. About 10 yards (9 m) past a mounting block on the left, look for a path going off at an angle right, take this and turn first right. You may then see the sign which should be at the bottom.

Coast Path continues
For the short route you need to turn left just after the house on your right beyond the kissing gate. If you have time the circular route out around Dennis Head is rewarding. To walk this, proceed ahead into the open field along a vestigial track towards a wood, keep to the left of the wood but close to it. Pass round the back of it where you will find a stile on your left; you can complete the circuit of the head returning to the stile and then back along the right hand hedge. You pass through several fields but then watch out for the sharp and partially concealed right turn into the wood. (Dogs must be kept under strict control.)

You come out by an old railed hound enclosure to bear slightly right and then go up a tarmac drive with grass in the centre. At the top turn right down the road, turn left up steps just as you get to the drive of a house called Traeth Cottage; it is easy to miss; if you get to the shore you have missed it!

Go along the back of the car park, down the road, crossing the first bridge over the creek. Turn right and go along past The Shipwright's Arms to the ferry point.

For the statistically minded, now that we have included the Isle of Portland within the whole of the total distance for the Coast Path, you will have passed the half-way point by the time you reach the ferry point.

42 | Helford to Falmouth (Ferry Terminal)   OS E103 (V) Helford

Grading: Moderate   Distance -   **16.1**   **539.4**   **10.0**   **334.6**

See also our Helford to Falmouth Path Description.

Helford to Helford Passage - use ferry, see details below. If the ferry is not running your alternatives are probably a taxi or a walk of 13 miles (21 km). This is mostly road but you can incorporate Frenchman's Creek. (Local taxis service - Autocabs 01326 573773).

Helford Passage (Helford River). Seasonal.	April 1st to October 31st. Departs hourly -
Helford River Boats, Helford Passage,	Helford Passage on the hour and Helford 10 mins.
Nr Falmouth Tel Mawnan Smith	past the hour. 9am to 5pm daily. Summer months
01326 250770	only (July and August) runs on demand from
	9am to 9.30pm. All crossings subject to
	weather conditions.

Helford to Helford Passage (Walking route) approx. 13 miles (21 km).

This moderate to easy route, on footpaths and minor roads, is as close to the Helford River as possible.

Take the path up the hill in front of the Shipwright's Arms; you will pass houses on your right and come down to Penarvon Cove. Back at the west side of the cove you will need to turn inland. Follow this track up a road where you turn right then left onto a farm track. This will lead you to the permissive path above Frenchman's Creek, eventually descending to continue alongside it through the woods. At the head of the creek you come to a definitive footpath. This is at the sign of the permissive path to Frenchman's Creek. Take the path on the right to Withan and Mudgeon past Frenchman's Pill cottage on the left, and across a footbridge over the river. Follow the waymarked route through the woods. When you get out of the woods, aim for the far left corner of the field and take the stile with the iron wheel gate on the left. Follow the boundary on the left and over the stiles past Withan Farm, from where you head in a westerly direction, until you reach a concrete-block stile to a farm lane where you turn left. Pass Mudgeon Farm on your right. When you reach a crossroads, turn right towards Mawgan. After a short distance, the path goes downhill.

Proceed uphill and you will join the road from St Martin where you turn right, passing the ancient settlement at Gear. Going downhill, you soon reach the narrow bridge over Mawgan Creek and on the next bend, you come to Bridge Farm. Turn left and proceed up the road. When you reach the main road, turn right. Just before the church turn left at the Gwarth-an-drea sign and left at the back of the bungalow called The Oaks. When you reach the road, turn right along Gweek Drive and follow this road until you meet a road on the left with a ford, and cross the bridge and follow the road to Gweek.

From Gweek, take the road opposite the Gweek Inn past the post office and take the footpath on the right through a wooden gate, just before light industrial units. The path runs parallel to a stream and it is not very clear. You join a bridleway at the ruins of a building and need to turn right, passing Kestle Dee farm. You will meet the road at Carwythenack Chase and need to take the Constantine / Port Navas road. Follow the field edge and cross the corner of the field to the stile by the signpost. Follow the road, crossing a stream and take the footpath on the left after the stream. Follow the field edge and go over the stile in the corner of the field behind the hut. Follow the road to Nancenoy and Polwheveral. You will now have to climb uphill.

Descend from the footpath junction towards Polwheveral. At the crossroads, turn right into the Port Navas road. After about 140 yards (128 m), take the left footpath into the corner of a field and cross the field to a stile left of the gate. Follow the field edge and cross the corner of the field to the stile by the signpost. Follow the road to Port Navas. We suggest you walk through Port Navas, exploring the creek and the quay. At Trenarth Bridge, by the post box, follow the Mawnan / Falmouth sign.

At the head of Port Navas Creek is a footpath on the left to Lower Penpol. Take the next footpath on the right, just past a turning to some houses. Cross the field to a stile left of a house. Continue right up the road past Budock Vean Golf and Country Club. Turn right at the road for Helford Passage. Turn right past Dring House. At the end of the road turn left onto a new definitive footpath before 'Ridifarne' and walk down to The Bar and turn left, following the coastal path to Helford Passage. You now reach the Ferry Boat Inn at Helford Passage, where the ferry from Helford would have put you down had it been operating.

Coast Path continues
At Helford Passage go along the beach eastwards to go up the steps at the end. At Durgan bear sharp right, when you reach the track, then bear left by the old school. Go up the road past a little grassy area with a seat on the right then DO NOT turn first right; it is the second turning you want.

At the next beach you come to Porth Saxon; you go in front of the boathouse, and the path is then at the back of the shore. At the following beach, Porthallack, the path in contrast stays in the fields to go on to the beach beyond a building.

The true coast path goes out round Rosemullion Head with its fine views, but there is a short cut across its neck. You come to the National Trust Nansidwell property and shortly into a big field; go downwards and across to join the bottom hedge. The exit is in the corner. There is another path better walked going ahead but it is the wrong path. The path does not go on the beach but bears left at the last moment.

You come out onto the road at Maenporth (refreshments in season). Turn right along the road, turning right again at the other end of the beach.

There follows a 1.5 mile (2.25 km) stretch past a golf course and around Pennance Point to the outskirts of Falmouth.

On reaching the road turn right for Swanpool, there walk across the back of the beach to continue on the coast path turning right at the first junction. At Gyllyngvase Beach turn right along the road; it will not be most people's favourite walking but it is quite rewarding looking back to where you have previously been.

When you get towards the end of the sea front passing the last big hotel, The Falmouth Hotel, do not go down right but continue on the pavement beside the road until you have passed the cul-de-sac notice, then you can bear right if you wish, away from the road. However presently you will need to cross the road for the safety of the pavement around Pendennis Point.

There is a path on the right from Pendennis Head towards the docks which you can take if you wish.

You come to a T junction where you turn right, there is then a town centre sign pointing left but that is the long way round for traffic so stay with us. Go ahead under the railway bridge. The road shortly bears left and there is a pub on the right which still proclaims it has hotel stables and a motor garage.

The road bears right passing a big car park and soon becomes a shopping street. Continue until Marks & Spencers, and the next turning on the right takes you to the ferry.

| 43 | Falmouth to Place House | OS E105 (T) Falmouth (Trains); (V) St Mawes |

| No Grading | | Distance - | 0 | 539.4 | 0 | 334.6 |

See also our Falmouth to Portloe Path Description.

In season you can cross by using two ferries, see details below. The only point to watch is that depending on conditions, the first ferry takes 20 to 30 minutes for the passage.

The ferry from Falmouth to St Mawes runs the whole year round except for winter Sundays. The scarcity of public transport in winter on Sundays combined with the fact that it is a long hike, makes us advise anyone arriving in Falmouth in winter on a Sunday to take it as a day off!

The ferry from St Mawes to Place only runs in season. If you are a purist there is a reasonable walking route round of 8-9 miles (13-14 km), two sections of which are very good walking indeed, see below for details. There are about a couple of buses a day from St Mawes to Gerrans, except on Sundays, or you could consider a taxi. If the ferry is not in service you can always ask. We have heard from walkers who have been lucky enough to get a lift from local boat owners.

Falmouth/St Mawes	All year round. Weather permitting.
St Mawes Ferry Co	Summer service every 1/2 hour, Winter service
75 The Beacon Falmouth TR11 2BD	every hour.
(01326) 313201 - Office	Sundays Departs Falmouth on the hour, departs
(01326) 313587	St Mawes 1/2 past the hour.

The St Mawes Ferry Co. is prepared to land pre-organized parties of 20 or more at Place House. To do this they would need prior knowledge to lay on an extra boat. This is also dependent on the state of the tide and weather.

St Mawes/Place House (St Anthony)	Seasonal
For information please write to:	Daily - 1 May-30 September, 2001.
Mr R Balcombe	St Mawes - Place 1/2 hourly
Turks Folly, Drump Road	from 1000 to 1630 hrs. No 1300 ferry.
Redruth TR15 1PR	Place - St Mawes 1/2 hourly from
Tel: (01209) 214901	1015 to 1645 hrs. No 1315 ferry.

Walking route around the Percuil River (approx. 9 miles / 14 km)
At St Mawes, on leaving the ferry from Falmouth turn left along the road. As you approach the castle, take a minor road going left, the most prominent sign being 'St Mawes Castle car park'. If you look carefully there is also a small footpath sign amongst the clutter. Follow this minor road until you come to the National Trust's Newton Cliff, which you enter. The route follows a very scenic path along the Carrick Roads with superb views across to Falmouth and the far shore. Ignore two minor stiles on the left which lead down to small coves. You come out on a minor tarmac road to turn right. Continue along this road bearing left at the junction to pass in front of a boatyard. Immediately after passing the boatyard buildings the path bears a few yards to the right to proceed along the bank above the shore.

You come to the gate leading to the churchyard with a large sign 'Dogs on Leads Please Consecrated Ground'. Go through this gate keeping left all the way to pass the church on your right. Ignore the turning right marked 'way out' but instead keep left through a lych-gate and pass a house called Lanzeague. After its second gate the path bears right up the hill. You go through a metal gate where there is a public footpath sign 'St Just Lane' and continue uphill with views of the creek to your left. You go through another gate into a lane, in parts muddy in parts green, to finally exit onto the road.

Turn left and walk along the road for about 150 yards (135 m), ignore the first footpath on the right immediately past a house, but take the second on the right shortly afterwards. For the first field you have the hedge on the right. For the second and third it is on your left, then for the fourth it is again on your right. Take care in this fourth field, as there is a temptation as you enter to turn right; do not do this but go straight ahead to continue with the hedge on the right. Look for the sharp right turn through the hedge a little before you come to the end of the field. Descend the bank to the road, where you turn right and proceed down to meet the main A3078 at Trethem Mill.

Turn left - this is on a bridge crossing the creek - and immediately turn right up some stone steps and ascend the footpath through a wood. Coming out of the wood, cross the field on a bearing of 110. In the next field bear right on 140 and leave by a wooded track. At the top there is a stile; cross it and bear 137 diagonally across the field to a hedge and follow this to the road. Turn right down the road.

At the next junction follow the road curving round to the right past Polhendra Cottage. Here almost immediately turn left through the second gate, a metal one. There is a footpath sign if you look for it, but it is not readily apparent. Aim across on 123 to descend to the bottom of the hedge which you can see on the opposite side of the valley. Here you will find a bridge, cross it and proceed up, with the hedge on your left. At the top ascend some stone steps and cross the next two fields on 125. On reaching the road turn right into Gerrans and walk down to the church.

At the church take the left fork (not left turn) into Treloan Lane. You walk via Treloan and Rosteague, at each junction keeping straight ahead. At the house just beyond Rosteague you pass through a pedestrian gate and the path unexpectedly goes right, through a hedge gap, before continuing in the same direction but with the hedge on your left. You cross an open field to enter an enclosed lane eventually coming to the road at Porth Farm about 1.5 miles (2.4 km) from Gerrans.

The slightly quicker way is then to turn right along the road and left where there is a sign 'Footpath to Place by Percuil River' to cross a wooden bridge. The pleasanter alternative, a few yards longer, is to go ahead on the road to turn right through the gates of the Trust's Porth Farm then turn right to come to the same bridge.

Over the bridge the path turns right to follow Porth Creek and then the Percuil River, down to the low tide landing point for the ferry and soon on to Place itself. This last stretch of walking is very scenic.

44 | Place House to Portscatho (The Quay)   OS E105

| Grading: Easy | Distance - | 10.0 | 549.4 | 6.2 | 340.8 |

See also our Falmouth to Portloe Path Description.

The St Anthony Peninsula, thanks to the National Trust, offers a very good half-day circular walk. Most people will start at Porth Farm, walk to Place as already described, and then follow the coast path round St Anthony's Head and on to Towan Beach, here turning back inland to Porth Farm.

Some maps show a definitive right of way across the front of Place House; this route however is not really practical except at very low tides.

The Coast Path continues up the road at Place passing the gates of the house and shortly turn right to go behind the church. You get back to the creekside, soon to leave it again to go over behind Amsterdam Point. The path then is superb with wonderful views across the Carrick Roads. After the footbridge across the top of a one-time dam turn sharp right. Shortly turn even sharper left to go up steps and turn right again at the top. Look for the very little path forking right up to the topograph for the best viewpoint.

The path then proceeds forwards without problems to Portscatho; however, owing to the lie of the land you do not see the village until the very last moment and it always seems to take longer than you think it should.

45 | Portscatho to Portloe (Post Office)   OS E105 (V) Portscatho

| Grading: Strenuous | Distance - | 12.0 | 561.4 | 7.5 | 348.3 |

See also our Falmouth to Portloe Path Description.

You leave Portscatho going through a couple of small fields; if the tide is out you have a choice. You can start down the steps then turn right and go down to cross Porthcurnick Beach - this is slightly shorter. The reward for not turning for the beach but going up the steps opposite is that you then pass a seasonal refreshment hut.

If the tide is out it is easier to walk along Pendower Beach to Carne Beach. You can look forward to see if this is feasible as you walk down by the car park before Pendower Beach.

Having ascended Nare Head, it is possible to short cut it by veering left but, unless the weather is poor, do not do this or you will miss out on the rewarding views. Study the way the first arrow is pointing and follow its direction along the edge of the gorse. There is an unmarked path going right to the head itself. Shortly afterwards there is a post with an arrow pointing left here on a bearing of 120 degrees; if you look carefully you will see a small path going forward into the gorse - take this. This path gives the best views of Gull Rock offshore. It winds back to join the main track, where you turn right.

At the other end of the track about 200 yards (185 m) on, where it opens up, there are little ventilators; bear across right to pick up the coast again; do not stay on the track.

Another place you can go wrong is after the very steep descent off The Blouth where the path bears left and then right over a stile. There is a sign but it is badly sited so it is easy to miss and as a result a lot of people go wrong here.

At The Straythe there is a pleasant surprise for those who walked this way some years ago. A well engineered path zigzags up to replace the old uncomfortable and nearly vertical flight of steps. At the top the route is well signposted through the gardens, but you do need to turn right in the field when you get there.

There is a long descent into Portloe but at least you can see it, unlike Portscatho. Watch for the sharp left turn just as you draw nearly level with a green seat on your right. Then you want the second turning on the left to pass in front of the public toilets and so down to Portloe.

46 | Portloe to East Portholland (Car Park)   OS E105

Grading: Strenuous   Distance -   3.8   565.2   2.4   350.7

See also our Portloe to Mevagissey Path Description.

This stretch is rewarding and will give you enjoyment for your efforts.

From the quay at Portloe you can turn first right, scramble along and up some steps, to rejoin the Coast Path that way. However the true Coast Path goes up the road, turns right along another road, and then shortly leaves it down some wide steps past cottages. The official route does have the advantage that it passes the Post Office which serves cream teas.

A new path has been made in the landslip area just before West Portholland.

You can, if you wish, avoid the road walk from West to East Portholland by going forward behind the beach at West Portholland and walking along the sea wall between the two settlements. This is a little rocky at the beginning but should present no problems to any surefooted walker.

47 | East Portholland to Gorran Haven (Beach)   OS E105

Grading: Moderate   Distance -   10.3   575.5   6.4   357.1

See also our Portloe to Mevagissey Path Description.

The path starts along a one time tarmac lane from East Portholland. Turn right at the end of this lane to descend a field and continue alongside the coast. There is a path forward but if you use it, you simply get a longer stretch of road to walk to get to Porthluney Cove.

There is a seasonal cafe behind the beach in front of Caerhays Castle. Note one point, on leaving the road you cross half the first field joining a rough track close to a projecting corner of waste land. The path does not stay on the track here but turns sharp right along the fence; the badly sited marker post is usually invisible in the long grass.

From Hemmick Beach via The Dodman to Gorran Haven, it is all good walking; there are wonderful views from The Dodman in the right conditions. You can look back on triumphs past and challenges still long to come! Just north of The Dodman Cross is an 18th Century coastguard watch-house which does prove useful shelter in heavy rain.

At Little Sand Cove there is an old path cutting the corner off Pen-a-Maen Point. We do not recommend it - you climb higher and will not have such good views.

You come into Gorran Haven on Foxhole Lane, turn right into Canton and just before the beach turn left into Church Street. Proceed up this; there is a footpath loop to the right if you want a brief and better look at the beach, and turn right at the top into Cliff Road.

Gorran Haven to Mevagissey (Harbour)   OS E105 (V) Gorran Haven

Grading: Easy   Distance -   **5.7**   **581.2**   **3.5**   **360.6**

See also our Portloe to Mevagissey Path Description.

This section starts happily enough but you are beginning to leave the most remote and least spoiled section of the South Cornish coast behind.

You go up past the old coastguard row and turn right again at the top, still Cliff Road. At its end Cliff Road turns left and you go over a stile into a field.

From Turbot Point you descend to Colona Beach passing the National Trust Bodrugan's Leap sign. Turn right to pass behind the beach, do not go left when the track bears left, but proceed ahead very shortly to cross the tarmac drive to continue ahead on a footpath across the grass. At its start you are heading in a straight line for Mevagissey harbour; later it veers a little left and you pick up a hedge on your right. Continue along this hedge until it goes up to join the road where you turn right.

At the end you will find the road is called Chapel Point Lane; turn right, bear left at the sea and follow the road round past the Rising Sun.

You bear right on entering Mevagissey on Polkirt Hill. You pass buildings on your right and then enter a park; proceed through this to the other end. Turn right down the first flight of public stone steps on the right to come out on the quay close to some public toilets.

 ## Mevagissey to Charlestown (Harbour)   OS E105 & E107 (V) Mevagissey; (V) Pentewan

Grading: Strenuous   Distance -   **11.6**   **592.8**   **7.2**   **367.8**

See also our Mevagissey to Fowey Path Description.

In Mevagissey walk along the back of the harbour to turn right and then very shortly bear up left veering away from, and up above, the quayside. You come out into open playing fields, go across but aim for the extreme right end of the terrace of buildings you see opposite. You now continue on a lovely new path, which was constructed in Spring, 1999, following the 1998 cliff fall here. We are very lucky to have this path here, as the cliff fall was severe, and other solutions were looked at, which did not meet with this Association's approval.

Continue along, avoiding the right turn down some steps. The path comes out again into a field and there is a steep descent to cross a bridge. Here, turn left. You descend from Penare Point to walk behind the ruins of Portgiskey, crossing three stiles to turn right. Ignore the next stile on the right but proceed, curving right up the hill to cross a stile just before the road, at which you turn right.

You come out on to the road close to the entrance of a massive caravan park. Here you have the choice of:

1.   turning left to the main road B3273, then right towards St Austell and first right again signposted Pentewan and called West End, which is the official route, or;

2.   turning right towards the sea, then left after the public toilets along the front, then go over a bridge across the St Austell River. You then make for a stone arch ahead, and turn right to go over a narrow wooden bridge.

This route avoids the shops at Pentewan, although there is a seasonal cafe on the campsite.

Do not leave Pentewan unrefreshed as you have a long tough section ahead.

You are then faced with another choice. You can either:

A.   continue on the road through Pentewan, and take the road to the left to follow the official path (you will need to walk back from the harbour if you followed option 2 above).

B. take the Association's preferred route by turning right off the road into the harbour area just after the public toilets, and walking along the harbour to the end of the cottages where you will see a path on your left going up through gardens to link up with the Coast Path behind the cottages. (If you followed option 2 above, simply pass the winding gear, turn right immediately in front of the Pentewan Beach sign to join the path going up through the gardens.) The path through the gardens is signed as a public footpath and does not look like a public right of way, but it is!

Back on the Coast Path put this book away; you will need your energies for other things! However take it out again when you have crossed a wooden bridge in a sizeable wood.

Having crossed the bridge, you soon cross another small stream and come to a T-junction. The right turn will take you down to Hallane Mill Beach, a lovely spot for a picnic with a waterfall. The Coast Path turns left soon to turn right again to start ascending to Black Head, a superb diversionary viewpoint on a clear day. It was once a rifle range but was purchased by the National Trust, helped in a small way with a donation from this Association.

The passage of the wood behind Ropehaven can give trouble if signing is not maintained. On entering the wood you turn right taking care on this rocky path which can be slippery when damp, then left at the seat. Avoid the right fork down to a cottage and turn sharp left at the top into a narrow walled lane. Turn right on to the narrow road. The path leaves it to go into a field just beyond the little car park/lay by. After the stile which follows the long climb to Silvermine Point, keep to the fence, and don't be tempted to follow the better defined track inland.

At Porthpean Beach the sign forward can be misleading - you do in fact go down on to the promenade to walk along past toilets and a seasonal cafe. Continue to the end; it does not look likely, but there is a steep set of steps at the end to get you back on track.

Just before Charlestown is a stile leading through a high wall; you get a slightly longer walk on the coast by using it.

50 | Charlestown to Par (Polmear)　　　　　　　OS E107 (V) Charlestown

| Grading: Easy | Distance - | 7.0 | 599.8 | 4.3 | 372.1 |

See also our Mevagissey to Fowey Path Description.

The official path does not go across the dock gate at the mouth of the harbour, but provided the gate is closed most people will go that way.

You come up from the harbour keeping to the right of a house called Salamander. It is at first a tarmac track and then goes into fields. Later you come out beside a road, walk a few yards along it to turn right and then fork left.

After passing the Carlyon Bay Hotel you come out by a car park area; keep to the right of this to cross the road and continue alongside a golf course.

The clay processing industrial complex gets nearer, and you turn left just before a wall/wire netting fence. The path continues through the complex itself, giving you a detailed look at one of Cornwall's major industries. Avoid the escape route left under a low railway culvert, but continue ahead along what looks like a dead end to the road and turn right to go past the entrance to the clay works.

Continue north on the road and go under a railway viaduct to turn first right signposted A3082 Fowey, cross a level crossing and under another railway bridge. The road forks, and you should keep right to enter Par Green, which is a one-way system, and brings you into the town of Par. You pass The Good Shepherd Church on your right and Welcome Home Inn on your left.

You can then take the second path off on the right, although the National Trail waymark indicates straight on along the road. To try and make this clearer, the beginning of the path has a low concrete wall and house No. 52 (Sandroy), on the right. It soon comes to a tidal stream; bear left to walk along it, cross a road and come out in a caravan site. Keep down the right hand side, to turn left and go along the seaward side of a blue roofed building. You pass a cafe, and finally come to Polmear, where you bear right to rejoin the official path.

If you miss all this you can simply walk along Par Green, then bear right at its end to get to Polmear by main road. It is less pleasant, gives less chance of refreshment but it gets you there just the same.

Grading: Moderate   Distance -   **9.6**   **609.4**   **6.0**   **378.1**

See also our Mevagissey to Fowey Path Description.

It is a fine walk out from Polmear via Polkerris around Gribbin Head to Menabilly and so on to Fowey. The availability of public transport from Par to Fowey makes this a very practical half day excursion with lovely views nearly all the way.

The path leaves the main road at Polmear just beside the eye-catching Rashleigh Cottages. For a very short while it is also The Saints' Way; see note below*. At the first junction keep right and at the second turn right, leaving the Saints to their own devices.

As you enter Polkerris you turn right. Go down to the beach and turn left, currently no sign, to proceed up the ramp and join a zigzag path to the top.

You should have no problem then until you enter the National Trust The Gribbin property through a field gateway. There is soon a junction; bear right and you come to a pedestrian gate. The official route goes to the Daymark and then sets off downhill inland. (There is a better alternative seaward; bear right along the fence from the pedestrian gate to presently go through a second pedestrian gate and the way forward is then obvious passing through a little wood; when you come out proceed downhill to join the official route. If you want the best route but also wish to make a closer examination of the Daymark itself bear left and go and find out. When you have satisfied your curiosity, proceed due south and you will come to the second gate already mentioned.)

If you are walking between mid-June and mid-September, it is worth planning your walk to arrive at the Daymark on a Sunday. The Daymark, now owned by the National Trust, is open to the public on mid-season Sundays, and the views from the top are memorable. The Trust provides torches, and there are guides at the bottom and the top of the tower, so it is thoroughly recommended, provided you are not anxious or do not have a head for heights.

You come down towards Polridmouth Beach and walk around close behind it; the path becomes concrete and there are even concrete stepping stones. This does not sound delightful but this is a lovely little stretch by the house and lake. The path goes steeply up bearing right through woods at the other side.

Again there should be no navigational problems until you reach Allday's Fields (memorial stone on your left). You enter a wood; first right is a loop path out towards the castle and there is a steep path dropping to the beach which can be used as a short cut when the tide is out. On entering the wood the more direct route is to go ahead at the first junction and to turn left at the next. This takes you down an increasingly rock cut lane which has a very sharp elbow about two thirds of the way down.

The path comes out at Readymoney Cove and it is then all road to Fowey. However if you are continuing along the Coast Path, watch for the ferry point on your right before you get into the town. It is down steps just after Fowey Hotel's tea garden (although if you are walking in low season, you may find that the ferry is operating from the Town Quay in Fowey itself).

*The Saints' Way is a long distance footpath from Fowey to Padstow and a guide book is available. Quite apart from being a walk in its own right, this could make a link enabling walkers to undertake a circular Cornish peninsula walk of approximately 220 miles (354 km).

Grading: Strenuous   Distance -   **11.5**   **620.9**   **7.1**   **385.2**

See also our Fowey to Looe Path Description.

This section is very good value for money in two senses of the word. Firstly there is a fine path all the way from Polruan to Polperro with magnificent sea views. Secondly, it is probably the toughest stretch of walking on the South Cornwall coast. (Leaving Fowey, if you have time on your side, you can go via the higher vehicular ferry to Bodinnick and walk The Hall Walk to Polruan [4 miles / 6 km]).

Fowey/Polruan (River Fowey)
Polruan Ferry Co. Ltd
Toms Yard
East Street
Polruan-by-Fowey
Cornwall
PL23 1PB
Tel: 01726 870232

All year round at 5-10 min intervals.
1st May - 30th Sept. Daily 0715 - 2300 hrs
except Saturday 0730 start, Sunday 0900 start.
1st Oct - 30th Apr. Daily 0715 - 1900 hrs.
except Saturday 0730 start, Sunday
1000 - 1700hrs. Closed Xmas Day

In winter months when the weather deteriorates you will find that the ferry operates to and from the Town Quay at Fowey rather than the from Whitehouse Quay lower down the harbour. There should be sign up to this effect.

Landing from the ferry in Polruan, go along the quay and up Garrett Steps just beside The Lugger and at the top turn right along West Street and then left when you get to Battery Lane. The path comes out in a grassy area; keep with the wall on your left going round the corner. The path goes right, just after an earth bank and then you proceed ahead across another open area with a small ruin up on your left. It joins the road beside a school; continue ahead to turn sharp right just before the notice saying 'Furze Park'.

When you reach the National Trust money box on the path, take the right, downward path.

About 2 miles (3 km) after leaving Polruan there is a considerable hill behind Great Lantic Beach. You can go all the way to the top and turn right there. The route we recommend turns right about 30 yards (28 m) before the top, goes over a stile and drops down again. Ignore the first two turnings right as these are beach paths. Presently a wide path, the other route, joins from the left (there is a gate on your right). Shortly after that is another path right - this is a spectacular, seaward path, and makes you appreciate the rugged beauty of Pencarrow Head even more.

Although a definitive right of way is shown below the Watch House, at the moment the practical route is the broad path above it. Assuming you are on this path, ignore the stile on your right which goes directly to the house. Just after this is another loop path right but it has little in views to compensate for the extra effort. After this you can either take the right turn, or keep to the upper path and then join the lower one to follow the path around the back of a cove.

When you come to Lansallos Cove, turn inland for the coast path: unless the tide is fully in, however it is more interesting to go ahead and turn right down to the beach through a small rock cut lane. Go left, cross the back of the beach and climb the little rock cut steps on the other side.

Later, as the first houses in Polperro come into view, there is a series of parallel paths all going to Polperro. You should take the rocky path on your right by an outcrop on your left, as you get a glimpse of some houses on the opposite cliff. This is the most seaward path and passes several seats and shelters to arrive at a rocky area overlooking the mouth of the harbour. From the rocky area turn left and the official route into Polperro is the first set of steps on the right.

53 | Polperro to Looe (Bridge)   OS E107 (V) Polperro

Grading: Moderate		Distance -	8.0	628.9	5.0	390.2

See also our Fowey to Looe Path Description.

This next section is particularly well walked and the local bus company is sufficiently commercially minded to put up bus times for cliff walkers between Polperro and Looe actually on the path!

In Polperro you have to walk behind the harbour crossing the Roman Bridge to turn right. Leaving Polperro there is a loop path right called Reuben's Walk. If you take this turn left again just before the miniature lighthouse.

When you are about three quarters of the way up the hill, take the right fork at the junction of two well-defined paths. This may seem obvious, but the sign here is frequently vandalised.

Note the spectacularly sited War Memorial on Downend Point. A little way past this is another beach path right which you ignore.

There are seasonal refreshments at Talland.

After the beach cafe go up the tarmac track, turn left to pass the toilets, and then right. Turn right at the Smugglers Rest cafe into a small car park to rejoin the path.

The walk to West Looe is pleasant and quite easy. However, there are often copious amounts of horse manure on the stretch from Talland as far as Hendersick.

On entering Looe at Hannafore, you have a choice. You can either follow the official path along the road, passing flower beds and a seasonal cafe, or you can take the first right to walk alongside the beach, ascending the steps in front of a black barrier and turn right. Either route will bring you to a stretch of road with no pavement. This drops into a dip and watch for a battlemented look-out platform on your right. Just past this are steps down to the harbour area of the river; that is the best way to go. This has a double advantage; it keeps you away from the traffic and takes you past the seasonal ferry to East Looe: certainly if you are walking straight through, this is the best way to go.

The ferry runs between West and East Looe generally during the mid and high season. It is, however, dependent on both the weather and tide, and you may find it running off-season if the weather is exceptional.

If you are walking, simply keep to the quayside in West Looe, cross the bridge, and turn right into the main street, Fore Street, in East Looe.

54 | Looe to Portwrinkle (Quay)   OS E107 & E108 (T) Looe (Trains); (V) Downderry

Grading: Strenuous - Moderate in parts	Distance -	12.2	641.1	7.6	397.8

See also our Looe to Plymouth Path Description.

This is a section with several difficulties. You leave East Looe by turning up Castle Street, cross a minor crossroads and continue up the hill. The road peters out becoming a pleasant high level path above the sea.

The path becomes a road again and at the first junction bear right into Plaidy Lane. Pass Plaidy Beach on your right, and continue on the road until just after it has veered left. Here a steep tarmac path takes off right just beyond a big electric cable post.

At the top of the path you come to a road again to continue ahead for a while until the road bears left but the path goes forward again between houses. Go down steps, do not turn left or right but continue nearly opposite to go ahead.

The path comes down to Millendreath (seasonal refreshments): pass behind the beach to go up the cul-de-sac road the other side. The road becomes a path in a sunken lane, but 150 yards (135 m) after you reach the road again, turn right into the National Trust's Bodigga Cliff property, keeping to the left of the picnic tables. This beautiful place is now accessible for people of varying abilities, including wheelchair users.

The path comes out on the road above Seaton, and you turn right down what is Looe Hill. Go down to the bottom and turn right into Bridge Road. If time presses, the quickest route is along the road to Downderry.

Beach Route (tidal)
However, at most states of the tide, there is a better alternative. (If there has been flooding in Seaton, which you will have noticed at the Seaton Nature Reserve, and / or the tide is high, this beach route will be very difficult to negotiate, and it is therefore recommended that you take the road option instead.) Where the road starts to go uphill opposite the post office and general store, there is a wall on the seaward side. Behind this wall is the beginning of coastal defence works with a path on top. After a while you have to go down to the beach and make a choice. The first left turn by a stream will bring you into the centre of Downderry for shops, toilets and seasonal refreshments. The next will bring you to the Inn on the Shore. If you don't need any facilities, you should continue on to the next stream and turn left up some concrete steps; this latter option will lessen the amount of road walking, and there is a lot to come in the next section. You come up beside a school to turn right along a road, and to rejoin the official route.

Coast Path continues
Continue with the road as it bears sharply inland at a hairpin bend. Take the waymarked turn off right, next to a house called Downderry Lodge, ignoring the right turn immediately after you have taken this path. The path zigzags uphill to come eventually into a field.

The Coast Path should then go right and many people have mistakenly done that finding it hard to believe that twenty eight years after the Cornish section of the Coast Path was opened it is still unfinished! However the dull bypass route goes forward through a few inland fields and then joins a road where you turn right. You then have a long tedious section on the road before turning right again just after a bungalow named 'The Bungalow' to go down to Portwrinkle to turn left.

The OS Explorer 108 map shows a coast path from Downderry Lodge, which runs through fields to Portwrinkle. At the time of writing the Official route is still on a dangerous road as described above. However, by the time you read this, our much sought-after route may have been installed, so watch out for new signs directing you along the path as shown on the OS map, or very near it. If you are fortunate and the new path has been installed, as you walk along it say a thank you to Cornwall County Council for the work involved and to this Association for 15 years of non-stop lobbying for it.

55 | Portwrinkle to Cremyll (for Plymouth)   OS E108 (V) Cawsand/Kingsand

Grading: Moderate   Distance -   21.4   662.5   13.3   411.1

See also our Looe to Plymouth Path Description.

(If the tide is out and there is no firing at Tregantle Fort, you can in fact walk along the beach the whole way to Polhawn Cove and some find this a better alternative to what is currently offered. If you do this you need the first path down right to the beach and be warned, the last mile before Polhawn becomes rocky.)

The Coast Path takes the second path on the right, opposite the entrance to the golf club. It is currently well marked except right at the end of the course, where you need to aim for the pedestrian gate seen on top of a rise.

You come out to the road but the path for a while is just inside the hedge. This travesty of a path ends by the road junction to Torpoint where you have to come down to the road and turn right along it. All this agony is caused by some bureaucrat in the MOD who refuses to let you walk through the rifle range when not in use; if it can be done elsewhere, including on a tank firing range in Dorset, with good will it could here.

However, back to the road: you pass the Tregantle Fort entrance, then the road bears left and shortly you turn right, signposted Whitsand Bay etc. The road shortly bears left to lead you to a National Trust path.

There is then another long stretch of road, until you see notices for Whitsand Bay Holiday Park on the left and the Coast Path starts again on the right; at this point even sharper left is a seasonal cafe. The Coast Path is now well marked and a great improvement over the road, but it does involve two steep climbs. (If time presses, you could stay on the road until you see Wiggle Old Farmhouse on the left. Turn right and you will rejoin the Coast Path within a few yards.)

The path continues to be well marked, and you should take the diversion onto the lovely Rame Head if time allows.

Continue along the tarmac avoiding the path turn off on the right. The road turns left with intermittent views ahead to Plymouth Sound Breakwater and presently, over a 0.25 mile (400 m) later, takes off into the wood right.

Traversing Cawsand/Kingsand the official and in fact easiest way is not straightforward and only some of it is signposted, so read the next paragraph carefully.

You enter Cawsand from Pier Lane, go across the square to pick up Garrett Street. As you come towards the end of this street look for the old Devon/Corn boundary mark on a house on your right. Then turn right in front of the Post Office. Soon you will approach a street called The Cleave. Just before you reach it, turn left. Then turn first right up what is Heavitree Road but you will not know this until you are a few yards up it. As you ascend you will presently see Lower

66

Row on your left; here turn right and enter Mount Edgcumbe Country Park.

When you come out on to a road at Hooe Lodge turn right, but look in 20 yards (18 m) for the path leaving the road on the left. You continue along a section of the one-time Earl's Drive but shortly after going under an old stone arch turn right. Follow the signs which direct you down to the foreshore for a very few yards but you soon go up again.

You continue through a high deer gate; you come out by a classical summer house and you should keep along right to pick up a concrete driveway, and later right again when the drive goes left to walk inside of a hedge. You pass an old blockhouse on your left.

If you are not too pushed for time, a visit around the gardens of Mount Edgcumbe is worthwhile, and free. A charge will be made if you wish to visit the House.

The path comes out by The Orangery (seasonal cafe); go through an arch then go forward to turn right through the park gates to the ferry point for Plymouth.

56 | Cremyll (for Plymouth) to Mountbatten Point   OS E108 (T) Plymouth (Trains)

Grading: Easy   Distance -   12.0   674.5   7.5   418.6

See also our Plymouth to Wembury Path Description.

The distance includes the walking route around to Mountbatten Point. If you use the water taxi service, then deduct approximately 5 miles (8 km).

Cremyll/Plymouth	All year round at $\frac{1}{2}$ hourly intervals.
Cremyll Ferry,	**Summer service** from 1st May to 18th Sept.
Cremyll Quay,	From Mt Edgcumbe Weekdays 0650 to 2015
Cremyll,	Saturdays 0815 to 2100, Sundays 0900 to 2100
Torpoint,	From Plymouth Weekdays 0720 to 2030
Cornwall. PL10 1HX	Saturdays 0845 to 2115, Sundays 0915 to 2115
Tel: 01752 822105.	**Winter service** from 19th September to 30th April
(Full timetable available - phone above no.)	From Mt Edgcumbe Weekdays 0650 to 1815,
	Saturdays 0815 to 1830, Sundays 1000 to 1700
	From Plymouth Weekdays 0720 to 1830,
	Saturdays 0845 to 1845, Sundays 1015 to 1715
	Closed Xmas, Boxing & New Year's Days

Plymouth's new Waterfront Walk has been installed. From stepping ashore at Admirals Hard, watch out for a variety of information plaques and pieces of artwork all relating to Plymouth's history.

On landing at Admirals Hard, walk up the road and turn second right into Cremyll Street, and continue to the massive gates of the Royal William Yard. Pass them on your right and continue on out to Firestone Bay. At the sea wall you have a fine view to Drake's Island and beyond towards Wembury. A slight excursion could be made by turning right to walk out to Western King's Point and Devil's Point, for River Tamar views, but you will have to return.

From the sea wall turn inland to walk into Durnford Street, continue along it and walk past the Royal Marine Barracks, turning right immediately after them. This will bring you into Millbay Road where you continue, passing the Dock Gates (east). Then you turn right into West Hoe Road. Keep to this road. You are now in the West Hoe area and the streets surrounding you have numerous B & B establishments. Fork right into Great Western Road.

As you approach a terrace of three storey small hotels, watch out for a path on your right known as Rusty Anchor. This is a slight diversion from the main road and provides a shore line walk.

On regaining the main road, turn right and continue along the Hoe foreshore. You stay on this promenade all the way around to The Barbican and Sutton Harbour. However, you could achieve grand views over Plymouth Sound by climbing steps opposite the former swimming pool up to the lighthouse, Smeaton's Tower, and passing that to cross The Hoe to have a look at Sir Francis Drake, still scanning the English Channel for the Armada.

Retrace your steps and continue your shore line walk to The Barbican. A small jetty on your right is of historic significance in that it is the site of the Mayflower Steps; of great interest to our US members.

Whatever you decide upon, ferry or the walking route, it is well worth exploring the ancient Barbican area before carrying on.

Sutton Harbour / Mountbatten
Two services are available:

Haven Water Taxi 07930 838614	All year round. 0800 - 2300 hrs. Except Mondays, Tuesdays and Wednesday in Winter 0800 - 1630 hrs.
Plymouth Water Taxi 0378 859284	All year round. As required between 0900 - 2330 hrs. Except Mondays, Tuesdays and Wednesday in Winter 0800 - 1830 hrs.

In the unlikely event of the water taxis not operating to Mountbatten Point, this is your walking Route from Sutton Harbour to Mountbatten Point. It is well marked with Plymouth's innovative signs and symbols.

Lock gates have now been installed at Sutton Harbour, so walk on across them into Teat's Hill Road. As you progress along Teat's Hill Road you will arrive at Breakwater Hill. Turn right here, but do not walk into the scrap yard unless you want to view vehicles being broken up. Carry on up the hill for a limestone, cliff top walk with views over the Cattewater. At a fork in the lane bear left and you will descend to the area of Cattedown Wharf. We will now just supply directions - continue on past warehouses into Maxwell Road, a new road will take you direct to Laira Bridge which you take to cross the River Plym. You now have pavements to walk upon. At the first roundabout turn right into Oreston Road.

After a small roundabout, you have a choice:-

(a) Across a piece of grass on your left you will find an old railway line which is now a cycle/walk route through to Radford Lake or,

(b) Keep on to the top of the road, bear right, then when you reach Rollis Park Road, turn right to descend to Oreston Quay. You are beside the water only for a couple of hundred yards, and at Plymstock Road turn left. Start climbing away from the estuary and at Lower Saltram turn right and carry straight on to Radford Lake.

The 'castle' through which you walk was once the lodge to a large house, now no more. Turning right after the causeway brings you to a path alongside the southern shore of Hooe Lake. At the time of writing it was not waymarked, but you should not go far wrong if you keep to this path. You will join a narrow road which leads to Hooe Lake Road.

Walk straight across the grassy area keeping to the shore and turn right along Barton Road, and by staying with this road you will come into Turnchapel. Continue on up St. John's Road to a car park on your right. In the corner is a signed route to Mountbatten Point.

NTG - Does not supply walking instructions for this 7 miles (11 km) of the Coast Path.

---

57 | Mountbatten Point to Wembury (Warren Point Ferry)   OS E108 & OL20

Grading: Easy   Distance -   11.8   686.3   7.3   425.9

See also our Plymouth to Wembury Path Description.

Due to the praiseworthy activities of Plymouth City Council you are about to step out onto welcome Coast Path realignments. Those who have walked this section before will be amazed at the difference and those who have been Association members for a while will realise that our efforts have been successful.

The path goes around Mountbatten Point then runs south climbing to Jennycliff.

Keep to the cliff edge and continue south, that is to the end of the grassy area where you will find a signed path entering woodlands.

This up and down new path is a delight and well below the dangerous road that we once had to walk. Within a 0.25 mile (400 m) this new path links in with the original Coast Path. Turn right for a scenic uncomplicated path to Fort Bovisand, one of the great forts that once defended Plymouth.

Those who have been this way before should now pause to reflect. Since Mountbatten Point you have not had to set foot upon a vehicular road! We congratulate all responsible for this improvement.

On the descent to a road the path can be seen ahead between hundreds of chalet/huts and the sea. At Heybrook Bay when you reach the road, turn right.

The path passes in front of the guns of HMS Cambridge. When firing is taking place you will certainly hear it. Red flags fly during the shooting and when it is about to commence. Do not walk seaward of them but follow a well marked diversion to the left. This path circles the property of the Royal Navy and will return the walker to the coast safely. Needless to say, if the red flags are not flying then the official coast path is yours, but do not loiter along the section.

There is a free telephone - 0800 833608 for prior information of firing times. Firing usually takes place between 0900 and 1800, rarely at night or at weekends and Bank Holidays. The gunnery school is closed at Christmas, Easter and for three weeks in August.

Now follows a low cliff top walk to Wembury Beach. The path passes seaward of the church and climbs to a level path that leads into the estuary of the River Yealm. At a small house, The Rocket House, once used for the storage of life saving apparatus, the official path takes off downhill diagonally towards the river and the ferry point. We suggest you walk down to the ferry point, even if the ferry is not running or you do not intend to use it, because you can take advantage of a scenic short circular walk back to the Rocket House. Once the ferry steps have been reached, carry on for a few yards then take a wooden stepped path on the left that climbs to good views over Newton Ferrers and Noss Mayo.

NTG - Map (page 83) the coast path now runs out and around Mountbatten Point and is now 'off road' at Staddon Heights Farm.

58 Wembury (Warren Point) to Bigbury-on-Sea (Car Park)   OS OL20

| Grading: Starts easy then strenuous | Distance - | 21.8 | 708.1 | 13.5 | 439.4 |

See also our Wembury (Warren Point) to Bigbury-on-Sea Path Description.

The first obstacle is crossing the River Yealm

Wembury (Warren Point) to Noss Mayo Ferry.
River Yealm

Bill Gregor,	Seasonal all week, on demand.
1 Underhaye,	16th April - 24th September
Yealmpton	1000 - 1100 and 1500 - 1600 hrs.
PL8 2JR.	
Tel: 01752 880079	

During fine weather and school holidays the ferry is operational between 1000 and 1600 daily - but please phone first. Mr Gregor is often there outside normal operating hours. There is a signal board to summon the ferryman by the steps at Warren Point or at the slipway at Noss Mayo. We suggest you might also telephone ahead to Mr Gregor to give him an idea of your estimated time of arrival.

If there is no ferry then this means a walk back to the Rocket House to follow the path described below into Knighton. There is an hourly bus service (number 48) to Plymstock and Plymouth where there is available an infrequent service to Noss Mayo (number 94). For a quicker conveyance around the estuary there are reasonably priced taxis available:-

Wembury Cabs - John Pitcher (01752 862151) and

Tim's Taxis - Tim Craig (01752 830225)

Walking route around the River Yealm.
From the Rocket House the track leads into a road. At Wembury House a stile leads to a field and to the footpath junction. The path you want is the one to the right which runs alongside a high wall. Follow it to the end of the wall where it goes through two successive kissing gates. It then

bears left approximately 330° across fields towards Knighton. As you leave the fields it goes down a few steps. Turn left and then first right. This will bring you out onto the road. Turn left and the bus stop is a little further along on the other side of the road just before the pub. The distance from ferry point to bus stop is 1.5 miles (2.5 km). Before reaching the bus stop you will pass a telephone box where you can call a taxi if you want.

Go across to a minor road opposite to descend and turn left and then right at the next road junction. Continue along the road for about 0.5 mile (800 m) ignoring all turnings and footpaths. At a major road turn left for a few yards to turn right on a footpath just by a bus stop. This is now a waymarked route, the Erme-Plym Trail. Stay with it down to Cofflete Creek and up the other side until you reach the main A379 road. Turn right and a mile of main road walking follows, the best pavement is at first on the left, then switches to the right leaving Brixton, then for a long stretch there is none at all but it restarts on the left. (There is a safer but longer alternative starting at Brixton Church, see below). Turn right down the road signed Newton Ferrers 3 miles. Go down to Puslinch Bridge and bear right up the hill. Nearly at the top, a footpath goes right cutting the corner to Wrescombe. Emerging onto the road turn right to continue along to The Butts and down the main road to Newton Ferrers. If you arrive within approximately two hours of low tide you can bear right down Yealm Road and turn down Newton Hill, to cross a tidal causeway to Noss Mayo and another across the inlet at Noss. If you are not so fortunate turn left down the road to Bridgend and Noss Mayo, being sure to turn first right as you enter Noss. Here those who have come around will have a picturesque riverside walk out to where those who have been fortunate enough with the ferry will disembark.

Alternative route - Brixton to Puslinch Bridge
At Brixton Church go up Old Road and follow the waymarked Erme-Plym Trail signs until you arrive on a minor road in the outskirts of Yealmpton. Here turn right and continue down the road ignoring the footpath left turn of the Erme-Plym Trail. At the main A379 road, cross over turning left and immediately right into Stray Park. At the bottom bear right along a tarmac footpath. This comes to a road; turn left along a stony track. At the footpath sign continue ahead to pass the entrance to Kitley Caves. The path eventually emerges in a car park. Leave this and turn left on the road to reach Puslinch Bridge. From here on the route is as described above.

Coast Path continues
From the ferry, the Erme Estuary is about 9 miles (14 km) ahead. You are the best judge of how long that will take you to get there for low tide, so plan your Noss Mayo departure accordingly. The well-marked path climbs through woodlands to pick up Lord Revelstoke's nine- mile drive, made for the carriages of his guests at Membland Hall, since demolished.

At Battery Cottage, just as you are leaving the woodlands, look out for a path going off to the right. You can take this down to Cellars Beach, for a swim maybe. It continues on around the back of the beach then climbs to rejoin the Coast Path at Brakehill Plantation where you turn right onto Lord Revelstoke's drive.

There is a definitive seaward path at Stoke Down at 560460 just after passing a single stone gate post on the left. Use this if you wish to visit the historic Church of St Peter the Poor Fisherman; this will mean an uphill road walk to regain the Coast Path. If you do not divert then the path crosses the Stoke Beach road to continue along, passing the ruined 'Tea House'.

You are now in for a very steep descent and further on a steep climb up to St Anchorite's Rock and you pass Bugle Hole. The section then to Mothecombe Beach provides superb views to the Erme estuary. It has been fairly described as England's most unspoilt river estuary: we certainly believe it to be the most attractive. At the beach do not turn inland but take the seaward path in the woods at Owen's Hill.

River Erme   No ferry

Low water is at about the same time as the Devonport Tide Table shown here.

It is usually possible to paddle across the river 1 hour each side of low water along the old ford. Great care should be taken because heavy rains or seas can make the crossing dangerous. On modern maps the old ford is not shown but this in fact ran from Ordnance map ref. 614 476 to map ref. 620 478. In other words, the old ford connected the road by the row of coastguard cottages with the end of the inland road to Wonwell Beach from Kingston.

Should you arrive at the River Erme at a time that promises a very long wait for low tide to enable you to wade across then there is an inland alternative. This alternative is of about 7 miles (11 km) with fairly steep up and down country lanes. You are the best judge of your rate of travel so the decision to wait for the tide or continue walking is yours.

Walking route around the River Erme
If you follow the riverside paths shown on OS map OL20 you will be trespassing on a private estate so follow the narrow country lanes to Holbeton village. Then continue on a northerly route to Ford and Hole Farm. Soon after passing Hole Farm take off on a public footpath on your right. From here to the main A379 road is about 0.75 mile (1.2 km). Turn right to cross the River Erme at Sequer's Bridge. Stay on the A379 for about 0.5 mile (0.75 km) but take care as this is an extremely busy road. You will see a road on your right signposted to Orcheton. Follow this road south towards the village of Kingston but before you reach that village you will see road signs to Wonwell Beach. Just before the slipway on to the sands you have a choice. If the tide now permits you can continue south along the beach or take to the waymarked Coast Path in the woodlands on your left.

Coast Path continues
Beyond the Erme the walking becomes tougher but the all round views will compensate for the effort. (There is an interesting low tide alternative at Westcombe Beach. Go onto the beach for a walk through the promontory to Ayrmer Cove via one or other of two 15 yard (14 m) long caves. You will walk on shingle through them but be a little careful on rocks that can be slippery once through the caves. This is a low tide diversion only.) The path passes Challaborough with its cafe and caravans to Bigbury-on-Sea, where the Bay View Cafe is open all day and the only establishment for evening meals.

Burgh Island can be visited by walking across the sands or by a 'sea tractor' if the tide is in. The pub is very old, the hotel is fascinating art deco modern and the hut at the top of the island stands on the site of a chapel. This hut was used by the 'huers' - pilchard fishermen on the lookout for shoals of fish.

| 59 | Bigbury-on-Sea to Hope Cove, Inner Hope (Lifeboat Station) | OS OL20 (V) Bantham; (V) Thurlestone |

Grading: Moderate   Distance -   9.2   717.3   5.7   445.1

See also our Bigbury-on-Sea to Salcombe Path Description.

There are riverside footpaths along both west and east banks of the River Avon to Aveton Gifford. This makes the inland walking route from Bigbury-on-Sea to Bantham and vice versa about 9 miles (14.5 km) in total. The OS OL20 map shows the riverside paths. What you have to watch is that the road between the two words 'Ford' is tidal and therefore is at times submerged. This route is described below.

Coast Path continues
The official route turns right at the bottom of the road on to what is called Clematon Hill at the western side of the mouth of the River Avon.There are good views here across the estuary but unfortunately you have to walk up the busy road to Mount Folly Farm afterwards. However, again there is compensation because the views southward across the estuary just after the farm are particularly spectacular.

Bigbury/Bantham (River Avon)   Seasonal - Monday to Saturday.
Neill Schroeter, Harbourmaster   from 9th April - 8th Sept.
Marsh Cottage, Fore Street,   1000 - 1100 hrs and 1500 - 1600 hrs.
Aveton Gifford, Devon TQ7 4LR   Sundays if pre-booked party of 10 or more.
Tel: 01548 561196

The ferryman is generally around, and can be called by waving. Low water is about the same time as the Devonport Tide Table. It is possible at low tide, when not rough, or the river is not in flood, to wade the river. However, we strongly stress we are not advising this as a cheap method of avoiding the ferry crossing. When the ferry is working, you are strongly advised to use it because wading is not easy and you may get a lot wetter than you expect. You will most likely be up to your thighs in water and in no circumstances should the crossing be attempted if conditions are wrong. The two guide points are just below the ferry crossing. On the true right bank - the western side - there is a well defined hedge running north and south with pine trees. On the left bank - the eastern side - there is a castellated building with battlements and a little flag pole in the middle. (This castle is just above the famous thatched boat house which is so well known from many pictures taken of the River Avon and Bantham.) However, if crossing from the true right to the left - in other words from west to east - take off at the hedge and wade towards the castle-like building. If going the other way, vice versa. Please note it is important that you do wade at this point. The river looks shallow in a number of other places but there are deeper channels and indeed soft sand patches which can make it extremely difficult. Further towards the sea, there is a considerable tidal ebb which can be exceedingly dangerous.

PLEASE NOTE WHEN THE FERRY IS NOT OPERATING A RECOMMENDED WAY TO REACH BANTHAM IS BY REASONABLY PRICED TAXIS:

Acorn Taxis (Telephone: 01548 531010 : Mobile: 07967 023336 / 7)

Adrian's Taxis (Telephone: 01548 854385 : Mobile: 0976 - 808756)

Arrow Cars - Mr Kemp - (Telephone: 01548 856120) and

D & C Taxis (Telephone 01548 852906).

It should always be borne in mind that the depth of water at low tide and consequently safe passage across is affected by natural conditions inasmuch that strong south west or westerly winds tend to bank up water in the English Channel and, therefore, there will be a greater depth of water than expected. This will also happen if there is a lot of rain in the catchment areas of the rivers, with consequently more water coming down. Caution: although we know several who have waded the River Avon we do not recommend it; great care is required, especially by those with backpacks.

VERY IMPORTANT - PLEASE TAKE NOTE

EVEN AT DEAD LOW WATER WE STRESS THAT YOU MUST CONSIDER VERY SERIOUSLY WHETHER YOU SHOULD WADE THIS RIVER. IT IS VERY DIFFICULT AND CAN BE DANGEROUS EVEN FOR TALL AND STRONG ADULTS. MANY OF OUR MEMBERS, INCLUDING YOUR SECRETARY WILL NOT VENTURE ACROSS. THEIR OPINION BEING - 'WHEN THE FERRY IS NOT RUNNING THEN THE *ONLY ALTERNATIVE IS TO GO ROUND'.*

Inland Walking Route - approx. 7 miles (12 km)

Much of this route has been waymarked 'Avon Estuary Walk' with a heron motif in blue and white.

When the tide is not low (and we urge you to read again our advice about wading) and the ferry is not available, the only way to the other side is an inland walk to Aveton Gifford and around. This is a pleasant 7 mile (12 km) diversion as it is mostly along country paths. Walking through agricultural land in deep country makes a change from the coast. The paths are shown on OS OL20 and are quite well marked but they are little used and are not always easy to follow. Allow plenty of time for some heavy walking, for straying off route or for a possible delay at the tidal road near Aveton Gifford.

Disregard the coast path where it turns right through Mount Folly Farm and descends to the ferry point, but proceed towards Bigbury for 60 yards (55 m) to the next footpath sign. Turn right into the field over a stone stile and walk along the field edge. Over a wooden stile will bring you onto the golf course where, after a short distance, you meet a surfaced track. Go northwards along the track towards the clubhouse for 200 yards (185 m), turning right at an entrance between two huts going down a track to Hexdown Farm. Pass left of the farmhouse to bear immediately right and then left. Bear right before the next gate to continue downhill with the boundary on your left. Proceed along a track through a timber gate. Follow the footpath sign slightly left along a tarmac drive, into woodland, then through Lincombe and on to the B3392 on a corner. Proceed northwards towards Bigbury for 350 yards (320 m) (be careful of the traffic) and turn right at the footpath sign to Aveton Gifford (via tidal road). Cross the field to a post and wire fence and enter the top of Doctor's Wood. Re-emerge into a field and cross due east to a wooden stile. Proceed along a high level path (beautiful views) then walk downhill to the tidal road which will bring you to Aveton Gifford. There is a viable alternative if the tide is over the road by walking north-westward to Foxhole then north-eastward to Waterhead and Aveton Gifford. The whole path is adequately waymarked.

Cross the Avon on the roadbridge (A379) towards Kingsbridge, and turn right at the end of the bridge into a cul-de-sac named Bridge End. Continue to a gate at a signpost, and straight on to a metalled road, where you turn right at a signpost.

Bear left at the road fork, following the footpath sign to a gate; turn right here and follow a fence on the right, and through another gate into a field.

Turn half right down to the bottom of the valley, and bear right to a gate with a waymark 'to Stiddicombe Creek'. Cross this and enter the wood on the right. Work steadily uphill to the top corner and follow the waymark signs along the top of the field with a hedge on the left (watch for herons by the river) to a stile by a gate; over another stile and continue. Bear right and cross a farm track to a gate between walls. Cross the stream ahead with stepping stones, and along to a stile and waymark signs, where you turn right and go straight on to Bantham, where you turn right and go through the village where you will see the ferry sign; here you would have stepped ashore had it been operating. The coast path is straight on towards the sea. Some of this walk is shown in the National Trail Guide.

Coast Path continues
You should take great care where the path proceeds along the seaward boundary of the Thurlestone Golf Course; watch out for golfers and where they hit the ball. We have had a report of a walker on this section who was hit in the mouth by a golf ball at close range, with resulting horrific damage to teeth and lips.

60 | Hope Cove, Inner Hope to Salcombe (Ferry)   OS OL20 (V) Hope Cove

| Grading: Strenuous | Distance - | 12.9 | 730.2 | 8.0 | 453.1 |

See also our Bigbury-on-Sea to Salcombe Path Description.

Excellent coastal walking, some of the finest in South Devon. Before leaving Inner Hope you ought to walk along the inland road to look at The Square and its attractive thatched cottages. It is well marked out to Bolt Tail where the remains of an Iron Age fort are marked by a dry stone wall and the remains of a ditch.

The path is obvious to Bolberry Down (refreshments available - Port Light Hotel) and on to a viewpoint overlooking Soar Mill Cove. There is a steep descent to the cove but the climb out is easier. We have heard of walkers going wrong as they near the splendid rocky Bolt Head. The correct route is the coast route; do not divert inland anywhere until the headland is reached. The path then runs due north into and around Starehole Bay.

From the bay the path joins the Courtenay Way which was cut out under rocky pinnacles. The way ahead is through woodlands to the roadway below the National Trust's Overbecks House and Youth Hostel. Follow the road to South Sands where, in season, a ferry can be taken to the main ferry point in Salcombe. If it is not running or you are a purist, the way ahead to the town and ferry for East Portlemouth is along the most seaward roads ahead.

OS - Outdoor Leisure Map 20. The Coast Path runs out onto Bolt Head. This is not shown on the map.

61 | Salcombe to Torcross (Car Park)   OS OL20 (T) Salcombe; (V) Beesands

| Grading: Strenuous | Distance - | 20.8 | 751.0 | 12.9 | 466.0 |

See also our Salcombe to Torcross Path Description.

This is first class walking, some of the best of the whole Coast Path.

Salcombe to East Portlemouth Ferry All year round.
The Salcombe Ferry,   Winter - $\frac{1}{2}$ hourly between 0800 - 1700 hrs.
Somerset House,   Summer - Continuous service 0800 - 1930 hrs.
Devon Road,   0830 hrs start weekends.
Salcombe
Devon TQ8 8HQ
Tel: (01548)842061/842364

Having crossed the estuary the path goes off to the right along the narrow road. Just after the National Trust car park at Mill Bay the path now goes uphill on the left through the trees. Refreshments are available at the Gara Rock Hotel if you want to climb the hill from the path.

The official route is to the very end of Prawle Point, to the Coastguard lookout. It is hoped that the National Trust will mark a path out to the point along the western side of the headland. The path is there and it is a better route than the one on the top. The official route is back inland again but near to the lookout on the east side of the point is a path descending a valley; this is the better one. Prawle Point is National Trust property and there is a true coast path along the top of low cliffs around Copstone Cove to link in with the official route at Western Cove.

It is easy walking for a while along the edges of fields on what is a 'raised' beach. The path then becomes rocky and up and down prior to Lannacombe Beach. About 0.5 mile (800 m) before Lannacombe, try to find time to take the new path that the National Trust has cut to the right, signposted to the previously hidden Woodcombe Sand beach. Until now the beach, a peaceful isolated spot, could only be reached through the grounds of Woodcombe House, and many people didn't even know it was there. The path twists and drops, and you have to come back the same way, but it is only about 100 yards (90 m) and well worth the effort.

The path is straightforward to Start Point and on to Torcross and has recently been rerouted following the purchase of land between Hallsands and Beesands by the National Trust - this is a distinct improvement. It is not currently possible to visit the old deserted village at Hallsands, and the latest news is that it is deemed to be unsafe. You can, however, get a glimpse of the ruins by taking the path to the village as far as the closure notice, which will not take long and is a very moving experience.

62 Torcross to Dartmouth (Lower Ferry)   OS OL20 (V) Torcross; (V) Strete; (V) Stoke Fleming

Grading: Moderate   Distance -   16.4   767.4   10.2   476.2

See also our Torcross to Dartmouth Path Description.

The Coast Path runs along the length of the shingle bank. You can walk either side of the road; the top of the beach for sea views or alongside the Ley for bird watching.

There is no true coast path from Strete Gate to Warren Point and virtually the whole route is inland and some on a busy main road. This is reckoned to be the worst section of the whole of the South West Coast Path and the Association continues its efforts to obtain an enormous improvement. WE CANNOT OVEREMPHASISE THE NEED FOR EXTREME CAUTION ON THIS SECTION, SOME OF WHICH IS ON DANGEROUS, BUSY ROADS.

If you intend to avoid the busy main road through Strete, then as you approach the village, look for Hynetown Road on your left and turn into this road to follow the official path to rejoin the main road on the other side of the village. After this follow the main road for about 200 yards (185 m) and then take care to fork left, signposted 'Southwood' - there is no coast path sign here. Immediately before the entrance to Blackpool Sands you must turn left by the cottages.

Follow the inland signed route to Stoke Fleming and the rest of the signs along this poor route. You have about another 2.5 miles (4 km) to go before you regain the Coast Path proper.

As you stand on the National Trust's Warren Point this is another occasion to pause and reflect. The beautiful path you see ahead of you towards the River Dart estuary could easily be continued behind you nearly all the way back to Slapton Sands, if it were not for landowners who do not like you and the Countryside Agency which refuses to support Devon County Council and this Association.

Dartmouth Castle commands the mouth of the River Dart and should be visited, time permitting. In season there is a regular ferry from the castle to Dartmouth and this can be utilised for a pleasant river trip, instead of walking down the road.

63 Dartmouth to Brixham   OS OL20 (T) Dartmouth; (V) Kingswear (Trains)
(King William of Orange Statue)

Grading: Strenuous   Distance -   17.3   784.7   10.8   487.0

See also our Dartmouth to Brixham Path Description.

Walkers will probably use the lower ferry to cross the River Dart but there are two other regular ferries which also run all year round. Nearby is the passenger ferry, which lands by the steam railway station, and which gives a more comfortable crossing, and if these two are not running then further up the river is the higher ferry taking pedestrians and vehicles. If you use the higher ferry you will then need to turn right along the railway line to the road, then turn right again and descend the hill to join the Coast Path by the lower ferry slipway.

Dartmouth/Kingswear
South Hams District Council, Lower Ferry, Lower Ferry Office, The Square, Kingswear TQ6 OAA
Tel: (01803) 752342

All year round, continuous between 0700 and 2300 hrs. Sundays start 0800 hrs.

On landing at Kingswear, by the lower ferry, pass through an arch on the right. Ascend Alma Steps then turn right along Beacon Road. In 1.25 miles (2 km) turn right down steps at Warren Woods.

When you reach the old Battery Buildings at Froward Point do divert inland to see The Daymark navigation tower nearby if time permits but then return to the Coast Path to continue. The sign here is 8.75 miles (14 km) to Brixham and the path descends steeply going right from the back corner of the derelict look out building and then passes through the World War II gun and searchlight positions. Next at Pudcombe Cove you can obtain access to the National Trust gardens at Coleton Fishacre if they are open.

Walking on above Pudcombe Cove and Ivy Cove to Scabbacombe Head, you will see the Scabbacombe Sands, Long Sands, Man Sands, Southdown Cliff and Sharkham Point before reaching St Mary's Bay. Taken together, the strenuous grading of this section is well justified.

Now you have a pleasant walk to Berry Head Country Park, a Nature Reserve with much of interest - do spend time there if you can. The Northern Fort, one of the two Napoleonic Forts, contains the Berry Head lighthouse and the old guardhouse is now a cafe, open in the season and sometimes out of season as well.

Having left Berry Head and descending Berry Head Road, when you are level with the Breakwater descend the steps to the new promenade which follows the water's edge past the new marina to the inner harbour.

64 | Brixham to Torquay Harbour   OS OL20 (T) Brixham; (T) Paignton (Trains)

Grading: Moderate   Distance -   **13.5**   **798.2**   **8.4**   **495.4**

See also our Brixham to Shaldon Path Description.

The path goes along the back of Broadsands, along the back of Goodrington Sands beach, around Roundham Head, along Paignton and Preston sea fronts and along the promenade at Torquay.

From Brixham to Elbury Cove the path is fair though not as scenic as one might hope. Thereafter it becomes more urbanised with the poorest section from Hollicombe to Torquay Harbour where you usually have quite heavy traffic nearby. Remember, in case of need, there is a very frequent bus service from Brixham to Torquay via Paignton! There is also a regular Brixham/Torquay seasonal ferry service.

When departing from Brixham leave by the new path running along the harbour, signposted Coastal Footpath to Oxen Cove and Freshwater Car Park. At the car park continue on past the Zeneca Brixham Environmental Laboratory and on to the Battery Gardens where you follow the lower path to Fishcombe Cove. Ascend from the cove and at the road junction turn right, signpost Public Footpath to Churston Ferrers.

At the far end of Elbury Cove ignore the more obvious path going inland and leave the beach by ascending the steps. Take care at Broadsands beach that you do not follow the path up the cliff at the eastern end, but turn left up the minor road, pass under the railway viaduct and then turn immediately right where the Coast Path is signposted.

At Goodrington turn right under a railway bridge, follow the promenade round and just before the end a zigzag path takes you up, through ornamental gardens on to Roundham Head.

At Hollicombe Head you can turn right and go through the delightful park that was once the gas works. Bear left to emerge through the main gate onto the road. Then turn right for Torquay.

CP - At Goodrington South Sands the path crosses back under the railway line. There is no road walking until Paignton Harbour.

65 | Torquay Harbour to Shaldon (Ferry)   OS E110 (T) Torquay (Trains)

Grading: Strenuous	Distance -	17.3	815.5	10.8	506.2

See also our Brixham to Shaldon Path Description.

You walk on round Torquay Inner Harbour, turning left up Beacon Hill and soon reach The Imperial Hotel. Turn in right here to pass in front of the main entrance to the hotel and then follow the scenic path to the grassy plateau of Daddyhole Plain, which you cross to find the path descending to Meadfoot Beach.

At the far end of Meadfoot Beach turn right through a small car park and ascend to Marine Drive where you turn right. There is some subsidence on this road but it does not affect pedestrians. Shortly, turn right at a signpost for the Coast Path, going towards Thatcher Point. However, at present, you will have to return on the same path as the footpath is closed between Thatcher Point and Thatcher Pines; this is because of a cliff fall which the path managers have yet to resolve. At the road turn right and shortly find a path above the left hand side of the road, and at the end of this cross the road and take the Bishop's Walk path signposted to Anstey's Cove.

As you join the road by the car park above Anstey's Cove you can, time and energy permitting, take the steep path down to the picturesque cove; however, you'll have to return the same way, as following repeated rock falls the adjacent Redgate Beach has been sealed off indefinitely by Torbay Borough Council, and it's no longer possible to cross the two beaches and regain the official route by the path up the cliffs. Instead, about 50 yards (46 m) beyond the turning down to Anstey's, take the path through the woods to the right signposted 'To Babbacombe & St Marychurch over the Downs', which takes you up to Walls Hill.

From Walls Hill the path will take you to the road descending to Babbacombe Beach, at the far end of which you traverse a wooden bridge structure to Oddicombe beach, where the path bears upwards just before the lower station of the Babbacombe Cliff Railway. Shortly you pass under the railway and then take care to turn right downwards at the start of a pleasant path leading to a grassy picnic area where you bear left uphill to join the track to Watcombe.

At the valley road linking the main Torquay/Teignmouth Road to Watcombe Beach, turn left and immediately right, signposted Maidencombe 0.75 mile (1 km) and follow a wooded path until you reach a path junction, where the signposting shows the inland route as the coast path and the more coastal path as an alternative path. We suggest you take the new more coastal path, which in time will become the official route, and then from the car park at Maidencombe go a few yards up the road and turn right, unless you wish to obtain refreshment in the village.

From here there are some quite stiff gradients until you reach the road at Labrador where you turn right and in a few yards leave the pavement to take a sunken path on your right and shortly enter a field on your right via a stile by a field gate.

You will get superb views now as you descend along the coastal side of the field system, then take the path round The Ness to Shaldon.

66 | Shaldon to Exmouth (Ferry)   OS E110 (V) Shaldon;
(T) Teignmouth (Trains); (T) Dawlish (Trains); (V) Dawlish Warren (Trains); (V) Starcross (Trains)

Grading: Easy	Distance -	12.7	828.2	7.9	514.1

See also our Shaldon to Sidmouth Path Description.

The above figures relate to the distance involved when the Starcross ferry is operating. If not, the walking route around the Exe is described below, and you should add approximately 10.6 miles (17 km).

This is a section where you may have problems depending on the time of year and state of the tide.

There is no ferry at winter weekends. Your walking route around is to continue along riverside roads from the ferry point and cross Shaldon Bridge. Immediately after crossing the railway line, exit from the bridge into Milford Park. Walk beside the railway line, through Bitton Sports

Ground into Park Hill, cross into Bitton Avenue at Clay Lane then turn right into Willow Street. At the end bear left then right which will bring you into Quay Road, into Osmond Street and then straight on to Harbour Beach and the ferry. Keep going on out onto `The Point', turn north east and once more you are upon the Coast Path.

Shaldon/Teignmouth (River Teign)
The Teign Ferry Ltd.
Little Coombe, 18 Haldon Avenue,
Teignmouth. TQ14 8JZ
Tel: 01626 776079 Fax: 01626 776669
E-mail: teignferry@eclipse.co.uk

All year round.
20 minute intervals.
Weekdays 0800 hrs - sunset
Weekends 1000 hrs - sunset

Coast Path continues
After crossing from Shaldon by ferry, follow the promenade past the pier and shortly you reach Eastcliff Walk forking up on your left and there you must make your first decision. The true route is ahead along the sea wall but at certain states of the high tide and particularly in bad weather it may be impossible after a 2 mile (3.2 km) walk to pass under the railway line at the end of the wall, and if this appears likely a detour is needed. You should ascend Eastcliff Walk which soon becomes a track and will eventually lead you to the A379 where you turn right and rejoin the Coast Path at the top of Smugglers Lane.

If conditions look right, enjoy the walk along the sea wall and at the end pass under the railway line and ascend Smugglers Lane to the A379. Now you have a short walk on this busy main road, although there is a footpath on the left hand side, and after about 150 yards (135 m) turn right into Derncleugh Gardens, then left into Windward Lane and take the path over a stile on your left. After a field section you are back on the road but immediately follow the Old Teignmouth Road on your right, until you reach the main road yet again, turn right and shortly by some railings turn right and follow the path which soon zigzags down to the boat cove and follow the sea wall to Dawlish Station.

From here it is possible at low tide to walk along the sea wall to Dawlish Warren, then at the start of the new promenade cross the railway by a footbridge to join the inland path and reach the main road. If the tide is high you must take the alternative route by turning left opposite the Railway Station and in 30 yards (27 m) turning right through an arch and ascending the steps. Continue forward, passing a new housing development on your left, and after passing through another two arches, you emerge onto the A379 road and continue forward. Shortly after passing the new Rockstone Flats turn right on the road signposted Dawlish Warren 0.75 mile (1 km) and immediately take the coastal footpath signed on your right to follow the Ladies Mile to Dawlish Warren. (You can in fact take a footpath immediately before the Rockstone Flats, although this is not signposted, then take the left fork to join the Coast Path.)

There is no official path along the Warren but if time and energy permit you can enjoy a circular walk round this sandy Nature Reserve.

You are now faced with crossing the River Exe and in the summer months there is a ferry from Starcross to Exmouth reached by walking along the road from Dawlish Warren. However this is a busy road and you can if you wish catch one of the frequent buses to Starcross.

Starcross/Exmouth (River Exe)
Mr B Rackley,
Starcross Pier & Pleasure Company
26 Marine Parade,
Dawlish.
Tel: (01626) 862452

April - end October.
Hourly, 7 days a week
from Starcross Pier
on the hour from 1000 hrs
from Exmouth, Ferry Steps.
on the half-hour from 1030 hrs.

Alternative routes around the River Exe

1. You can catch a train at Dawlish Warren changing at Exeter and going back down to Exmouth.

2. You can do the same thing using the frequent bus services, changing over routes at either Countess Wear or in Exeter.

3. You can use the all year round ferry at Topsham to cross the River Exe. From Starcross continue by road to Powderham Church where a footpath follows the river and then the canal to a bridge across the canal where the ferry then crosses the river. (This ferry is dependent on tide and weather and does not operate at lunchtime or on a Tuesday.)

4. **Exe Water Taxis** (Easter to end October) will pick up passengers and take them to Exmouth - contact Bob or Jenny Killick, 60 High Street Topsham EX3 ODY (01392 873409). This is an evening telephone number so you will have to call them the day before you intend to cross. The water taxi leaves from the far end of the spit at Dawlish Warren.

Topsham Ferry (River Exe)	All year round on request.
Exeter City Council Canals & Rivers Dept.	Apr. - Sept. Daily except Tuesdays, from 1100 to
Tel: (01392) 274306 (Office)	1700 hrs. Oct - Mar. Saturdays, Sundays and
Tel: (0780) 120 3338 (Site)	Bank Holidays 1100 to 1700 hrs or sunset.

Once across the river you have to get to Exmouth and we are inclined to suggest the frequent bus service, but failing this the walk as far as Lympstone will be on the road except for a small footpath section between Clyst Bridge and Ebford. From Lympstone there is a riverside path to Exmouth, now part of the East Devon Way - look for the mauve markers featuring a foxglove.

67 Exmouth to Budleigh Salterton (River Otter Car Park)   OS E115 (T) Exmouth (Trains)

Grading: Moderate   Distance -   9.9   838.1   6.2   520.3

See also our Shaldon to Sidmouth Path Description.

No real problems here for walkers but keep inland of the range at Straight Point.

68 Budleigh Salterton to Sidmouth (River Sid)   OS E115 (T) Budleigh Salterton

Grading: Moderate then strenuous   Distance -   11.1   849.2   6.9   527.2

See also our Shaldon to Sidmouth Path Description.

The start is along a raised path inland to the River Otter Bridge at South Farm, then a riverside path back to the coast.

The path around High Peak is well marked but it does not unfortunately go over the top as you, and many others in the past, obviously expected. If you do battle your way to the top you will certainly not be disappointed with the views. The path on the top of Peak Hill immediately west of Sidmouth has been improved to give better seaward views.

The descent from Peak Hill towards Sidmouth takes you down through a wood and out on to the road. Turn right and keep to the right hand side of the road to pass through two kissing gates, then bear right through a gap in the hedge on to parkland for the descent into Sidmouth. At the bottom of the lawn, make your way onto the zigzag path which leads down between beach huts onto the small esplanade. Turn left and continue at sea level on the Clifton Walkway to the main esplanade.

69 Sidmouth to Seaton (River Axe)   OS E115 & E116 (T) Sidmouth

Grading: Severe then strenuous   Distance -   16.7   865.9   10.4   537.6

See also our Sidmouth to Lyme Regis Path Description.

Please note that there are a number of quite considerable ascents and descents on this section, so do not judge the effort required purely on the distance. There are one or two places in this stretch where it is easy to come off the route but one is not likely to come to any severe harm.

On leaving Sidmouth, dramatic cliff falls are the cause of a diversion, which is well marked.

After Branscombe Mouth there are alternative paths. The one over Hooken Cliffs gives superb views and is probably easier to walk. The undercliff path, apart from the beginning among the caravans is scenically better and we would recommend this if the weather is good. You have the interesting undercliff itself, the massive cliffs to the left, interesting rock formations ahead, and good views to seaward. At most states of the tide it is possible to walk along the beach from Seaton Hole to Seaton, avoiding some road work.

WATCH THE TIDE - YOU CAN GET CUT OFF

CP - Between Weston Cliff and Branscombe Mouth, the path is nearer the coast than the map suggests.

NTG - From Branscombe Mouth to Beer Head the map does not show the path along the top of Hooken Cliffs, only through Under Hooken. It is mentioned in the text, and both routes are official.

70 | Seaton to Lyme Regis (Town Car Park)   OS E116 (T) Seaton

Grading: Moderate   Distance -   11.0   876.9   6.8   544.4

See also our Sidmouth to Lyme Regis Path Description.

You leave Seaton across its concrete bridge over the River Axe and have to turn inland. Go up the road to the golf course, then walk due east across the fairway into a lane, which you go along, turning to the coast in less than 0.25 mile (400 m).

The section through the Landslip is in a National Nature Reserve and can be very rewarding to some but extremely frustrating to others. Views are extremely limited and the path in places puts on a fair imitation of a corkscrew or helter-skelter; you are unlikely to get lost but most unlikely to know where you are. Suggested times to walk the Landslip range from 1.5 hours to 4 hours, but we are told that the standard time is about 3 hours.

The path into Lyme Regis has now been improved and you can take a path directly down to The Cobb without having to come into the car park, and then down the road.

71 | Lyme Regis to Charmouth (River Char)   OS E116 (T) Lyme Regis

Grading: Moderate   Distance -   4.4   881.3   2.7   547.1

See also our Lyme Regis to Abbotsbury Path Description.

From Lyme to Studland the geology is such that the cliffs are vulnerable to slippages - you may encounter temporary diversions around such sections.

From Lyme Regis town centre take Church Street and Charmouth Road (A3052) until you reach Lyme Regis Football Club on the right, beyond which you will find a stile at the corner of a lane and take the footpath across fields to a lane where you turn left (yes west!) for 100 yards (90 m). At a finger post sign turn right up through the wood and near the top turn onto the path that runs between the cliff edge and the golf course. A diversion is in place around a landslip at Raffey's Ledge, just west of Charmouth. Until negotiations for a new path are finalised, use the map opposite. **Late news** - large cliff falls east of the River Char, diversion marked.

Alternatively at the end of the new promenade at Lyme Regis you may choose to walk along the firm sand on the beach to Charmouth, if the tide is well out. DO NOT attempt to walk upon the surface of the grey mud slide, and be aware of the state of the tide before starting out.

72 | Charmouth to West Bay (Bridport Arms)   OS E116 1 mile to (V) Charmouth

Grading: Strenuous   Distance -   11.2   892.5   7.0   554.1

See also our Lyme Regis to Abbotsbury Path Description.

This is a section of interesting walking with spectacular views from Golden Cap, the highest mainland point on the south coast of England, and later from Thorncombe Beacon. However, be warned, your good views are not obtained without effort!

When you get to what looks like the top of Golden Cap you have to turn left and go a little higher to the trig. point to find your way down, which starts at the north end before later bearing east again. There is a car park and a pub at Seatown.

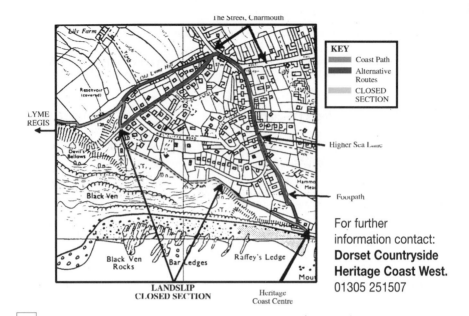

The Street, Charmouth

KEY
Coast Path
Alternative Routes
CLOSED SECTION

LYME REGIS

Higher Sea Lane

Footpath

Black Ven

Devil's Bellows

Black Ven Rocks   Bar Ledges   Raffey's Ledge   Mou

LANDSLIP
CLOSED SECTION

Heritage
Coast Centre

For further
information contact:
**Dorset Countryside
Heritage Coast West.**
01305 251507

73 West Bay to Abbotsbury (Swannery Car Park)   OS OL15 (V) West Bay; (V) Abbotsbury

---

Grading: Moderate   Distance -   15.2   907.7   9.4   563.5

See also our Lyme Regis to Abbotsbury Path Description.

SEE SECTION 80 FOR DETAILS OF THE ALTERNATIVE INLAND COAST PATH FROM WEST BEXINGTON TO OSMINGTON MILLS.

WARNING: If you intend to walk the whole length of Chesil Bank rather than going to Abbotsbury and along the edge of the Fleet (section 74), you should telephone Major Hazard on 01305 783456 ext. 8132, to check whether the bank is safe to walk. There may be some firing at Chickerell Rifle Range and it is not unknown for the odd bullet to mis-target, and travel as far as the Bank. As a result, walkers will be sent back despite having walked half this gruelling hike.

After you have walked round the back of West Bay harbour, pass to the right of St. John's Church and ahead to the West Bay Hotel, opposite which is the coast path sign pointing across to the foot of surprisingly steep cliffs.

Watch for the inland loop at Burton Freshwater. When the river is low you can 'cut the corner' across the beach, but this is not at all possible when the river is flowing strongly. As you start to descend to the caravan park you can look across and see if the river is not reaching the sea, then it is up to you.

At Burton Beach, just east of the hotel, there is a cafe / toilet (open all year).

At Burton Mere, unless you are particularly interested in maritime flowers, the definitive route goes inland of the Mere, rather than going along the seaward side: you will get quite enough pebbles later.

There is a fair weather cafe and all year round toilets at West Bexington, and seasonal snack wagons in the car park where the road turns inland past Abbotsbury Gardens. Walkers, however, should continue on the beach for another 200 yards (185 m).

There are refreshments, shops and B & B's in Abbotsbury. If you have time, the climb up to St Catherine's Chapel is worth the effort.

There is an alternative path to the south of Chapel Hill avoiding Abbotsbury village.

80

Grading: Easy. Chesil Beach: Strenuous   Distance -   17.5   925.2   10.9   574.4

See also our Abbotsbury to Weymouth Path Description.

Presumably you must have wanted to go into Abbotsbury if you did visit the village, but it is worth mentioning that the path does not really go there at all, but only close to it. Therefore, the correct, and sometimes quieter, way out is by the footpath going south to Nunnery Grove, and not the road by Mill Farm.

The inland path is well marked and enjoyable to walk; part of it goes along a ridge and has some good views. You do not get back to the shores of the Fleet until Rodden Hive.

On the outskirts of Abbotsbury after Horsepool Farm keep going up the ridge; beguiling, much better tracks go round the hill to the right, but they will not bring you to the stile you need at the top. In about 1 mile (1500 m) turn south off to the ridge and turn sharp left after Hodder's Coppice. A track goes forward, but this is NOT the one you want. After you have crossed a minor road, the official path follows the field headland east and then south to the north east corner of Wyke Wood as signposted, and not in a direct line as shown on some maps. Take particular care as you approach Rodden Hive - the path suddenly dives through a hedge on your left. There is an apparent track and even a marker post which might make you think that the path goes to the right of the stream, but it does not.

At Tidmoor Point, follow the red and white posts unless you have to divert as firing on the range is in progress across the definitive right of way. A deviation has been made inland at Wyke Regis around a Service Establishment.

An alternative for the tough walker who wishes to stay on the coast is to use the Chesil Beach; you can do this by going onto the beach where the path turns inland at Abbotsbury but note you cannot 'get off' again until you reach the causeway from Wyke Regis to Portland. This is only a walk for the fit and not one to be attempted at times of severe gale! Please note that the Chesil Bank is closed to visitors from 1st May-31st August for the Schedule 1 bird nesting season. During the nesting season please keep to the seaward side of the beach so as not to interfere with nesting birds.

Weymouth Harbour   All year round.
Weymouth & Portland Borough Council,   Apr. - Oct. Daily.
Harbour Master's Office,   Nov. - Mar. Monday & Friday only.
Municipal Offices, North Quay,   Additional sailings in December.
Weymouth, DT4 8TA
(01305-206423 or 01305 206278) Ask for Dep. Borough Engineer.

75 | **The Isle of Portland**   **OS OL15 (T) Portland**

Grading: Moderate   Distance -   21.3   946.5   13.2   587.6

See also our Isle of Portland Path Description.

The total distance includes walking Portland Beach Road (A354) twice (there and back).

A circuit of the Isle of Portland is well worth the extra effort. It is a fine walk, with much of interest along the rugged coast, which can be spectacular in rough weather. The Island and Royal Manor of Portland still quarries its famous limestone, still 'hosts' H. M. Prison Services, but is replacing the Ministry of Defence with new port and tourism facilites, so you may be lucky enough to find a new route around the North East section.

From Ferry Bridge you have a number of choices, none of them of much merit, for the first 2 miles (3 km). Using the footway beside the busy A354 road; crossing over the car park beyond the Chesil Beach Centre to slog along the pebbles of Chesil Beach; or catching a bus to the roundabout at the south end of the causeway to alight at the Royal Victoria Lodge. Fourth, and probably best, is to cross the bridge to beyond the boatyard and on the eastern bank, walk along the raised bed of the old railway to near the end of the causeway, before returning to the A354 road. You come to Fortuneswell where you need to cross the road and follow signs for the Chesil

Beach Gallery, turning left before the public toilets. Continue past the Cove House Inn and bear right up onto the promenade. Towards the end of this and just before the `grassy walls', bear left and immediately left again up a zigzag path; then right past the school and up the steep path in the grass incline to the steps to the terraced path that was the old A354 road.

Bear off right onto the coast path running between old quarry banks and the cliff face. 3 miles (5 km) of spectacular and airy cliff top walking brings you to Portland Bill with the Pulpit Rock and lighthouse (refreshments). Continue around the end of the low headland and pass to the seaward of wooden chalets to follow a winding path along the top of low cliffs to join a road above Freshwater Bay after about 1.5 miles (2.5 km).

Turn right up the road for 600 yards (550 m), past Cheyne Weares Car Park to a finger post on the right. Follow the zigzag path down into the rugged undercliff area, and follow the waymarks through the disused quarry workings down to Church Ope Cove.

Before the 'West Cliff' and 'Coast Path' signs, turn right through a gap in the hedge with a 'Crown Estate' sign on to the undercliff path. Continue to seaward along the rugged path to Durdle Pier and bear up left to turn right onto a wide firm path (old track bed of the former Weymouth to Easton railway line). Continue along the track to just before a 'rockfall' sign, where it is necessary to turn left over a bank to follow a rocky path that climbs up the cliffs to an isolated chimney seen above on the skyline. A word of warning here - although the track continues northwards and appears to be well used, do not be tempted to continue as the way forward is eventually blocked by the perimeter security fence of the former MOD Establishments and there is no other route up the high cliffs.

Our preferred route is to turn sharp right at the chimney to go along a prison road, and follow a tarmac road northwards through a gap in a high wall. At the next road turn right and bear downhill toward the gates of the former MOD establishment, but shortly go left at a fork through a barrier gate. Continue forward to a left hand bend, and carry on ahead on a grassy path towards a large pinnacle of rock after which, at the 'rock falls' sign, bear left steeply up on to the higher escarpment heading for a large communications mast. At the high wire perimeter fence turn left and follow the fence along and then around to the north to the entrance of Verne Prison. Take a path through a little gap to the left of the entrance, passing beside railings and down steep steps. Bear right along a path that traverses under the grassy banks and by a waymark post, bear left down to a haripin bend in the road.

Turn left and past house number 90 to take a footpath down left. Emerging onto a road bear left, and take the path beside a `No Entry' sign to Ventnor Road. Walk down to Fortuneswell Road, and cross the road to a path through a park and turn right onto the road to the roundabout by the Royal Victoria Lodge. From here retrace your steps for 2 miles (3 km) to Ferry Bridge.

76 Ferry Bridge to Lulworth Cove (Visitor Centre)   OS OL15 (T) Weymouth (Trains)

Grading: This section runs the gamut from easy to moderate to strenuous. Distance - 22.7 969.2   14.1   601.7

See also our Weymouth to Lulworth Cove Path Description.

SEE SECTION 80 FOR DETAILS OF THE ALTERNATIVE INLAND COAST PATH FROM WEST BEXINGTON TO OSMINGTON MILLS.

A footpath sign shows you where to continue on to Weymouth, but leave the old railway line at the north end of the shallow cutting to get back to the Coast Path.

Pass the sailing centre and continue into Old Castle Road; opposite Castle Cove Sailing Club bear right onto a tarmac footpath. Continue on paths close to the coast to Nothe Fort and bear sharp left down to the harbourside which is followed to the Town Bridge, which is crossed and the opposite side of the harbour is followed back to the Pavilion Complex. Here bear left to join The Esplanade. In summer a little ferry may run across the harbour to shorten the route.

Leave Weymouth along the new promenade and at Overcombe, go up to the minor road to Bowleaze Cove. However, after passing the Spyglass Inn it is best to cross the grass public open space and follow the cliff edge to the Beachside Centre. Beyond the holiday camp, the path leads to a stile at the eastern end of the establishment shown as Short Lake House on maps, and it is important that you follow the sign. It does in fact point in the right direction; compass carriers check it - it's about 72 degrees. You go up over the hill apparently going inland - you do not follow the cliff edge.

On the downhill approach to Osmington Mills the route avoiding the landslide bears away from the cliff edge over a stile and down the right hand side of a field. At the bottom it joins the inland Route just before it crosses two stiles to meet the narrow road that is followed down to the coast.

At Ringstead you are taken slightly inland, because the path shown on maps seaward of the houses does not exist. At the old coastguard cottages at White Nothe, be careful to take the left fork of the two yellow arrows, that being the correct route. From White Nothe onwards you will find that there are some quite severe gradients to be traversed before you reach Lulworth.

However, some people turn even further inland than they need. Some signposts indicate 'Youth Hostel-Coast Path' and contain the acorn emblem. These signs are intended to indicate the route to the Youth Hostel at East Lulworth and are not the continuation of the coast path.

The newly stonepitched path will lead you down through the car park and past the Heritage Centre, and onto a tarmac road to the cove.

Those who wish to arrive at Lulworth by a quieter non-car park route should, on Hambury Tout, turn right and take the old track down on the right hand side of the fence. This links with the beach path to St Oswald's Bay; on reaching this turn left. Presently it comes to a tarmac road which you can follow into Lulworth.

77   Lulworth Cove to Kimmeridge, Gaulter Gap (Beach car park) OS OL15 (V) Lulworth

Grading: Severe   Distance -   **11.8**   **981.0**   **7.3**   **609.0**

See also our Lulworth to Kimmeridge Path Description.

The coastal path through the Army ranges is open at the times shown below, and is a very fine walk indeed, but a tough one. If closed, two alternative routes are shown opposite.

The path behind the beach cafe has been permanently closed and there is some negotiation about the permissive path beside Bishops Cottage - but this will be clearly signposted when resolved. Tide permitting, the beach route is the better option. At most states of the tide, it is perfectly possible to walk along the pebble beach at Lulworth Cove, going up the path which rises diagonally on the far side of the beach. At the top of the steep ascent off the beach, the best route proceeds seawards and there the path turns south eastwards along the coast to the beginning of the Army Ranges, just by the Fossil Forest.

If time is of the essence, when you have crossed the beach and gone up the path, do not turn right but go straight ahead. This way you will come to the Bindon Gate into the ranges, and you can go ahead here, arriving at the coast again at Mupe Bay - shorter, but less scenic.

The village of Tyneham, church, school and historical information are worth going inland to see, between 1000 - 1600 hrs.

RAC Gunnery School Lulworth Ranges: No Firing and Firing Periods

1. *NON FIRING PERIOD.* The Range Walks will be open to the public during the following holiday periods, all dates are inclusive.:

EASTER 2001	13 APR - 22 APR 2001
SPRING 2001	26 MAY - 3 JUNE 2001
SUMMER 2001	28 JULY - 2 SEPT 2001
CHRISTMAS/NEW YEAR 2001/2002	22 DEC 2001 - 1 JAN 2002

2. *FIRING PERIODS.* The Range Walks are normally open to the public every Saturday and Sunday except for some weekends in the year. For 2000 they have reserved the following 6 weekends for firing:

FIRST WEEKEND	3 - 4 JAN 2001
SECOND	10 - 11 MAR 2001
THIRD	12 - 13 MAY 2001
FOURTH	16 - 17 JUN 2001
FIFTH	13 - 14 OCT 2001
SIXTH	24 - 25 NOV 2001

3. Experience has shown that it is sometimes possible to avoid firing on some of these reserved weekends and if this is the case, the Range Walks will be opened. Should this occur in 2001 we will make every effort to publicise the fact.

4. Tyneham Church and the School are normally open for viewing 1000 hrs-1600 hrs when the walks are open.

5. Information is also available by ringing 01929 462721 ext 4819, which is a 24 hour answering service

Alternative Route when Lulworth Range Coast Path is unavailable: Lulworth Cove to Kimmeridge, Gaulter Gap.

Option 1 - approx. 13.5 miles (22 km) on a safer, quieter but more strenuous route using mainly rights of way, and permissive paths through Lulworth Park (pre-plotting of given grid refs. onto a map will assist navigation).

Leave the Cove and take the 2nd road on the left (825807).100 yards (90 m) on the right, a footpath leads north for 0.75 mile (1.2 km); turn right (east) and after 100 yards (90 m) turn left (north) to pass Belhuish Coppice and Belhuish Farm, and then across the B3071 at 835832.

At 844(5)828 eastern boundary of Burngate Wood, use the permissive (blue) path north-east past Park Lodge, and go across the road (855832) onto a bridleway.

(The permissive red path across the stile, just up on the left, loops around the lake - if you're ready for a peaceful stop - and meets this bridleway further up at 861(5)834.)

Continue NE along the bridleway to 865839 where it veers north, and later north-east through the Highwood to meet the road at 872862. On the road walk east, fork right (signposted Stoborough) at 882855; over the crossroads at 886855 east for further 1.5 miles (2.4 km) along Holme Lane to walk east 912855.

(*) Turn right just before a railway bridge onto Dorey Farm bridleway at 912855. After 1.25 miles (2 km) turn right onto Creech Road leading south-southwest towards the Purbeck Ridge. After another 1.5 miles (2.4 km) of road, walk up a steep gradient to a viewpoint car park. Beyond the car park 905817 take the left road that turns back and down over the ridge to Corfe. (A short cut bridleway 905817 zigzags down to meet the same road.) As the road levels out at a left hand bend 907812, take the bridleway ahead that leads out south through Steeple Leaze Farm.

200 yards (185 m) south of the farm, a footpath leads south crossing another ridge bridleway, down a steep path, and across a field to Higher Stonehips, and on to Gaulter Gap, the easterly point of the range walks.

Option 2 - approx. 12 miles (19 km).

This route is mainly road walking, and care is needed on narrow bends. Leave the Cove to West Lulworth on the B3070, and then turn right to East Lulworth at 835816 to continue on the B3070. After 3 miles (5 km), turn right (east) at grid reference 886855 along Holme Lane, and then continue from * above, at 912855.

78 | Kimmeridge, Gaulter Gap to Swanage (The Pier) OS OL15

| Grading: Severe and then moderate | Distance - | 21.4 | 1002.4 | 13.3 | 622.3 |

See also our Kimmeridge to South Haven Point Path Description.

From Gaulter Gap, Kimmeridge, the path is straightforward although care may be needed where small sections have slipped, cracked or may be close to the cliff top; after descending Hounstout and going inland to Hill Bottom cottages, the path turns south again, and beyond the gate climbs left up to a high level route which is well signposted. The climb up West Hill is away from the views, but as you gain height along Emmett's Hill, the views back along the Dorset coast are very good. The Royal Marines memorial is just to the left of the path.

From St Aldhelm's Head, there is fine high level walking all the way to Durlston Head, but not much accommodation along this stretch.

There is only minimal signing in the Durlston Country Park. However, you keep on the low level path all the way round Durlston Head but as you come up on the north side of it you take the second turning right, not the first which is a dead end into a quarry.

The section of the Coast Path through Swanage is not well signed, and is being constantly diverted temporarily to accommodate drainage works. You are unlikely to go far wrong, and will soon be walking along the sea front promenade.

CP - the map suggests that the Coast Path enters Worth Matravers; it does not, but turns sharply through the word 'Farm' of Renscombe Farm.

79 | Swanage to Sandbanks (South Haven Point) OS OL15 (T) Swanage; (V) Studland

| Grading: Moderate | Distance - | 12.2 | 1014.6 | 7.6 | 629.9 |

See also our Kimmeridge to South Haven Point Path Description.

At Ocean Bay Stores at the north end of Swanage Sea Front, tide permitting, you may prefer to keep along the pedestrian promenade to the end and then walk 200 yards (185 m) along the beach turning up some steps to the official route. At high tide you have to leave the seafront on the main road (Ulwell Road) and where it bears left into a one-way system continue ahead into Redcliffe Road. At the sub post office turn sharp right into Ballard Way and at the end do not be put off by the signs 'Ballard Private Estate'. Carry forward into the chalet estate and follow signs for the coast path to emerge on to a grassed area on the cliff edge.

From Ballard Down the path is obvious all the way to Handfast Point and the much photographed rocks of Old Harry.

When you reach a road junction by a public toilet, turn right. You will then pass two footpaths to the right but do not take either of them. Carry on up the road passing the Bankes Arms pub. After passing the Manor House Hotel, take the track / road down to the beach, and go left at the beach. When the tide is out, this is firm, but when it is in more effort will be required.

Further up the beach, maybe we should mention there is a naturist beach, so you must not be put off if you find that on this last lap that you are the only one wearing clothes! The National Trust has also provided an alternative route, The Heather Walk, through the dunes, and this is marked by yellow topped posts.

Despite any notices you may see, dogs on leads may accompany Coast Path walkers along the shore line, but be sure to clean up after your dog if necessary.

Studland/Sandbanks (Mouth of Poole Harbour) Bournemouth-Swanage Motor Road & Ferry Company, Shell Bay, Studland. BH19 3BA.
Tel: Studland (01929) 450203.

All year round. Daily every 20 mins. Sandbanks 0700 - 2300 hrs
Shell Bay 0710 - 2310 hrs
Closed for 2 - 3 weeks in November 2001 for refit (phone for info).

Wainwright at the end of his work on the Pennine Way said it all, and said it better, of a shorter path. Ward & Mason in the old Letts Guide simply say 'That's it'. We will add whether you have been lucky enough to walk the whole way from Minehead at one go, or simply, as most of us have, in bits and pieces over a period, nonetheless you will be glad you walked and have just finished Britain's longest and finest footpath. It's a longer step than most take in their lifetime!

80 | Alternative Inland Coast Path: West Bexington to Osmington Mills OS OL15

Grading: Moderate   Distance - 27.0   16.8

See also our alternative Inland Route Path Description.

Although this is certainly not a coastal path it is an enjoyable walk along a well-marked path with good views seaward from the ridges. Because it is inland a more detailed route is given. When walking this section bear in mind that we found no place for obtaining refreshments between the start of the walk, where there is a cafe, and the village of Osmington.

At West Bexington car park turn inland up the road signposted 'Inland Route - Coast Path', and where the road turns left, continue forward up a stony track, signposted 'Hardy Monument $5^1/_2$ miles'. At top of the hill the footpath briefly joins the main road but you immediately leave again over the stile on the right through the field, signposted `Hardy Monument 5 miles'. Take care, as the way across this field is not clear and should, at first, keep parallel to the road and then you bear right to a waymarked post. After you have crossed the wall, you can start to bear upwards to the left to the further signpost near the road, marked with the acorn symbol and the words 'Inland Route'. After about 300 yards (275 m) continuing through the field and by the corner of a wall there is a further signpost 'Hardy Monument $4^1/_2$, Osmington Mills 15'. Continue forward, very shortly emerging on to the B3157 road which you cross and leave through a gate, signposted `Hardy Monument $4^1/_2$'.

You now approach Abbotsbury Castle and where the path in front divides, take the upper right-hand fork along the top of the south side of the Fort past the trig point, from where you can get superb views in all directions, and you should be able to see the Hardy Monument clearly in the distance. Proceed eastwards and cross the minor road now and go forward, signposted `Hardy Monument 4'. Proceed in an approximate easterly direction along the ridge of Wears Hill and the crest of White Hill for about 2 miles (3.2 km) following the signposts and waymarks. However be careful not to follow signs with the acorn symbol incorrectly that indicate routes down to the village of Abbotsbury lying in the valley below, with the old chapel clearly visible. At the east end of White Hill bear north-east as signposted and leave in the inland corner through a gate on to a minor road. Turn left along the road for approximately 50 yards (46 m) and then turn right, signposted 'Inland Route - Hardy Monument 2'.

Follow the bridleway marked with blue arrows along the wire fence above the scrub to a path junction; where the bridleway carries on forward take the yellow waymarked footpath to the left and cross a stile. At the far side of the field the track then leads approximately 50 yards (46 m) to a further gate with a stile and waymark. Immediately adjacent to this gate is a stone circle which is an ancient monument and there is a sign to this effect. You now continue forward, leaving a small wood to the left, to reach the road from Portisham to Winterbourne Steepleton. Turn left along the road for approximately 60 yards (55 m) and then turn right into a field over a stile, signposted `Hardy Monument $1^1/_2$ - Osmington Mills 13'. On the far side of the field proceed forward, signpost `Hardy Monument 1'. At this point there is a signpost forking right to Hellstone only, with a return possible on a different path.

At Blackdown Barn turn left to climb up through the woods, signposted `Hardy Monument $^1/_2$'. At the monument you will find a small signpost 'Inland Route - Osmington Mills 11 miles' with a blue arrow indicating the way forward. Cross the road to a further signpost with the acorn symbol and now descend through the bracken. You shortly reach the road again, turn left and in a few yards ignore the signpost on the right, cutting back indicating 'Bridleway to Coast Path' and continue forward, (signposted 'Coast Path East') and in another 100 yards (90 m) turn right, signposted 'Inland Route to Courton Hill' on one side of the sign and 'Osmington 12 - Courton Hill 2' on the other. Now there is a good ridgeway path without navigational problems for some 3 miles (4.8 km) and good views to seaward in the distance. After passing the radio mast you come to the B3159 marked by the Borough of Weymouth boundary stone and continue across the road, signposted 'Inland Route East'.

On reaching the A354 turn right immediately before the main road down the signposted track and after just over $^1/_4$ mile (400 m) you will find a stile in the hedge on your left. The path leads across a narrow field to cross the busy A354. Before the farm with its adjacent radio mast take care to go through the gate on the right, marked with a blue arrow. After crossing the field, leaving two tumuli to your left, you reach a metalled road. Turn right and at the next junction there is a signpost surmounted by a symbol 'Dorset - Came Wood' which, unusually, carries the six-figure map reference of the locality (687857). Here you turn right at the signpost 'Bridleway to Bincombe'. At the end of the path join a metalled lane and at the junction turn left, signposted 'Inland Route East'.

Drop down the road into the village of Bincombe and where the road turns right take the track forward leaving a small church on your right. Where the path splits take the left hand fork signposted again with a blue arrow and the acorn symbol. After the overhead high-voltage power lines pass through a small signposted wooden gate and then proceed forward through one field into the next to the footpath sign. Here turn left, following the line of the old indistinct curving grassy track until it meets the road at the bottom of Combe Valley. Turn left here and follow the road until you reach the Combe Valley road sign to 'Sutton Poyntz' and take this turn to the right. After 70 yards (64 m) turn left through a gate, signposted 'White Horse Hill - Osmington Mills'. The path now is easy to follow with extensive views to seaward over Weymouth and Portland. On passing a ruined building on your left you reach a broad track and turn right, signposted 'Osmington $1^1/_2$' and after about 200 yards (185 m) go through a gate, signposted 'Inland Route Osmington'. You will shortly pass the trig point on your right and at the next field gate bear left and follow the field boundary along White Horse Hill. Just beyond the next gate fork right, signposted 'Osmington 1, Lulworth 8'.

Descend to the village of Osmington and follow the signs through the village. When you reach the main Weymouth road at the Sun Ray Inn turn left and in about 250 yards (230 m) turn right at a signpost, over a stile and footbridge, and follow the field boundary on the left through two fields and at the top look back to see the Hardy Monument in the distance and also the white horse on the hillside. Go over the stile to the footpath sign, then turn half right to cross the field at an angle to a further stile. Cross it and turn left along the hedge side to the bottom. At the end of the field there is a very short length of enclosed footpath to the road; turn right along it, descending to Osmington Mills.

ACCOMMODATION

This list of accommodation has been prepared in path order.

The following letter code is used.

Facilities

O	=	Open All Year	D	= Drying facilities for wet clothes
EM	=	Evening Meal	PL	= Packed Lunches
CP	=	Car Parking	LSP	= Long Stay Parking
DW	=	Dogs Welcome	KT	= Kit Transfer
PD	=	Pick Up/Drop Service		

Room Codes

D	=	Double	T	= Twin
S	=	Single	F	= Family
ES	=	En Suite		

Please note: The figure in brackets denotes the number of en-suite rooms e.g. 4d[2] = 4 double rooms, two of which are en-suite.

KT - Kit Transfer. A service being offered by some of our accommodation providers is to transfer your kit to your next accommodation. This could prove useful to you. Naturally a fee may be levied for this service.

Distance from Path. Please remember these are only approximate and may not be accurate.

PD - Pick Up/Drop. This code appears following the distance from the path and denotes a facility whereby your host is prepared to collect and return you to the coast path within reasonable distance. No fee should be charged for this service.

The part of the address in CAPITALS is an aid to location; it does not signify the postal town. The extreme left-hand column refers to the appropriate section in the 'Trail Description'; we feel it may help you to find addresses quickly. The amount quoted gives an **indication of the starting rate** for bed and breakfast, and may well rise. If working on a tight budget, it is best to ask first.

Tourist Information Centres can be an additional source of accommodation addresses. We have provided a list of TIC's along the coast path for your use on page 137.

The majority of our B & B addresses have been submitted by members. The fact that they are included in this book does not indicate a recommendation by The South West Coast Path Association. Their inclusion is merely for information purposes; they are there, if you want them. We cannot, for financial and practical reasons, introduce vetting, inspection or any form of `Star' rating. We do have a system whereby addresses can be removed from the list.

We wish to develop this list especially for many 'sparse' areas. Suggestions for inclusion in our next list will be welcome. Details of any new accommodation should be addressed to the Administrator. Our list is not comprehensive and walkers will find many B&B's in towns and villages along the coast path that are not recorded in this book.

It would not be out of place here to add a word of thanks from those who walk, to those who kindly board. How many times have we been thankful for a friendly welcome and good 'digs'? Maybe a note we had from one of our accommodation addresses puts it well. 'We have had quite a lot of walkers this year and we have usually managed to dry them out - and feed them up.'

Although there are a lot of addresses that state they are 'open all the year', some of these close for the Christmas period. Walkers should remember that during the holiday season many of our accommodation addresses could be fully booked up in advance by holidaymakers staying for a week or two. Conversely a walker could book for one night only in good time, thus preventing a guest house proprietor from taking a week or more booking later on. Accommodation problems can be frustrating to all parties concerned so bear these facts in mind when bed hunting **for one night only**.

Important If having booked ahead, and for any reason you are unable to get to your accommodation address, please telephone and explain your absence to your intended host. We have known instances where the host has become so worried about the non-appearance of walkers that they have informed the emergency services. The last thing we want is Police, Coastguards and Royal Navy helicopters out on a wild goose chase.

Sect.	Name and Address	Tel. No. Fax. No. Web / Email	Map Reference Opening Times	Distance from Path Starting Price Facilities Accommodation
1	Mr & Mrs D Sanders 1 Glenmore Road MINEHEAD TA24 5BQ	01643 706225		700 mtr £16.50 O PL CP LSP KT 2D[1] 1T[1] 2S 1F[1]
1	Mrs D Morris Badgers 38 Summerland Road MINEHEAD TA24 5BS	01643 704583		400 mtrs £16.00 O D PL CP LSP 1D 1T 1S 1F
1	Mrs S Phillips The Old Ship Aground Quay Street MINEHEAD TA24 5UL	01643 702087 01643 709066 oldship.aground@virgin.net		500mtrs £25.00 O D EM PL CP LSP DW KT 1D 2T 1S 3F ALL ES
1	Mr B Rutland 11 Glenmore Road MINEHEAD TA24 5BQ	01643 705253 / 702287 brucerutland@supanet.com		1km £15.00 O D 1D 3F
1	Mr & Mrs J Segenhout Mayfair Hotel The Avenue MINEHEAD TA24 5AY	01643 702719		800 mtrs £24.00 D EM PL CP KT 5D 2T 2S 4F ALL ES
1	Mr R Brooker 23 Chestnut Way Alcombe MINEHEAD TA24 6EB	01643 709913	972 452	1 km PD £15.00 O D EM PL CP KT 1D 1T[1]
1	Mrs J Tice Cotswold 19 Tregonwell Road MINEHEAD TA24 5DU	01643 703102 01643 703399 blizicebandb@aol.com	970 467	PD £18.00 O D EM PL CP LSP KT 2D[2] 2T[2] 1S
1	Mr J Murray Marston Lodge Hotel St Michael's Road MINEHEAD TA24 5JP	01643 702510		400 mtrs £28.00 O D EM PL CP 6D 1T 2S 2F ALL ES
1	Mrs A Green 24 Ponsford Road MINEHEAD TA24 5DY	01645 703945 greenfinial@lineone.net	973 467 Mar-Oct	800 mts PD £16.50 D PL CP LSP KT 1D 1T ALL ES
1	Mr & Mrs R A Robbins Rosanda House 2 Northfield Road MINEHEAD TA24 5QQ	01643 704958 www.rosanda.co.uk rosanda.house.virgin.net		100 mts O D CP 2D 1T ALL ES
1	Mrs S Coombs Hurlstone Sparkhayes Lane PORLOCK TA24 8NE	01643 862650	887 469	On path £18.00 O D PL CP DW 1D 1T
1	Mrs J Robinson The Ship Inn High Street PORLOCK TA24 8QD	01643 862507 01643 863244 jrtheship@hotmail.co.uk		On path PD £25.00 O D EM PL CP LSP DW KT 11D 1S ALL ES
1	Mr & Mrs T V Stiles-Cox Leys The Ridge PORLOCK TA24 8HA	01643 862477 01643 862477	892 469	2 kms PD £19.00 O D PL CP 1D 2S
1	Ms K Stickley Alderton Bed & Breakfast DOVERHAY PORLOCK TA24 8LJ	01643 863344 01643 863344 karen.stickley@virgin.net		£17.50 O D EM PL DW 1D 2T

Sect.	Name and Address	Tel. No. Fax. No. Web / Email	Map Reference Opening Times	Distance from Path Starting Price Facilities Accommodation
1	Mr R G Steer Myrtle Cottage High Street PORLOCK TA24 8PU	01643 862978 01643 862978 www.smoothhound@chelsoftdemon.com bob.steer@talk21.com		100mtrs £22.50 O D CP DW 3D 2T 2F ALL ES
1	Mr & Mrs R G Thornton Lorna Doone Hotel High Street PORLOCK TA24 8PS	01643 862404 01643 863018 lorna@doone99.freeserve.co.uk	888 468	1.5 km PD £22.00 O D EM PL CP DW 3D 8T 3S ALL ES
1	Mrs B Starr Sea View Cottage PORLOCK WEIR TA24 8PE	01643 862523	864 478	On path £18.00 O D PL CP DW KT 1D(1) 1T
2	Mrs E J Richards Silcombe Farm PORLOCK TA24 8JN	01643 862248	833 482	On path PD £18.00 O D EM PL CP LSP KT 2D[1] 1T 1S
2	Mr & Mrs C Parker-Clifford Tregonwell Riverside Guest House 1 Tors Road LYNMOUTH EX35 6ET	01598 753369		400 mtr £22.00 O D PL CP LSP DW KT 7D[5] 1T 1S 1F[1]
2	Mrs J Pile Oakleigh 4 Tors Road LYNMOUTH EX35 6ET	01598 752220	Mar-Nov	400 mtr PD £20.00 D PL CP LSP DW KT 5D 2T 2S
2	The Bath Hotel 01598 752544 LYNMOUTH EX35 6EL	01598 752238 www.torslynmouth.co.uk bathhotel@torslynmouth.co.uk	Easter-Oct	20mtrs £29.00 D EM PL CP DW 12D 8T 1S 3F ALL ES
2	Mr & Mrs J McGowan The Denes Longmead LYNTON EX35 6DQ	01598 753573 01598 753573 www.thedenes.com j.e.mcgowan@btinternet.com		1km PD £16.00 O D EM PL CP KT 2D[1] 3T[1] 3F[1]
2	Mrs Mari Kirk 12 Crossmead LYNTON EX35 6DG	01598 753288		400 mtrs £17.00 O D EM PL CP DW 1D 1T 2S
2	Mrs P E Morgan Kingford House Longmead LYNTON EX35 6DQ	01598 752361		£19.00 O D EM PL 4D 1T 2S ALL ES
2	Mr & Mrs D Keen St Vincent House Castle Hill LYNTON EX35 6JA	01598 752244 01598 753971 keenstvins@lineone.net		80 mtrs PD £17.50 O D EM PL CP DW KT 4D 2T 1S 1F ALL ES
3	Mrs Dallyn Mannacott Farm Nr Hunters Inn MARTINHOE EX31 4QS	01598 763227	662 481 April to Oct	800 mtrs £15.50 D PL CP PD 1D 1T
3	Mrs M Mangnall Moorlands HOLDSTONE DOWN COMBE MARTIN EX34 0PF	01271 883463	625 477	200mtrs £18.00 O D EM PL CP DW EM by arrange. 1D 1F ALL ES
3	Mr & Mrs F J Barry Glendower King Street COMBE MARTIN EX34 0AL	01271 883449 frankjbarry@netscapeonline.co.uk		100 mtrs £15.00 O D PL CP LSP KT PD 3D[2] 3T[2] 2S[2] 1F[1]

Sect.	Name and Address	Tel. No. Fax. No. Web / Email	Map Reference Opening Times	Distance from Path Starting Price Facilities Accommodation
3	Mrs J Bosley Hillview Guest House The Woodlands COMBE MARTIN EX34 OAT	01271 882331 hillviewgh@appleonline.net	575 469 Easter to Sept	200 mtrs £16.00 D PL CP LSP KT 2D[2] 1T
3	Mr & Mrs R Atkinson Mellstock House Woodlands COMBE MARTIN EX34 0AR	01271 882592 01271 882090 combemartin-touristinformation.com/mellstock.htm mellstockhouse@leos.org.uk	472 573	300 mts £18.00 O D EM PL CP LSP KT 3D[3] 1T[1] 1S 1F
3	Mr R Leonard The Fo'c's'le Seaside COMBE MARTIN EX34 0DJ	01271 883354 01271 883354 www.focsleinn.co.uk		100mtrs £25.00 O D EM PL CP LSP DW 8D 1T 4S 1F ALL ES
3	The Saffron House Hotel King Street COMBE MARTIN EX34 0BX	01271 883521	581 469 Mar-Oct	500mtrs £20.00 D EM PL CP 4D(3) 1T 4F(4)
3	Mrs A Waldon Idlehour Borough Road COMBE MARTIN EX34 OAN	01271 883217		20 mtr £13.00 D CP DW 2D 1T 1S
3	The Wild Pear Centre King Street COMBE MARTIN EX34 0AG	01271 882579 01271 883086	581 470	500 mtrs £14.00 O D 2D 4T 4F
3	Mr & Mrs Parkes Crimond Guest House COMBE MARTIN EX34 0BS	01271 882348 01271 882348	583 468	500mtrs PD £16.50 O D PL CP DW KT 1D 1T 1S 1F ALL ES
4	Mr G Greenway 31 Beach Road HELE BAY ILFRACOMBE	01271 866007		on path £15.00 O EM PL CP 2D 1T 1F ALL ES
4	Mr & Mrs A G Furber Slipway Cottage 2 Hierns Lane, The Harbour ILFRACOMBE EX34 9EH	01271 863035 01271 863035		On path £17.50 O D EM PL CP LSP DW 3D[2] 1T
4	Mr & Mrs W J Millington Sherborne Lodge Hotel Torrs Park ILFRACOMBE EX34 8AY	01271 862297 01271 865520 www.smoothhound.co.uk/hotels/sherborn.html 113121-222@compuserve.com		200mtrs £16.00 O D EM PL CP LSP DW 6D[5] 3T[2] 1S 1F[1]
4	Mr & Mrs C D Hewitt Norbury House Hotel Torrs Park ILFRACOMBE EX34 8AZ	01271 863888		200mtrs PD £20.00 O D EM PL CP LSP DW KT 2D[2] 2T[2] 1S 4F[4]
5	Mr T Wright Glen Tor Hotel Torrs Park ILFRACOMBE EX34 8AZ	01271 862403 01271 862403 www.glentorhotel.co.uk info@glentorhotel.co.uk	512 473	80 mts £21.00 O D EM PL CP LSP 4D 1T 1S 1F ALL ES
5	Mr & Mrs I Welsh Greyven House Hotel 4 St James Place ILFRACOMBE EX34 9BH	01271 862505 www.greyvenhouse.co.uk greyvenhouse@btinternet.com	571 429 Mar-Nov	50mts PD £19.50 D EM PL CP DW KT 3D[2] 1T[1] 1S 2F[1]
5	Mrs M P Newcombe Sunnyside LEE NR ILFRACOMBE EX34 8LW	01271 863189		50mtrs PD £18.00 O D PL CP PD 1D 1T 1S

Sect.	Name and Address	Tel. No. Fax. No. Web / Email	Map Reference Opening Times	Distance from Path Starting Price Facilities Accommodation
5	Mr & Mrs M Rogers The Blue Mushroom LEE NR ILFRACOMBE EX34 8LR	01271 862 947	489 467	On Path £22.00 O CP LSP 2D ALL ES
5	Mrs F Nustedt The Grampus Inn LEE NR ILFRACOMBE	01271 862906 jnustedt@globalnet.co.uk	464 483	250 mtr £21.00 O D EM PL CP LSP DW KT 1D 1T 1F ALL ES
5	Mrs G Potts The Orchard LEE ILFRACOMBE EX34 8LW	01271 867212		PD £23.00 O D PL CP KT 2D 1T 1S ALL ES
5	Mrs S Tod Fuschia Valley House LEE BAY EX34 8LW	01271 866857		500mtrs £18.00 O D PL CP DW KT 2D[1] 1T 1F
6	Mr T Cole Lundy House Hotel Chapel Hill MORTHOE EX34 7DZ	01271 870372 01271 871001 www.lundyhousehotel.co.uk info@lundyhousehotel.co.uk	Closed Jan	20 mtrs PD £22.50 D EM PL CP DW KT 4D 1T 3F ALL ES
6	Mrs A Braund Clyst House Rockfield Road WOOLACOMBE EX34 7DH	01271 870220	March to Oct	100 mtrs £20.00 D EM PL CP 1D 2T
6	Mr & Mrs H J Riley Camberley Beach Road WOOLACOMBE EX34 7AA	01271 870231 01271 871199 camberley@tesco.net	465 438	600 mtrs £19.50 O D PL CP KT 3D 2T 1F ALL ES
7	Mrs G Adams Combas Farm PUTSBOROUGH CROYDE EX33 1PH	01271 890398	449 396	900 mtrs £19.00 D EM PL CP LSP 2D[2] 1S 2F[2]
7	Mr & Mrs C Gedling West Winds Guest House Moor Lane CROYDE BAY EX33 1PA	01271 890489 01271 890489 www.westwindguesthouse.co.uk chris@croydewestwinds.freeserve.co.uk	March to Nov	On path £27.00 D PL CP DW KT 3D 1T 1S ALL ES
7	Mrs J Windsor Chapel Farm Guest House Hobbs Hill CROYDE EX33 1NE	01271 890429 www.chapelfarmcroyde.co.uk	Easter-Oct	500 mtrs £18.00 D PL CP 3D ES
7	Mr & Mrs G Casban Leadengate House CROYDE EX33 1PN	01271 890373	443 388	800 mts £20.00 O D PL CP LSP DW EM by arrange. 2D 1T 1S 1F ALL ES
7	Mr & Mrs A Baretta Shuna Down Road CROYDE EX33 1QE	01271 890537 01271 890537		100mtrs O PL CP LSP KT 4D 1T ALL ES
7	Mr & Mrs P Davis Moorsands Moor Lane CROYDE EX33 1NP	01271 890781 www.croyde-bay.com/moorsands.htm	441 395	450mtrs £24.00 O D CP KT 2D 1T 1S 1F ALL ES
8	Mrs R C Saunders Stockwell Lodge 66 South Street BRAUNTON	01271 814338	486 362	200mtrs PD £15.00 O D PL CP LSP DW KT 4D[2] 4T[2] 1S 2F[2]

Sect.	Name and Address	Tel. No. Fax. No. Web / Email	Map Reference Opening Times	Distance from Path Starting Price Facilities Accommodation
8	Mrs J Watkins North Cottage 14 North Street BRAUNTON EX33 1AJ	01271 812703	485 367	200mtrs £16.00 O D EM PL CP DW KT 2D[1] 1T 1S 1F
8	Mr R Tatman St Helens Priory Hobbs Hill BRAUNTON EX33 1NE	01271 890757		800 mtrs PD £22.50 O D EM PL CP LSP DW KT 4[4] 2T
8	Mr & Mrs R F Tyson Crossways Braunton Road BARNSTAPLE EX31 1JY	01271 379120	553 336	200 mtrs £16.00 O D PL CP LSP DW 2D[1] 3T[1] 2F
8	Mr & Mrs J Harrison Cresta Guest House Sticklepath Hill BARNSTAPLE EX31 2BU	01271 374022 01271 374022 www.crestaguesthouse.com.uk		800mtrs £18.00 O D PL CP DW 3D[3] 1T[1] 2S 2F[2]
9	Mrs D E George Oakwood 34 Yelland Road FREMINGTON EX31 3DS	01271 373884		2.5kms £14.00 O D EM PL CP DW 3D 2T 1F
9	Mr & Mrs C Chatwin Pepperlea The Holt BIDEFORD EX39 5DG	01237451496	380 230	300mtr PD £16.00 D EM PL CP LSP KT 1D 1T 1S 1F
9	Mrs H Laugharne Mount Hotel Northdown Road BIDEFORD EX39 3LP	01237 473748		500 mts PD O D PL CP LSP KT 2D 2T 2S 1F ALL ES
9	Mr & Mrs N George Bude House 28 Bude Street APPLEDORE EX39 1PS	01237 476608	467 305	100 mtrs £17.50 O D CP 1D 1T ALL ES
9	Mrs D Cope Conkers Durrant Lane NORTHAM EX39 2RL	01237 474794 www.enterprise.conkers.co.uk		350 mts PD £26.00 O D EM PL CP LSP KT 1D[1]
9	Mr & Mrs M Federl Locksley House 1 Tower Street NORTHAM EX39 1JL	01237 474885		1.5 kms £14.00 O D PL CP DW 1D 1T 2S
9	Mrs Clegg Mayfield Avon Lane WESTWARD HO! EX39 1LR	01237 477128		400 mtrs PD £14.00 O D PL CP LSPKT 3D 1T 1S
9	Mr & Mrs P Snowball Brockenhurst 11 Atlantic Way WESTWARD HO! EX39 1HX	01237 423346 01237 423346 snowball@brockenhurst1.freeserve.co.uk	432 290	200 mtrs PD £22.50 O D PL CP LSP DW KT 2D 1T 3S ALL ES
9	Mr & Mrs R Sharratt Eversley 1 Youngaton Road WESTWARD HO! EX39 1HU	01237 471603		200 mtrs £15.00 O D CP DW 1D 1T 1S 1F[1]
9	Mrs M Brocklesby The Puffin Inn 123 Bay View Road WESTWARD HO! EX39 1BJ	01237 473970 01237 422815 thepuffins@breathemail.net		500 mtr £21.00 O D EM PL CP LSP DW 2D 2T 1F ALL ES

Sect.	Name and Address	Tel. No. Fax. No. Web / Email	Map Reference Opening Times	Distance from Path Starting Price Facilities Accommodation
9	Mrs C Pile Culloden House Hotel Fosketh Hill WESTWARD HO! EX39 1JA	01237 479421 01237 475628 culloden.house@ukgateway.net		200 mtr £25.00 O D EM PL CP LSP DW KT 5D[4] 9T[7] 2F[2]
10	Mr & Mrs D May Maecroft, Acre Road Horns Cross PEPPERCOMBE, Bideford EX39 5DH	01237 451786 brimacombe@ondigital.com		1km £16.00 O D CP 2D[1] 1T
10	Mr & Mrs K.W Ryder The Old Mill BUCKS MILL EX 39 5	01237 431701 01237 431701 kryder 1 @ compuserve.com	355 237	On path £19.00 O D EM PL CP LSP 2D 1T 1S
10	Mrs M Dunn 55 The Quay CLOVELLY EX39 5TF	01237 431436 01237 431919 www.westcountry-walking-holidays.com mick@westcountry-walking-holidays.com		500mtrs £20.00 O D PL CP DW KT PD 1D 1T
10	Mrs C Giddy Temple Bar High Street CLOVELLY EX39 5TE	01237 431438		on path £20.00 D CP LSP 1D 1T 1S
10	The New Inn High Street CLOVELLY EX39 STQ	01237 431303 01237 431636 newinn@clovelly.co.uk		£34.25 O D EM PL CP LSP 7D 1S ALL ES
10	Ms L.J Simms Donkey Shoe Cottage 21 High Street CLOVELLY	01237 431601		200mtrs £19.00 O D PL CP LSP KT 2D 1T 1S
10	Mr & Mrs T D Curtis Fuchsia Cottage Burscott Lane HIGHER CLOVELLY EX39 5RR	01237 431398 www.clovelly-holidays.co.uk tomsuecurtis.fuchsiacot@currantbun.com	313 242	1km £16.00 O D PL CP LSP KT PD 1D[1] 1S 1F[1]
10	Mrs B May Boat House Cottage 148 Sierra Hill HIGHER CLOVELLY EX39 5ST	01237 431209	553 124	800 mtrs £16.00 O D PL CP LSP DW KT 1D 1T 1F
10	Mrs D L Vanstone The Old Smithy Sierra HIGHER CLOVELLY EX39 5ST	01237 431202	310 250	500 mts £16.50 O D PL CP LSP 3D[2] 2T[2] 2F[2]
10	Mrs P Vanstone High Banks Cottage Sierra Hill HIGHER CLOVELLY EX39 5ST	01237 431752		750 mtrs £17.50 O D PL KT 1S
11	Mr & Mrs J W George Gawlish Farm GAWLISH HARTLAND EX39 6AT	01237 441320 01237 441320		500mtrs PD £18.00 O D EM PL CP LSP KT 2D[1] 1T[1]
11	Mrs Y Heard West Titchberry Farm WEST TITCHBERRY HARTLAND POINT EX39 6AU	01237 441287 01237 441287	242 271	250mtrs £16.00 O D EM PL CP LSP KT PD 1D 1T 1F
11	Mr & Mrs N Johns Hartland Quay Hotel HARTLAND QUAY EX39 6DU	01237 441218 01237 441371	March to Nov	on path £22.00 D EM PL CP LSP DW KT 5D[4] 5T[4] 2S[1] 2F[2]

Sect.	Name and Address	Tel. No. Fax. No. Web / Email	Map Reference Opening Times	Distance from Path Starting Price Facilities Accommodation
11	Mrs H Davey Stoke Barton Farm Stoke HARTLAND EX39 6DU	01237 441238 Easter to Sept		500mtrs £17.00 D PL CP LSP DW KT 1D(1) 1T(1)
11	Ms C Meincken 2 Morwenna Cottages HARTLAND EX39 6AF	01237 441927		2kms PD £17.00 O D EM CP PD 1D 1T
11	Mrs B Slee Homeleigh Stoke HARTLAND EX39 6DU	01237 441465	235 247 Feb-Oct	£16.00 D PL CP LSP KT 1D 1T
11	Mr & Mrs S Yeomans Golden Park HARTLAND NR BIDEFORD EX39 6EP	01237 441254 Mobile 07974 465786	232 202	1.6kms PD £18.00 O D EM PL CP LSP KT 2D[1] 1T[1]
11	Mrs M Loveridge 2 Harton Manor The Square HARTLAND EX39 6BL	01237 441670	258 245	4 kms PD £15.00 O D PL CP LSP DW KT 1D[1] 1T 1S
11	Mr & Mrs M Miller Linton Hills WELCOMBE BIDEFORD EX39 6HE	01288 331609 01288 331609 milmalc@earthling.net		3.2 kms PD £20.00 O D PL CP LSP KT 1D 2T[1]
12	Mrs Heywood Cornakey Farm CORNAKEY MORWENSTOW EX23 9SS	01288 331260		500mtrs £18.00 O D EM PL CP LSP DW 2D[1] 1T
12	Mrs J Hudson Little Bryaton MORWENSTOW BUDE EX23 9SU	01288 331755 www.little.bryaton.dial.pipex.com little.bryaton@dial.pipex.com	221 156	1.2 kms PD £20.00 O D EM PL CP LSP DW KT 1D 1T 1F ALL ES
12	Mrs D Hobbs Meadow Park MORWENSTOW EX23 9ST	01288 331499	Mar-Nov	1.5 kms PD £17.00 D EM PL CP LSP 1D 1T 1F
12	Mr & Mrs L Heard Dene Farm MORWENSTOW EX23 9SL	01288 331330		2.5kms £18.00 O D EM PL CP LSP KT PD 3D[3] 1F
12	Mr & Mrs Cole Jays, WOOLLEY MORWENSTOW BUDE EX23 9PP	01288 331540 www.members.tripod.co.uk/jaysbarn/jaysbarn cole.jays@talk21.com	254 168	4km PD £18.50 O D EM PL CP LSP KT 1D 1T 1S 1F ALL ES
12	Mrs S Trewin Lower Northcott Farm LOWER NORTHCOTT POUGHILL, BUDE EX23 7EQ	01288 352350 sally@coast-countryside.co.uk	223 077	1km PD £18.00 O D EM PL CP LSP DW KT 2D 1T 1S 1F ALL ES
12	Mrs S Weston Willow End 3 St Annes Hill BUDE EX23 0LT	01288 353294 Mobile 07977 569516	213 048	PD £18.00 O D PL CP LSP KT 1D[1]
12	Mr P Lancaster Blue Whale Guest House 23 Downs View BUDE EX23 8RG	01288 352202		300 mtr O D EM PL CP LSP KT PD 9D[6] 4T[2] 2S[1] 2F[2]

Sect.	Name and Address	Tel. No. Fax. No. Web / Email	Map Reference Opening Times	Distance from Path Starting Price Facilities Accommodation
12	Mrs J Rouse Corisande Hotel 24 Downs View BUDE EX23 8RG	01288 353474 01288 353474 www.bude-cornwall.co.uk/corisande janerouse@compuserve.com		600 mtrs PD £16.00 O D PL CP LSP DW KT 4D[3] 1T[1] 1F[1]
12	Mrs E W Luxton Wyvern House 7 Downs View BUDE EX23 8RF	01288 352205 01288 356802		400mtrs £15.50 O D EM PL CP LSP 3D[2] 1T 1S 1F[1]
12	Mr M E Payne Pencarrol Guest House 21 Downs View BUDE EX23 8RF	01288 352478 Closed Dec		300 mtrs £18.00 D PL CP LSP 4D[3] 1T[1] 2S 1F[1]
12	Mr & Mrs M Fly 8 Downs View BUDE EX23 8RF	01288 355059		300 mtrs £14.50 O D EM PL CP LSP DW 5D[4] 1T[1] 1S 1F[1]
12	Mr & Mrs B G Hatwell Baradine 3 Morwenna Terrace BUDE EX23 8BU	01288 352945		500 mtr £15.00 O D PL CP LSP 1D 1T 1S
12	Mr & Mrs M Curtis Atlantic Calm 30 Downs View BUDE EX23 8RG	01288 359165 01288 359165 www.atlantic-calm.bude-cornwall.co.uk mikec@talk21.com	206 071	200 mtrs PD £16.00 O D EM PL CP LSP DW KT 3D 2T 2S 1F ALL ES
12	Mr G Dockrill Link's Side Guest House 7 Burn View BUDE EX23 8BY	01288 352410 north-cornwall.co.uk/bude/client/linkside linksidebude@north-cornwall.co.uk	209 068	200 mtrs £16.00 O D PL CP DW 5D[4] 2T[1] 1S 1F[1]
12	Mrs E Abbott St Merryn Coast View BUDE EX23 8AG	01288 352058 01288 359050 st.merryn@ukonline.co.uk		1.6km PD £14.00 O D CP DW 1D 1T 1S 1F
13	Mr Ball The Meva-Gwin Hotel UPTON BUDE EX23 OLY	01288 352347	201 049	100 mtrs £22.00 D EM PL CP LSP 5D(5) 3T(3) 3S(1) 2F
13	Mr & Mrs M Fly Fairway House 8 Downs View BUDE EX23 8RF	01288 355059 www.smoothhound.co.uk fairwayhouse@kfly.freeserve.co.uk		200 mts PD £15.00 O D EM PL CP DW KT 6D[4] 2T[2] 1S 1F[1]
13	Mr & Mrs J Thorne Upton Cross UPTON BUDE EX23 0LY	01288 355310 01288 355310		150mtrs £19.00 O D PL CP DW KT 2D 1T 1F ALL ES
13	Bay View Inn 01288 361273 Marine Drive WIDEMOUTH BAY EX23 0AW	01288 361273 www.bayviewinn.co.uk enquiries@bayviewinn.co.uk	201 022	100 mtrs £17.00 O D EM PL CP LSP DW 3D[2] 2T[1] 3F[3]
12	Mrs A Short 5 Penkenna Close HIGHER CRACKINGTON BUDE	01840 230648		1.6km PD £15.00 O D PL CP 1T 1S
13	Mrs R Crocker Lower Tremorn Farm CRACKINGTON HAVEN EX23 ONU	01840 230667 01840 230667	157 977	500 mtrs PD £20.00 O D EM PL CP LSP 5D ALL ES

Sect.	Name and Address	Tel. No. Fax. No. Web / Email	Map Reference Opening Times	Distance from Path Starting Price Facilities Accommodation
13	Mr & Mrs J Cooper Coombe Barton Inn CRACKINGTON HAVEN EX23 0JG	01840 230345 01840 230788	March to Oct	on path £20.00 D EM PL CP LSP KT PD 4D[3] 1T 1S 1F[1]
14	Mrs J Horwell High Pennycrocker Farm ST JULIOT BOSCASTLE PL35 0BY	01840 250488 01840 250488 jackiefarm@aol.com	127 927	1km PD £17.00 O D PL CP LSP 1D 1T 1F ALL ES
14	Mr & Mrs G Crown Tolcarne House Hotel Tintagel Road BOSCASTLE PL35 0AS	01840 250654 01840 250654 www.milford.co.uk/go/tolcarne.html crowntolhouse@eclipse.co.uk	Feb to Nov	800 mtrs £26.00 D EM PL CP LSP DW 4D 2T 1S 1F ALL ES
14	Ms J Jones & Ms J Rhodes Lower Meadows House Penally Hill BOSCASTLE PL35 0HF	01840 250570 www.north-cornwall.co.uk/client/lower-meadows-htm	101 913	200mtrs £20.00 O D PL CP KT 2D 1T 1F ALL ES
14	Mr & Mrs G Mee Bottrraux House Hotel BOSCASTLE PL35 0BG	01840 250231 01840 250170 www.boscastlecornwall.co.uk bothotel@dircon.co.uk		800 mtrs £25.00 O D EM PL CP LSP 4D 3T ALL ES
14	Mrs C Nicholls Treosewill Farm Paradise BOSCASTLE PL35 0DL	01840 250545 01840 250545 ipl.co.uk/treosewill Nicholls@Trerosewill.telme.com	096 905	500mtrs PD £23.00 D PL CP LSP KT PD 3D 1T 2F ALL ES
14	Mrs D Johnson Tremorvah BOSCASTLE PL35 0AU	01840 250636 01840 250616 www.cornwall-online.co.uk/tremorvah drawingboard@compuserve.com	096 915	200mtrs PD £16.00 O D PL KT 1D 1T 1S
15	Mrs A Jones Grange Cottage BOSSINEY TINTAGEL PL34 0AX	01840 770487	065 888 Mar-Nov	200mtrs £17.00 D PL CP KT 2D(1) 1T(1) 1S 1F
15	Mr L N Leeds Willapark Manor Hotel BOSSINEY NR TINTAGEL PL34 0BA	01840 770782		100mtrs £28.00 O D EM PL CP DW 7D 2T 2S 2F ALL ES
15	Mrs P Tinney Bossinney Cottage BOSSINEY NR TINTAGEL PL34 0AY	01840 770327	066 888	600 mtrs PD £16.00 O D EM PL CP LSP KT 2D 1F
16	Mrs C West Chilcotts BOSSINEY TINTAGEL PL34 0AY	01840 770324 01840 770324	070 890	150mtr PD £16.00 O D PL CP LSP DW KT 1D 1T 1F[1]
15	Mrs Y Clark Bosayne Guest House Atlantic Road TINTAGEL PL34 0DE	01840 770514 www.clarky100.freeserve.co.uk clark@clarky100.freeserve.co.uk	890 050	30 mtr £16.00 O EM PL CP DW KT PD 3D[3] 1T[1] 3S 2F[1]
15	Mr & Mrs N Lamont The Riggs Guest House Bossiney Road TINTAGEL	01840 770427 01840770427 ala9413603@aol.com		£19.00 O D EM PL CP 1D 1T 1S 1F ALL ES
15	Mr R D Howe Pendrin House Atlantic Road TINTAGEL PL34 0DE	01840 770560 01840 770560 pendrin@tesco.net	056 888 Mar-Nov	400 mtrs £16.00 D EM PL CP 4D[2] 2T 1S 2F[1]

Sect.	Name and Address	Tel. No. Fax. No. Web / Email	Map Reference Opening Times	Distance from Path Starting Price Facilities Accommodation
16	Mrs A. May Challock Guest House TREKNOW TINTAGEL PL34 0EN	01840 770273	057 867 Easter-Oct	400mtrs £18.00 D PL CP DW 2D 1T
16	Mr & Mrs M Holden Mill House Inn TREBARWITH TINTAGEL PL34 0HD	01840 770932/770200 MILLHOUSE36@hotmail.com	058 864	800 mtrs PD £25.00 O EM PL CP LSP DW KT 5D 2T 1S 1F ALL ES
16	Port Gaverne Hotel 01208 880151 PORT GAVERNE, N PL29 35Q	01208 880244 pghotel@telinco.co.uk		200 mtrs D EM PL CP DW 8D[8] 2T[2] 2S[1] 5F[5]
16	Mr & Mrs J Andrews The Bay Hotel 1 The Terrace PORT ISAAC PL29 3SG	01208 880380	003 808	On Path £20.50 D EM PL CP LSP DW 3D[2] 1T 2S 4F[2]
16	The Castle Rock Hotel 4 New Road PORT ISAAC PL29 3SB	01208 880300 01208 880219 infor@castlerockhotel.co.uk		
16	Old School Hotel Guest House & Restaurant PORT ISAAC PL29 3RB	01208 880721 01208 880271 www.cornwall-online oldsch.hotel@eclipse.co.uk		£20.00 O EM PL CP LSP DW KT 6D[5] 8T[5] 2F[2]
16	Mrs L S Von Lintzgy Fairholme 30 Trewetha Lane PORT ISAAC PL29 3RW	01208 880397 01208 880189	001 805	200 mtrs £17.00 O D EM PL CP LSP DW KT 2D[1] 1T 2F[1]
16	Mrs M Andrews Hathaway Bed & Breakfast Roscarrock Hil PORT ISAAC PL29 3RG	01208 880416 www.cornwall-online.co.uk/hathaway marionandrews@talk21.com	Easter-Oct	30 mts £18.00 CP 1D 3T[2] 1S
16	Mr & Mrs D Jennings Courtyard CafE Pendragon House New Road PORT ISAAC PL29 3SB	01208 880715	998 809	100 mts PD £19.00 O D EM PL CP LSP KT 1D 1T ALL ES
16	Mr & Mrs R Vernon Trethoway 98 Fore Street PORT ISAAC PL29 3RF	01208 880214	Mar-Dec	200mtrs £20.00 D PL CP 2D[2] 1F
16	Messrs D & Goodbourn Compass Rose 56 New Rd PORT ISAAC PL29 3SD	01208 880767 compassrose@portisaac.fsnet.co.uk	808 995	300mtrs PD £17.00 O D PL CP KT 1D 1T
17	Mr & Mr M Pashley Pentire View Guest House POLZEATH PL27 6TB	01208 862484		100 mtrs £17.00 O D EM PL CP LSP DW 1D 2T 1S 1F
17	Mrs P White Seaways POLZEATH PL27 6SU	01208 862382 pauline@seaways99.freeserve.co		500mtrs £20.00 O D EM CP 2D[1] 1T[1] 1S 1F
18	Mr M Martin Silvermead ROCK NR WADEBRIDGE PL27 6LB	01208 862425 01208 862919	936 758	300mtrs £20.00 O D EM PL CP LSP DW 2D[2] 3T[1] 2S 2F[2]

Sect.	Name and Address	Tel. No. Fax. No. Web / Email	Map Reference Opening Times	Distance from Path Starting Price Facilities Accommodation
18	Roskarnon House Hote Mar-Oct ROCK NR WADEBRIDGE PL27 6LD	01208 862785		100mtrs £25.00 D EM CP 4D 5T 2S 1F ALL ES
18	Mr E. Champion Estuary Views 8 Treverbyn Road PADSTOW PL28 8DW	01841 532551		1km £20.00 O D CP DW KT PD 2D 1T 1S
18	Mrs M R Romer 23 Barry's Lane PADSTOW PL28 8AU	01841 532178	917 754 April-Nov	500mtrs £17.00 D KT 1D 1T[1] 1S[1]
18	Mr P A Tamblin Hemingford House 21 Grenville Road PADSTOW PL28 8EX	01841 532806 www.padstow-bb.co.uk peter@ptamblin.freeserve.co.uk	913 751	1km £22.50 O D PL CP DW DW By Arrang. 2D[1] 1T
18	Mrs J Cullinan 4 Riverside PADSTOW PL28 8BY	01841 532383 peter@petercullinan.fsnet.co.uk		on path £22.50 O DW 2D[2] 1T
18	Mrs M Spratt North Point Hill Street PADSTOW PL28 8EB	01841 532355		300mtrs £23.00 O D CP 2D 1T[1]
19	Mr & Mrs J Stock Woodlands Close TREATOR PADSTOW PL28 8RU	01841 533109 www.cornwall-online.co.uk/woodlands-close john@stock65.freeserve.co.uk		1km PD £17.00 O D CP LSPPD 1D[1] 1T[1] 1S
19	Mrs S Smith Tregudda Guest House West View NR PADSTOW PL28 8RD	01841 521191 01841 521191 gulli@clara.co.uk		50 mtr PD £18.00 O D EM PL CP LSP DW KT 3D 2S 1F ALL ES
19	Mrs S Hamilton Trevone Bay Hotel TREVONE NR PADSTOW PL28 8QS	01841 520243 01841 521195 hamilton@trevonebay.demon.co.uk	892 755 Easter to Oct	400mtrs £24.50 D EM PL CP DW 4D 3T 3S 2F ALL ES
19	Mrs J Loosemore Caradon Windmill NR PADSTOW PL28 8QS	01841 520120	896 752	1.2kms £14.00 O D CP LSP 1D 1T 1S 1F
19	Mrs S A Mills Well Parc Hotel TREVONE NR PADSTOW	01841 520318 sally@wellparc-demon.co.uk		PD £20.00 O D EM PL CP LSP KT 4D[2] 1T 1S 4F[4]
19	Mr & Mrs A Woosnam Mills Mother Ivey Cottage TREVOSE HEAD PADSTOW PL28 8SL	01841 520329 01841 520329 woosnammills@compuserve.com		On Path £22.50 O D EM PL CP LSP DW 2T 1F ALL ES
20	Treyarnon Bay Hotel 01841 520239 TREYARNON BAY PL28 8JN	01841 520235		100mtrs £22.50 O EM PL CP LSP 4D[3] 2T[2] 3F[3]
20	Mr & Mrs A.S. Etherington The Waterbeach Hotel TREYARNON BAY NR PADSTOW PL28 8JW	01841 520292 01841 521102 waterbeach@aol.com		150 mtrs £32.00 D EM CP LSP DW 5D[5] 5T[3] 3S[3] 7F[7]

Sect.	Name and Address	Tel. No. Fax. No. Web / Email	Map Reference Opening Times	Distance from Path Starting Price Facilities Accommodation
20	Mrs S Shadbolt Trelooan Treporth PORTHCOTHAN BAY PL28 8LS	01841 521158	858 716	300mtrs £15.00 O D PL CP LSP KT 1D 1T
21	Mr M Ward Malmar Hotel TRENANCE MAWGAN PORTH TR8 4DA	01637 860324 01637 860324 malmar@connexions.co	851 679	400 mtrs £21.00 O D EM PL CP DW 5D[4] 3T[2] 2S[1] 1F[1]
21	Mrs L Bennett The Merrymoor Inn MAWGAN PORTH TR8 4BA	01637 860258 01637 860258		45 mtrs £17.50 EM PL CP LSP DW KT 5D 1T 1S ALL ES
21	Mrs J Cook Quoit Treburrick ST EVAL PORTHCOTHAN BAY PL27 7UR	01841 540935	858 716	1.5 km PD £16.00 O D EM PL CP LSP KT 2D
21	Mr & Mrs D Cross Sea Vista Hotel MAWGAN PORTH TR8 4AL	01637 860276 1 Mar-31 Oct www.seavistahotel.co.uk crossd@supanet.com		500mtrs £18.00 EM PL CP DW 5D(2) 3S(1) 1F(1)
21	Mr & Mrs J N Parry White Lodge Hotel MAWGAN PORTH TR8 4BN	01637 860512 01637 860512 www.white-lodge-hotel.co.uk parryj@btconnect.com		50mtrs £24.00 O D EM PL CP LSP DW 8D[4] 8T[8] 2S[1] 8F[8]
21	Mr P Carthew Shore-Leas MAWGAN PORTH NR NEWQUAY TR8 4BA	01637 860851 pcarthew@tinyonline.co.uk	851 670	100 mtrs £16.00 O D CP LSP 1T[1]
21	Mr & Mrs R Brake Bre - Pen Farm BRE-PEN MAWGAN PORTH TR8 4AL	01637 860420	849 667	300 mtrs £18.00 O D EM PL CP LSP KT 3D[2] 1T
21	Mrs T Smith Kendra 20 Arundel Way NEWQUAY TR7 3BB	01637 878935		50 mts PD £18.00 O D PL CP LSP DW KT 3D 1T
21	Mr G Stevenson Trevalsa Hotel Watergate Road PORTH, NEWQUAY TR7 3LX	01637 873336 01637 878843		35 mtr D EM PL CP LSP DW 14D[13] 5T[5] 5S[4] 4F[4]
21	Mr & Mrs P Wright The Towan Beach Hotel 7 Trebarwith Crescent NEWQUAY TR7 1DX	01637 872093 01637 872093 towanbeach@hotmail.com		£18.00 O D PL 2D 2T 1S 1F ALL ES
21	Mr N Pedlar The Homestead Porthbean Road NEWQUAY TR7 3LU	01637 876918 neilpedlar@hotmail.com	830 627	20 mtrs £15.00 O D PL CP KT 1D 1T 1S
21	Mr & Mrs A Palmer Springvale Guest House 112 Henver Road NEWQUAY TR7 3EQ	01637 873857 david.ball@ifacom.net	829 621	300 mtr PD £13.50 O D EM PL CP LSP KT 4D[3] 2T 2F[1]
21	The Corisande Manor Hotel Riverside Avenue Pentire NEWQUAY TR7 1PL	01637 872042 www.corisande.com david@corisande.com		On Path £64.00 O D EM PL CP LSP 5D 3T 1S ALL ES

Sect.	Name and Address	Tel. No. Fax. No. Web / Email	Map Reference Opening Times	Distance from Path Starting Price Facilities Accommodation
21	Kallacliff Hotel Lusty Glaze NEWQUAY TR7 3AD	01637 871704		4 mtrs £18.50 D EM PL CP LSP 7D[6] 1T[1] 1S 3F[3]
21	Mrs S R Harper Chichester Guest House 14 Bay View NEWQUAY TR7 2LR	01637 874216 01637 874216 www.freespace.virgin.net/sheila.harper sheila.harper@virgin.net	813 614	750mtrs £16.50 O D EM PL CP 2D[2] 2T[2] 2S 1F[1]
21	The St Mawes Hotel Springfield Road NEWQUAY TR7 1RT	01637 872754		£16.00 O D PL LSP DW 5D[3] 3T[1] 5S[1] 3F[2]
21	Mr C Goss Porth Beach Hotel Beach Road NEWQUAY TR7 3NE	01637 872447 01637 872469 www.porthbeach-hotel.co.uk enquire@porthbeach-hotel.co.uk	830 627 Easter-Oct	20mtrs £20.00 D EM PL CP LSP KT 12D 1T 10F ALL ES
21	Mrs P Williams Roma Guest House 1 Atlantic Road NEWQUAY TR7 1QJ	01637 875085	803 616	500 mtr £14.00 O D EM PL CP LSP KT 4D[1] 1T 1S 1F[1]
54	Mrs T.J. Smith Kendra 20 Arundel Way NEWQUAY TR7 3BB	01637 878935		25 mtrs £15.00 D PL CP LSP DW 1D 1T
22	Mr & Mrs R Boston Highfield Lodge Hotel Halwyn Road CRANTOCK TR8 5TR	01637 830744		PD £18.00 O D EM CP LSP KT 8D[8] 1T 2S
22	Mr & Mrs S Wrigley Tregenna House West Pentire Road CRANTOCK TR8 5RZ	01637 830222 01637 831267	605 788	800 mtrs PD £18.00 O D EM PL CP LSP DW KT 6D[4] 3T[2] 7S 4F[2]
22	Mr & Mrs D Eyles Crantock Bay Hotel WEST PENTIRE CRANTOCK TR8 5SE	01637 830229 01637 831111 stay@crantockbayhotel.co.uk	777 607	£53.00 D EM PL CP LSP DW 10D 13T 9S 1F ALL ES
22	Mrs J Robinson St Marys West Pentire Road CRANTOCK TR8 5RZ	01637 830257 01637 830257 joyrobinson@compuserve.com		400 mts PD £15.00 O D EM PL CP LSP KT 2D[1] 1F[1]
21	Mrs V Banks Yellow Sands Ponsmore Road PERRANPORTH TR6 0BW	01872 573960		On Path PD £15.00 O D EM PL CP DW KT Self Catering flats avail. 2D[2]
23	Mr & Mrs W Woodcock Chy An Kerensa Cliff Road PERRANPORTH TR6 0DR	01872 572470	755 543	20 mtr £17.00 O D PL CP LSP DW KT 2D[1] 2T[1] 2S[1] 3F[3]
23	Mrs M Crofts Tremore Liskey Hill Crescent PERRANPORTH TR6 0HP	01872 573537 01872 573537 www.tremore.co.uk tremore@totalise.co.uk		400mtrs £19.00 O D PL CP LSP 2D[2] 1T[1] 5S[3]
23	Mrs S Wells 44 Tywarnhayle Road PERRANPORTH TR6 0DX	01872 572380		200 mtrs £13.50 O D EM PL CP LSP DW KT 1D[1] 1T[1] 1S 1F

Sect.	Name and Address	Tel. No. Fax. No. Web / Email	Map Reference Opening Times	Distance from Path Starting Price Facilities Accommodation
23	Mr & Mrs R Honey Perranova Guest House Cliff Road PERRANPORTH TR6 0DR	01872 573440	Jan-Oct	100 mtr £18.00 D EM PL CP KT 1D 1T 1S 1F
23	Mrs A Snow Gull Rock 25 Tywarnhayle Road PERRANPORTH TR6 0DX	01872 573289 0870 1312570 www.gullrock.co.uk holiday@gullrock.co.uk	755 544	100 mtr £16.00 O CP DW 1D 1F ALL ES
23	Mrs P Shoebridge Bolenna Court Hotel Perrancombe Road PERRANCOMBE PERRANPORTH	01872 572751 01872 572372		600 mts PD £20.00 O D EM PL CP DW 2D 1T 1S 1F ALL ES
24	Dorothy Gill-Carey Penkerris Penwinnick Road ST AGNES	01872 552262 01872 552262		1 km £15.00 O D EM PL CP LSP DW 3D[3] 3T[3] 2S 3F[3]
24	Mrs F Appleton Glen Cottage Quay Road ST AGNES TR5 0RP	01872 553546		500 mtrs PD £15.00 O D EM PL CP LSP DW KT 2D 1T 1S 1F
24	Mrs Glover Beach Cottage Quay Rod ST AGNES TR5 0RS	01872 553802		£17.00 D PL CP 3D[1] 1T 1S 1F
24	Mr & Mrs G Treleaven Driftwood Spars Hotel Trevaunance Cove ST AGNES TR5 ORT	01872 552428 01872 553701 driftwoodspars@hotmail		on path PD £30.00 O D EM PL CP LSP DW KT 8D 1T 1S 5F ALL ES
24	Mrs Harrison Ten-Re-Vras POLBERRO ST AGNES TR5 0SS	01872 553519	714 513	150 mts £15.00 O PL CP LSP 1D[1]
24	Mr & Mrs R Williams 2 Pen Mor Bolster ST AGNES	01872 552362	715 500	1 km £17.50 O D PL CP DW KT 1D
25	Mrs V Parkinson Buzby View Forthvean Road PORTHTOWAN TR4 8AY	01209 891178 01209 891178 www.chycor.co.uk/bnb/buzby/index.htm buzbyview@freenet.co.uk	691 473 Easter-Oct	500 mtr £19.00 D PL CP KT 2D 1T 1S
25	Mr & Mrs T Evans Botrea Guest House Beach Road PORTHTOWAN TR4 8AA	01209 890572 gevans@towan2001		500 mtrs PD £18.50 O D EM PL CP LSP KT 3D 1F ALL ES
25	Mrs S Hardwick The Beach Hotel PORTHTOWAN TR4 8AE	01209 890228 www.thebeachhotel.net colinehardwick63.freeserve.co.uk		On Path PD £18.00 O D EM PL CP LSP KT 5D[4] 3T[2] 1S[1] 2F[1]
26	Mr & Mrs P Allen Sycamore Lodge Primrose Terrace PORTREATH TR16 4JS	01209 842784		400 mtrs PD £17.50 O D PL CP LSP KT 2D 1T 1S
26	Mr & Mrs A Keast Fountain Springs Glenfeadon House PORTREATH TR16 4JU	01209 842650 01209 842650	Feb to Dec	50mtrs £18.50 D PL CP LSP DW 5D[5] 2T 1S[1] 1F[1]

Sect.	Name and Address	Tel. No. Fax. No. Web / Email	Map Reference Opening Times	Distance from Path Starting Price Facilities Accommodation
26	Mr & Mrs C J Healan Cliff House The Square PORTREATH TR16 4LB	01209 842008	656 455	On path £17.50 O D PL LSP DW KT PD 3D 1T ALL ES
26	Mr & Mrs I B Austin Portreath Arms Hotel The Square PORTREATH TR16 4LA	01209 842259 portreatharms@aol.com		100 mtr £20.00 O D EM PL CPDW 4D[4] 3T[1]
26	Mr & Mrs P Smythe Benson's 1 The Hillside PORTREATH TR16 4LL	01209 842534 01209 843578	Easter & Jun-Sept	On path D PL CP LSP 1D 1T 2S ALL ES
26	Mr C Symonds Suhaili 14 Forth-an-Nance PORTREATH TR16 4NQ	01209 842110		on path PD £18.00 O D PL CP DW KT PD 1D(1) 1T(1) 1F
26	Mrs A Ellis Vellynsaundry Pendarves CAMBORNE TR14 0RS	01209 712983	639 381	PD £15.00 O D CP LSP KT 1D[1] 1T[1] 2S
27	Mrs L Davies Nanterrow Farm GWITHIAN HAYLE TR27 5BP	01209 712282	599 412	1.5km £17.00 O D PL CP LSP KT PD 1D 1T 1S 1F
27	Mrs P Bailey Calize Country House Prosper Hill GWITHIAN TR27 5BW	01736 753268 01736 753268 calizebb@talk21.com	587 409	1 km £16.00 O D PL CP LSP DW 3D[2] 2T[1]
27	Mrs J Cooper 54 Penpol Terrace HAYLE TR27 4BQ	01736 752855		500mtrs D PL CP LSP 1D 1T 1S
27	White Hart Hotel 10 Foundry Square HAYLE TR27 4HQ	01736 752322 01736 752322		1km £25.00 O EM PL CP DW 5D 6T 2S 1F ALL ES
27	Mrs McLeod Wheal Merth, Heather Lane CANONSTOWN HAYLE TR27 6NQ	01736 740553	531 355	3 kms PD £15.00 O D EM PL CP LSP DW KT 1D 1T
28	Mr & Mrs D O'Sullivan Hindon Hall LELANT ST IVES TR26 3EN	01736 753046 01736 753046 hindonhall@talk21.com	543 369	on path £24.00 O D PL CP LSP 4D ALL ES
28	Mr & Mrs D Mason Kandahar 11 The Warren ST IVES TR26 2EA	01736 796183 www.kandahar11.com	519 403 Easter, May-Oct	On Path £23.00 CP LSP 3D[2] 1T 2F[2]
28	Mrs L Bowden Carlill 9 Porthminster Terrace ST IVES TR26 2DQ	01736 796738 www.travelcheck/hotel/1518.htm lynne@lgpa9.freeserve.co.uk		250 mtrs £18.00 2D[1] 2T[1] 2S 2F[1]
28	Ms L Dean-Burrows Ten Steps 11 Fish Street ST IVES TR26 1LT	01736 798222 01736 798222		1.5km £20.00 O D PL 2D 1T 1F ALL ES

Sect.	Name and Address	Tel. No. Fax. No. Web / Email	Map Reference Opening Times	Distance from Path Starting Price Facilities Accommodation
28	Mr D S Tremelling Chy-An-Creet Hotel Higher Stennack ST IVES TR26 2HA	01736 796559 01736 796559 www.saint-ives.com walk@saint-ives.com	507 399 Jan-Nov	1km PD £21.00 D EM PL CP LSP DW KT 4D 2T 1S 2F ALL ES
28	Mrs S Martin 6 Barnoon Terrace ST IVES TR26 1JE	01736 793172		50 mtr £15.00 O D PL 1D 1T[1] 1S[1]
28	Mr R Smith St Ives Backpackers The Gallery ST IVES	01736 799444 01736 799444 www.backpackers.co.uk st-ivesbackpackers@dial.pipex.		100mtrs £8.00 O D 3D 3T 10 DORMS
28	Ms K Daines Chy Lelan Bunkers Hill ST IVES TR26 1LJ	01736 797560 01736 797560 chylelan@dainesk.fsnet.co.uk		800 mtrs £18.00 O LSP 4D[4] 1T[1] 2S 1F
28	Mr & Mrs S Norris Kynance The Warren ST IVES TR28 2EA	01736 796636 www.kynance24.co.uk	Mid Mar-Oct	On Path £21.00 CP 3D 1T 1F ALL ES
28	Mrs Clifford Seagulls Guest House Godrevy Terrace ST IVES TR26 1JA	01736 797273 01736 799297 www.seagullsstives.co.uk seagullsstives@hotmail.com		20 mts £18.00 O D PL CP LSP 6D[4] 1T[1] 2S[2] 1F[1]
29	Mrs N Mann Trewey Farm TREWEY ZENNOR TR26 3DA	01736 796936	454 384	1.5kms £18.00 O D PL CP DW 2D 1T 1S 2F
29	Mr P Whitelock The Old Chapel Backpackers ZENNOR TR26 3DA	01736 798307 01736 798307 www.backpackers.co.uk zennorbackpackers@btinternet.com	455 385	500mtrs PD £10.00 O D EM PL CP LSP KT 1F 5 DORMS
29	Mrs A B Prowse Trewey Vean Farm TREWEY VEAN ZENNOR TR26 3DA	01736 796919	Mar-Dec	1.2 kms £19.00 D PL CP LSP DW 2D 3F
29	Dr Gynn Boswednack Manor BOSWEDNACK ZENNOR TR26 3DD	01736 794183	443 378 Apr-Oct	1 km £19.00 D PL CP LSP 2D[2] 1T 1S 1F
29	Mr & Mrs I Hamlett Rosmorva BOSWEDNACK ST IVES TR26 3DD	01736 796722	443 378	900 mtr £16.50 O D PL CP LSP 1D 1S 1F[1]
29	Mrs Berryman Treen Farm GURNARDS HEAD ZENNOR TR26 3DE	01736 796932	436 377 Mar-Oct	400 mtr £18.50 D PL CP LSP DW KT PD 1D 1T 1S
29	Mrs J Kell The Gurnards Head Hotel TREEN ZENNOR TR26 3DE	01736 796928 01736 795313 enquiries@gurnardshead.free-online		800 mtr £22.50 O D EM PL CP LSP DW 4D 1T 1F ALL ES
29	Mrs J Davey Pendeen Manor PENDEEN TR19 7ED	01736 788753 01736 788753 janetdavey@fsmail.net		250mtrs £18.00 O D PL CP LSP DW KT PD 2D[1] 2T[1] 1S 2F[2]

Sect.	Name and Address	Tel. No. Fax. No. Web / Email	Map Reference Opening Times	Distance from Path Starting Price Facilities Accommodation
29	Mrs M P W Cass The Radjel Inn PENDEEN TR19 7DS	01736 788446	385 344	850mtrs PD £18.00 O D EM PL CP LSP KT 1D 1T 1S 1F
29	Mr H Rutter The Smugglers Haunt 1 Church Road PENDEEN TR19 7SG	01736 788310		1km PD £18.00 O D PL CP KT 2D[1] 1T[1]
29	Mrs S M Russell Bojewan House PENDEEN TR19 7TR	01736 787312 01736 787242 sheila-russell@compuserve.com	393 347	1 km PD £17.00 O D EM PL CP KT 1D[1]
29	Mr Thompson & Ms Bailey Quiddles BOSCASWELL DOWNS PENDEEN TR19 7DW	01736 787278	383 344	1.6kms PD £12.00 D EM PL CP LSP KT 2D[1] 1T 1F
29	Mr & Mrs T Dymond The Old Count House BOSCASWELL DOWNS PENDEEN TR19 YED	01736 788058	383 344 March to Oct	1.2kms £16.00 D PL CP LSP 2D
30	Miss V A Bailey Field House TREWELLARD PENDEEN TR19 7ST	01736 788097 01736 788097 fieldhousetrewellard@talk21.com	338 377	1.5kms £18.00 O EM PL EM April-Sept 2D[1] 1T
30	Mrs Bailey Trewellard Manor Farm TREWELLARD PENDEEN TR19 7SU	01736 788526 01736 788526	374 339	1 km £20.00 O D PL CP LSP 2D(2) 1T
30	Mr R Harvey Rannick Studio HIGHER TREWELLARD PENDEEN TR19 7TE	01736 787335	385 337	2.5 km PD £15.00 O D EM PL CP LSP DW KT S/C CARAVAN SLEEPS 4
30	Boswedden House Hote CAPE CORNWALL ST JUST TR19 7NJ	01736 788733 01736 788733 www.boswedden.org.uk relax@boswedden.org.uk	359 318	200 mts £20.00 O D PL CP LSP DW 2D 3T 2S 1F ALL ES
31	Mrs J Cargeeg Manor Farm BOTALLACK TR19 7QG	01736 788525		300 mtrs £25.00 O CP LSP 1D[1] 1T[1] 1F[1]
31	Mrs E Lawry Llawnroc 1 Truthwall Villa ST JUST TR19 7QL	01736 788814		400 mtrs £15.00 O D EM PL CP KT 3D 2T 1F
31	Mrs A D Eddy Trethewes Carrallack Terrace ST JUST TR19 7LP	01736 788528	May to Oct	1.5 km £16.00 D PL CP LSP 2D 1S 1F
31	Mrs V Prentice The Retreat 13 Boswedden Terrace ST JUST TR19 7NF	01736 788221	364 315	800 mts £18.00 O D EM PL CP LSP KT 1T 1S
31	Mr & Mrs D Gwilin Boscean Country Hotel Boswedden Road ST JUST TR19 7QP	01736 788748 01736 788748 www.bosceancountryhotel.co.uk boscean@aol.com		500mtrs PD £22.00 O D EM PL CP LSP KT 5D 5T 2F ALL ES

Sect.	Name and Address	Tel. No. Fax. No. Web / Email	Map Reference Opening Times	Distance from Path Starting Price Facilities Accommodation
31	Mr & Mrs P Michelmore 2 Fore Street ST JUST TR19 7LL	01736 787784 01736 787784	372 313	1.5 kms £17.50 O PL Dogs by Arrang. 1D 1T 1F
31	Mrs C Collinson Bosavern House BOSAVERN St Just in Penwith PENZANCE TR19 7RD	01736 788301 01736 788301 www.bosavern.u-net.com marcol@bosavern.u-net.com	371 305	1 km PD £19.00 O D PL CP LSP DW KT 2D[2] 2T[1] 1S[1] 3F[3]
31	Mr & Mrs D Gallie Polwyn Cottage Old Coastguard Row SENNEN COVE TR19 7DA	01736 871349	350 264	On path £16.50 O D CP LSP DW KT 1D(1) 1T
31	Old Success Inn 01736 871457 SENNEN COVE TR19 7DG	01736 871232 www.sennen-cove.com		on path £28.00 O EM PL CP DW 7D[7] 2T[2] 2S[1] 1F[1]
31	Mr & Mrs M Adams Homefields MAYON SENNEN TR19 7AD	01736 871418 01736 871666 homefield/BandB@AOL.com		500 mts £15.00 D PL CP LSP DW 4D[4] 2T[1] 1S 1F[1]
32	Mr T Ellison Whitesands Lodge SENNEN TR19 7AR	01736 781776 01736 871776 www.whitesandslodge.co.uk info@whitesandslodge.co.uk	366 264	400 mts £10.00 O D EM PL CP DW 2D[1] 1T 1S 2F[1]
32	Mr & Mrs R Davis Sea View House The Valley PORTHCURNO TR19 6JX	01736 810638 www.seaviewhouseporthcurno.com seaview.porthcurno@tinyworld.co.uk	383 227	350mtrs £20.00 O D EM PL CP LSP DW KTPD 4D[3] 1T[1] 1S[1]
32	Mr & Mrs T Goss The Porthcurno Hotel The Valley PORTHCURNO TR19 6JX	01736 810119 01736 810711 www.porthcurnohotel.co.uk porthcurnohotel@netscapeonline.co.uk		250 mtrs PD £18.00 O D EM PL CP LSP DW KT 4D[2] 6T[3] 1S 1F[1]
32	Mrs R Thomas Grey Gables PORTHCURNO TR19 6JT	01736 810421 01736 810421	Apr-Oct	100mtrs £18.50 D EM PL CP 3D[3] 2T[1]
32	Mrs J M Green Mariners Lodge Hotel PORTHCURNO TR19 6JU	01736 810236 01736 810840 www.marinerslodgehotel.co.uk themarinerslodge@aol.com	386 220	200mtrs P D £18.00 O D EM PL CP LSP DW KT 3D[1] 2T[1] 3S 1F
32	Mrs E Crow Seabreeze PORTHCURNO PENZANCE TR19 6JS	01736 810796	222 385	200mtrs £20.00 O D CP 1F ES.
33	Mrs E Jilbert Penver Houses Farm TREEN NR PORTHCURNO TR19 6LG	01736 810778 01736 810778	394 231 March to Oct	750mtrs £16.50 D PL CP LSP DW KT 1D[1] 1T 1S
33	Mrs P Hall Treen Farmhouse TREEN NR PORTHCURNO TR19 6LF	01736 810253	394 231	PD £15.00 O D PL CP LSP DW KT 1D[1] 1T 1S

Sect.	Name and Address	Tel. No. Fax. No. Web / Email	Map Reference Opening Times	Distance from Path Starting Price Facilities Accommodation
33	Mrs D Hardy Pridden ST BURYAN PENZANCE TR19 6EA	01736 810801 01736 810054 www.priddenfarm.co.uk diana.hardy@virgin.net	415 265	8 kms PD £16.00 O D EM PL CP LSP DW KT 1D 1T[1] 1F[1]
33	Mr & Mrs Rowley Lamorna Guest House LAMORNA NR PENZANCE TR19 6XL	01736 731367 01736 731367	Feb-Oct	800mtrs £23.00 D PL CP 4D[3] 1T[1] 1S 1F[1]
34	Mr M Male Lowenna Raginnis Hill MOUSEHOLE TR19 6SL	01736 731077	468 262	On path £17.50 O D PL 1F(1)
34	Mrs M Maiden 1 Paul Lane MOUSEHOLE PENZANCE TR19 6TR	01736 731406 01736 731406	Mar-Mid Dec	250 mts £16.00 D PL 1D 2T
34	Mrs Buswell Penalva Alexandra Road PENZANCE TR18 4LZ	01736 369060 01736 369060	298 468	500 mtrs £15.00 O D CP LSP 2D[2] 1T[1] 1S[1] 1F[1]
34	Mr & Mrs P Schofield Chy-an-Gof 10 Regent Terrace PENZANCE TR18 4DW	01736 332361 01736 332361 piran@vision-arts.demon.co.uk		PD £22.00 O D CP LSP 2T 2S ALL ES
34	Mr & Mrs J Maddern The Tarbert Hotel & Restaurant Clarence Street PENZANCE TR18 2NU	01736 363758 01736 331336 www.tarbert-hotel.co.uk reception@tarbert-hotel.co.uk	819 325 10 Feb-22 Dec	1 km £29.00 D EM PL CP 7D 1T 2S 2F ALL ES
34	Mr & Mrs D Glenn Trewella Guest Hse 18 Mennaye Road PENZANCE TR18 4NG	01736 363818	March to Oct	150mtrs £17.50 CP 4D[4] 2T[2] 2S
34	Mr & Mrs J Hopkins Woodstock Guest House 29 Morrab Road PENZANCE TR18 4EZ	01736 369049 01736 369049 www.ivaccommodations.com/woodstock.html wooodstocp@aol.com	472 300	100 mtr £12.50 O PL DW KT 3D[2] 3T[2] 2S[1] 3F[1]
34	Mr & Mrs J Leggatt Cornerways 5 Leskinnick Street PENZANCE TR18 2HA	01736 364645 01736 364645 www.penzance.co.uk/cornerways enquires@cornerways-penzanse.co.uk	Feb-Dec	800mtrs £19.00 D EM PL CP LSP DW 1D 1T 1S 1F ALL ES
34	Mr & Mrs R Stacey Lynwood Guest House 41 Morrab Road PENZANCE TR18 4EX	01736 365871 01736 365871 www.penzance.co.uk/lynwood-guesthouse lynwoodpz@aol.com		200 mtrs £13.50 O D PL DW KT 2D[1] 2T 2S[1] 2F[2]
34	Mr P R Taylor Penzance Backpackers Blue Dolphin PENZANCE TR18 4LZ	01736 363836 01736 363844 www.penzancebackpackers.ndirect.co.uk pzbackpack@ndirect.co.uk	467 299	400 mtr £9.00 O D 2D 4DORMS[3]
34	Mr & Mrs M Russell Chy-an-Mor 15 Regeant Terrace PENZANCE TR18 4DW	01736 363441 01736 363441 www.chyanmor.co.uk mikeandjan@chyanmor.co.uk	475 298 Feb-Nov	100 mts £25.00 D CP LSP 5D 4T 1S ALL ES
34	Mr J Smalley Chy Bowjy CHY SAUSTER PENZANCE TR20 8XA	01736 368815 01736 363440 jj@jj-associates.co.uk	350 470	4.5 kms PD £15.00 O D EM PL CP LSP DW KT 1D 1S 1F PRIV FACIL.

Sect.	Name and Address	Tel. No. Fax. No. Web / Email	Map Reference Opening Times	Distance from Path Starting Price Facilities Accommodation
36	Mrs M Foy Mzima Penlee Close PRAA SANDS TR20 9SR	01736 763856	588 281	800mtrs £17.00 O D PL CP KT PD 1T 1F
36	Mrs G Garragham Bodeeve PRAA SANDS TR20 9TQ	01736 763246 01736 763246 gillieg75541410		On path £13.00 O D PL CP LSP 2T
36	Mrs P Williams 2 Penlee Close PRAA SANDS TR20 9SR	01736 762785	578 288	600mtrs £12.50 O D CP LSP 2D
36	Mr & Mrs E Sharp Gwynoon Chy-An-Dour Road PRAA SANDS TR20 9SY	01736 763426		50 mtrs PD O D CP LSP 2D 4S 2F ALL ES
37	Mrs C Cookson Pentre Peverell Terrace PORTHLEVEN TR13 9DZ	01326 574493 pentre@eurobell.co.uk	630 255	200 mtr PD £16.50 D PL CP LSP DW KT 1D 1T 2S
37	Mr F P Hallam Seefar Peverell Terrace PORTHLEVEN TR13 9DZ	01326 573778 www.cornwall-online.co.uk seefar@talk21.com	March to Nov	200mtrs £16.00 D PL CP DW KT 2D[2] 1T[1] 1S
37	Mr & Mrs P Ingham Anchor Cottage Cliff Road PORTHLEVEN TR13 9EZ	01326 574391	629 254	On Path £17.50 O D CP KT 1D[1] 1T
37	Miss S Kelynack An Mordros Hotel Peverell Terrace PORTHLEVEN TR13 9DZ	01326 562236 01326 562236 sanmordros@aol.com		On Path £17.00 O D EM PL KT 3D[2] 1T 1F[1]
37	Mrs C Budd Sandpipers Loe Bar Road PORTHLEVEN TR13 9EL	01326 564542	April to Sept	On path £18.00 D 1D 1T 1S
37	The Tye Rock Hotel Loe Bar Road PORTHLEVEN TR13 9EW	01326 572695 01326 572695 tyerockhotel@compuserve.com		On path £40.00 D EM CP 4D 3T ALL ES
38	Mrs J Lugg Tregaddra Farm Cury Cross Lanes HELSTON TR12 7BB	01326 240235 01326 240235 www.tregaddra.freeserve.co.uk holidays@tregaddra.freeserve.co.uk	700 218	4.8 kms £25.00 O D EM CP LSP 2D 1T 2F ALL ES
38	Mr & Mrs T Tucker Lyndale Guest House 4 Greenbank, Meneage Road HELSTON TR13 8JA	01326 561082 01326 565813 www.lyndale1.freeserve.co.uk enquiries@lyndale1.freeserve.co.uk		4.5 kms PD £16.50 O D EM PL CP LSP DW KT 3D[2] 1T[1] 1S 1F
38	Mrs J Tyler-Street Trenance Farmhouse MULLION TR12 7HB	01326 240639 01326 240639 www.cornwall-online.co.uk/trenance-farm trenancefarm@cwcom.net	673 185 Apr-Sept	500mtrs £20.00 D PL CP LSP DW 3D 1T ALL ES
38	Mr & Mrs T Valender The Old Vicarage Nansmellyon Road MULLION TR12 7DQ	01326 240898 01326 240879		750 mtrs £18.50 O D CP LSP KT 2D 1T 2F ALL ES

Sect.	Name and Address	Tel. No. Fax. No. Web / Email	Map Reference Opening Times	Distance from Path Starting Price Facilities Accommodation
38	Mr & Mrs M Wood Trenance Barton MULLION TR12 7HB	01326 240893 01326 240893		800 mtrs £18.00 O D EM PL CP LSP 1D 1T ALL ES
38	Mr & Mrs P Dann Ridgeback Lodge Hotel & Nansmellion Road MULLION TR12 7DH	01326 241300 01326 241330 www.business.thisiscornwall.co.uk/ridgeback Ridgebacklodge@compuserve.com	677 185	100mtrs £19.50 O EM PL CP LSP DW KT 4D[2] 1T 1S 2F[2]
38	Mr M Bolton Criggan Mill MULLION COVE TR12 7EU	01326 240496 0870 1640549 www.crigganmill.co.uk info@crigganmill.co.uk	667 180	200 mtrs £17.00 O D EM PL CP KT 25D 16T 25S 16F ALL ES
39	Mrs I Sowden The Most Southerly House LIZARD POINT TR12 7NU	01326 290300 01326 290300	702 115 Feb-Nov	on path £18.00 D PL CP LSP KT 2D[1] 1T
39	Mr & Mrs P Brookes Parc Brawse House Penmenner Road. THE LIZARD TR12 7NR	01326 290466 01326 290466 www.smoothhound.co.uk/hotels/parcbraw lindabrookes@cwcom.net		300mtrs £16.00 O D EM PL CP LSP DW KT 5D[4] 3T[2] 2S[1]1F[1]
39	Mrs P James Carmelin Pentreath Lane THE LIZARD TR12 7NY	01326 290677 01326 290240 pjcarmelin@aol.com	699 126	500 mtrs PD £15.00 O D PL CP DW KT 1D(1)
39	Mrs K Thirlaway Green Cottage THE LIZARD TR12 7NZ	01326 290099		750mtrs £15.00 O D PL CP LSP DW KT 2D
39	Mrs G Rowe Trethvas Farmhouse THE LIZARD HELSTON TR12 7AR	01326 290720 01326 290720	709 136 Mar-Oct	300mtrs £18.00 D PL CP LSP 1D[1] 1T 1F[1]
39	Mr & Mrs T Rowland 2 Gulveal Villas Penmenner Road HELSTON TR12 7NW	01326 290225		500 mtrs PD £16.00 D PL CP LSP KT 1D 1T
39	Ms S Thompson Penmenner House Hotel Penmenner Road HELSTON TR12 7NR	01326 290370		300 mtrs £20.00 O D EM PL CP LSP 4D[3] 1T[1] 1S[1]
40	Cadgwith Cove Inn CADGWITH	01326 290513 01326 291018 www.cadgwithcoveinn.com enquiries@cadgwithcoveinn.com		On Path £19.50 O EM PL CP DW 5D 2T
40	Mr & Mrs D Reeves RUAN MINOR HELSTON TR12 7JR	01326 290244	715 155	1.2km PD £16.00 O D PL CP LSP DW KT 2D
40	Mrs R Whitaker Wych Elm PONSONGATH COVERACK TR12 6SQ	01326 280576	756 179	1 km PD £18.00 O D EM PL CP LSP DW KT 1T ES
40	Mrs T Carey Tamarisk Cottage COVERACK TR12 6TG	01326 280638	Easter to Oct	On path PD £17.00 D CP LSP DW 1D 1T 1S

Sect.	Name and Address	Tel. No. Fax. No. Web / Email	Map Reference Opening Times	Distance from Path Starting Price Facilities Accommodation
40	Mr P Cheze-Brown The Croft Lowland Lane COVERACK TR12 6TF	01326 280387 01326 280384 www.cornwall-online.co.uk/the.croft	783 187	On Path PD £16.50 O D EM PL CP LSP DW KT 3T[2]
40	Mrs L Goldsworthy The Bay Hotel COVERACK TR12 6TF	01326 280464 01326 280464		O D EM PL CP LSP DW
40	Mrs M E Daw Bakery Cottage Polcoverack Lane COVERACK TR12 6TD	01326 280474		On path £17.50 O D EM PL CP LSP DW 1D 1T
40	Mrs W Watters Boak House COVERACK TR12 6SA	01326 280608	Mar-Nov	50 mts £18.50 D CP DW KT 1T 1S 2F
41	The White Hart Inn The Square ST KEVERNE TR12 6ND	01326 280325 whitehart@easynet.co.uk	791 212	1 km £25.00 O EM PL CP LSP DW 1D 1T ALL ES
41	Mr N Prouse The Paris Hotel COVERACK TR12 6SX	01326 280258 01326 280774		On Path £25.00 O EM PL CP LSP Local taxi avail. 3D 1T ALL ES
41	Ms S Sharpe Parc-an-Grouse ST KEVERNE HELSTON TR12 6QS	01326 280259 www.parcangrouse.atfreeweb.com sue@parcangrouse.fsnet.co.uk		200 mtrs £18.00 O D PL CP LSP KT PD 3D[2] 4T[3] 1F[1]
41	Mrs R Kelly Trevinock PORTHOUSTOCK ST KEVERNE TR12 6QP	01326 280498	802 216 Mar-Oct	1.5kms PD £18.50 D EM PL CP LSP DW KT PD 2D[1] 2S
41	Ms A Strickland Gallen-Treath Guest House PORTHALLOW TR12 6PL	01326 280400 gallentreath@btclick.com	797 232	150mtrs PD £22.00 O D EM PL CP LSP DW KT evening meal winter only 2D 1T 1S 1F ALL ES
41	Mrs P Hawthorne Valley View House Porthallow Cove ST KEVERNE TR12 6PN	01326 280370 01326 280370 www.smoothhound.co.uk/hotels/valleyvi.html hawthorne@valleyviewhouse.freeserve.co.uk	796 232	20 mtrs pd £19.00 O D EM PL CP LSP KT 2D[2] 1T
41	Tregildry Hotel Gillan MANACCAN HELSTON TR12 6HG	01326 231378 01326 231561 www.tregildryhotel.co.uk trgildry@globalnet.co.uk	Mar-Oct	250 mts EM PL CP DW 7D 3T ALL ES
41	Mrs L Jenkin Landrivick Farm MANACCAN HELSTON TR12 6HX	01326 231686		1.6 kms PD £21.00 O D EM PL CP LSP 1D[1] 1T 1S
41	Mrs P Julian Landrivick Farm LANDRIVICK MANACCAN TR12 6HX	01326 231686		1.6kms PD £21.00 O D CP LSP PD 1D 1T
41	Mrs J Jane Higher Roscadden Vicarage Lane MANACCAN HELSTON TR12 6JH	01326 231423	767 252	On Path £18.50 O D PL CP DW 2D 1T PRIV FACILITIES

Sect.	Name and Address	Tel. No. Fax. No. Web / Email	Map Reference Opening Times	Distance from Path Starting Price Facilities Accommodation
41	Mrs J Davies Pengwedhen HELFORD TR12 6JZ	01326 231481 nigeguy@onetel.net.uk	755 265 Easter to Oct	500 mtrs £22.00 D PL CP LSP 2D[1] 1T 2S
41	Mrs P Royall POINT Helford NR HELSTON TR12 6JY	01326 231666 www.helfordcottages.co.uk info@helfordcottages.co.uk	758 262	10 mts £23.00 O D CP 1T[1]
42	Mr & Mrs T Cooke Hideaway Rosevear MAWGAN TR12 6AZ	01326 221392	697 245	2kms PD £16.00 D CP LSP 2D(1) 1T
42	Mrs C Spike Carwinion Vean Grove Hill MAWNAN SMITH TR11 5ER	01326 250513		1.6 km £20.00 O D PL CP LSP DW 3D[1] 3T[2] 1F
42	Mrs S P Annan Chynoweth Carwinion Lane MAWNAN SMITH TR11 5JB	01326 250534 01326 251010 sannan@compuserve.com	781 283	800 mtrs PD £20.00 O D PL CP KT 2T[1]
42	Mrs Dugdale Trevean MAWNAN SMITH NR FALMOUTH TR11 5JD	01326 250100 01326 250543	781 283	800mtrs £25.00 O D PL CP DW 1D[1]
42	Mr & Mrs P Cork Grove Hotel Grove Place FALMOUTH TR11 4AU	01326 319577 01326 319577		On path £22.50 O D M PL 4D[4] 4T[4] 2S 5F
42	Mr J Walker Ambleside 9 Marlborough Road FALMOUTH TR11 3LP	01326 319630		800 mtrs £17.00 O D EM CP LSP DW 3D 1T 1S 1F
42	Mr & Mrs I Carruthers The Clearwater 59 Melvill Road FALMOUTH TR11 4DF	01326 311344 www.claerwaterhotel.co.uk clearwater@lineone.net	Feb-Dec	500mtrs £20.00 D EM PL CP LSP 5D[4] 2T 1S 2F[1]
42	Mr & Mrs J Appleyard Rosemary Hotel 22 Gyllyngvase Terrace FALMOUTH TR11 4DL	01326 314669 01326 314669 www.cornwall-online.co.uk/rosemary rosemaryhotel@lineone.net	810 318 Jan-Oct	50mtrs £21.00 EM PL CP 6D 1T 1S 2F ALL ES
42	Mr & Mrs R Picken The Lerryn Hotel De Pass Road FALMOUTH TR11 4BJ	01326 312489 www.thelerrynhotel.co.uk thelerrynhotel@tesco.net		20mtrs £26.00 O EM PL CP LSP DW 7D 8T 3S 2F ALL ES
42	Mr & Mrs P Crocker The Dolvean Hotel 50 Melvill Road FALMOUTH TR11 4DQ	01326 313658 01326 313995 www.dolvean.co.uk reservations@dolvean.freeserve.co.uk	809 319	300 mts £23.00 O D CP 7D 3T 1S
43	Mrs K Moseley Braganza Grove Hill ST MAWES TR2 5BJ	01326 270281 01326270281 braganzak/@aol.com		300 mtrs £25.00 O D PL CP KT 2D[2] 1T[1] 1S
44	Mrs J Milnes Bohurrow Farmhouse Bohortha ST ANTHONY IN ROSELAND PORTHSCATHO TR2 5EY	01872 580966		800 mts £18.00 O D CP LSP DW KT 1D 1T 1S ALL ES

Sect.	Name and Address	Tel. No. Fax. No. Web / Email	Map Reference Opening Times	Distance from Path Starting Price Facilities Accommodation
44	Mrs J.C Smith Maraval 4 Parc An Dillon PORTSCATHO TR2 5DU	01872 580310		£18.00 O D CP 1T[1]
44	Mr & Mrs C G Evans Tregerein Guest House PORTSCATHO TR2 5HD	01872 580336	877 358	On path £19.50 O D PL CP LSP 1D 1T ELL ES
44	Mr & Mrs R Hart Hillside House 8 The Square PORTSCATHO TR2 5HW	01872 580526 01872 580527	353 877	30 mtrs PD £17.50 O D PL DW KT 2D 1T 2S 1F
44	Mr Haywood Trewince Manor PORTSCATHO TRURO TR2 5ET	01872 580289 01872 580694 bookings@trewince.com.uk		1km £18.00 O D EM PL CP LSP DW 4D[4] 8T
44	M J Davis Harberton House Churchtown House PORTSCATHO TR2 5DZ	01872 580598 01872 580789		400 mtrs £20.00 O D PL CP LSP 1D 1T
44	Mr & Mrs A Sievwright The Royal Standard Inn 5 The Square GERRANS NR TRURO TR2 5EB	01872 580271 01872 580271		800 mts £16.00 O EM CP LSP 1D 1S
44	Mrs A Palmer Trenestrall RUAN HIGH LANES PORTSCATHO TR2 5LX	01872 501259	Feb-Nov	2.5km PD £17.00 D PL CP DW 1D 1T 1F
45	Mr & Mrs K Righton Broom Parc CAMELS TRURO TR2 5PJ	01872 501803 01872 501109	930 390	On Path £23.00 O D PL CP LSP DW 1D 2T[2]
45	Mr & Mrs M Rawling Treverbyn House Pendower Road VERYAN TRURO TR2 5QL	01872 501201 www.cornwall-online.co.uk/treverbyn mike-ali@treverbyn.fsbusiness.co.uk		2 kms PD £20.00 O D PL CP 1D 1T 1S 1F ALL ES
45	Mrs C Holdsworth Tregain Tea Room & Restaurant The Post Office PORTLOE TR2 5QU	01872 501252	937 395	On Path £22.00 D EM PL DW 1T 1S
45	Mr & Mrs R Dasent Cliff Garden PORTLOE NR TRURO TR2 5QZ	01872 501751 01872 501807 rdasent736@aol.com		On path £22.50 D PL CP LSP 2D(1)
47	Mr & Mrs A Freeman Llawnroc Inn GORRAN HAVEN ST AUSTELL PL26 6NU	01726 843461 01726 843461 www.llawnroc.mevagissey.com llawnroc@mevagissey.com		100 mts O D EM PL CP LSP DW 4D 4T 2F ALL ES
47	Ms G Mott Piggy Pantry The Willows GORRAN HAVEN	01726 843545 piggyspantry@hotmail.com		200 mtrs £20.00 O D PL CP DW 1D 1T
47	Mr & Mrs R J Smith 'Homestead' 34 Chute Lane GORRAN HAVEN PL26 6NU	01726 842567		On Path £25.00 O CP 1D 1T ALL ES

Sect.	Name and Address	Tel. No. Fax. No. Web / Email	Map Reference Opening Times	Distance from Path Starting Price Facilities Accommodation
47	Mrs J L Lucas Mount Pleasant Farm GORRAN HIGH LANES GORRAN HAVEN PL26 6LR	01726 843918 jlucas@mpfarm.fsnet.co.uk	987 432 25 Mar-4 Nov	1.6km PD £16.00 D EM PL CP LSP KT 2D[1] 1F
47	Mr & Mrs D Youlden Steep House PORTMELLION COVE PL26 6PH	01726 843732		On path PD £18.00 O D PL CP LSP KT 2D[2] 2T 1F
48	Ms J Connolly Mandalay Hotel School Hill MEVAGISSEY PL26 6TQ	01726 842435 joe@jconneely.freeserve.co.uk		300mtrs £18.00 O D EM PL CP LSP DW KTPD 5D 1T 1S 2F ALL ES
48	Mr & Mrs A Parsloe Tregorran Guest House Cliff Street MEVAGISSEY PL26 6QW	01726 842319 www.bedbreakfastcornwall.com/members/tregorra patricia@parsloep.freeserve.co.uk		100mtrs £18.00 O D PL CP LSP DW KT by arrangement 4D[3] 1T[1] 1F[1]
48	Mrs C J Avent Wild Air Polkirt Hill MEVAGISSEY PL26 6UX	01726 843302		On path PD £22.50 O D PL CP KT PD 3D[2]
49	Mrs A Arnold Treveglos Church Road CHARLESTOWN PL25 3NS	01726 61424		£19.00 D PL CP DW 1D 1T 1S
49	Mr M.I Christie T'Gallants Guest House 6 Charlestown Road CHARLESTOWN PL25 3NJ	01726 70203		200mtrs £22.50 O PL CP LSP 6D 2T ALL ES
49	Mr & Mrs R Callis Ardenconnel 179 Charlestown Road CHARLESTOWN PL25 3NN	01726 75469		400mtrs £17.00 O D PL CP LSP KT 2D[1] 2T[1] 2S[1] 2F[1]
49	Miss S Mathieson Coastguard House 11 Coastguard Terrace ST AUSTELL PL25 3NJ	01726 72828 01726 73954	039 515	30 mtrs PD £15.00 O D PL CP LSP DW PD KT 1D 1T
49	Mrs D A Best Broad Meadow House Quay Road ST AUSTELL PL25 3NX	01726 76636 01726 76636 neildeb.broadmeadow@tinyworld.co.uk	039 517	150mtrsPD £20.00 O D PL CP LSP KT 1D[1]
49	Mr & Mrs M Neill 34 Quay Road CHARLESTOWN ST AUSTELL PL25 3NX	01726 73607		100 mts £16.00 O D CP LSP KT 2D 1S
49	Mrs B A Mackenzie Trethowel Mill Bodmin Road St AUSTELL PL25 5RR	01726 74741		2.5 miles PD £15.00 O D PL CP LSP LT 1D 1T 1S
49	Mrs G Avery Piskey Cove 3 The Square ST AUSTELL PL26 6DA	01726 843781 01726 843781		On path PD £20.00 O D EM PL CP LSP DW 2D 1T 1F ALL ES
50	The Cliff Head Hotel Sea Road CARLYON BAY PL25 3RB	01726 812345 01726 815511 www.cornishriviera.uk/cliffhead cliffheadhotel@btconnect.com	053 520	on path £35.00 O EM PL CP LSP 20D 19T 18S 3F ALL ES

Sect.	Name and Address	Tel. No. Fax. No. Web / Email	Map Reference Opening Times	Distance from Path Starting Price Facilities Accommodation
50	Mrs M.H Ball Polbrean House Woodland Ave, Tywardreath PAR PL24 2PL	01726 812530		2 kms £17.50 O D PL CP 2D 1S
50	Mrs B D Burgess 55 Polmear Road PAR PL24 2AW	01726 812967	086 535	500mtrs £15.00 O D CP LSP 1T 2S
51	Mr & Mrs R M Bullock Trevanion Guest House 70 Lostwithiel Street FOWEY PL23 1BQ	01726 832602 01726 832602 www.usersglobalnet.co.uk/~trefoy/fowey.htm trefoy@globalnet.co.uk	124 518 March to Oct	800 mtr £22.50 D CP 2D[1] 1T[1] 1F[1]
51	The Ship Inn Trafalgar Square FOWEY PL23 1AZ	01726 832230 01726 832230	125 515	On path £20.00 O D EM PL LSP DW 4D [1] 2T
51	Ms M Evans The Dwelling House 6 Fore Street FOWEY PL23 1AQ	01726 833662 01726 833662	125 515	200mtrs £20.00 O D PL DW 2D 1F ALL ES
51	Mr & Mrs D Turner Topsides Esplanade FOWEY PL23 1HZ	01726 833715	123 515	50mtrs £17.50 O D PL DW 2D
51	Mrs C Eardley St Keverne 4 Daglands Road FOWEY PL23 1JL	01726 833164 www.fowey.com/stkeverne.htm carol@stkeverne1.fsnet.co.uk	124 518 Feb-Nov	500mtrs £20.00 D PL 2D ALL ES
51	Miss H E Smith Seahorses 14 Fimbarrus Road FOWEY PL23 1JJ	01726 833148 01726 833148 www.users.globalnet.co.uk/~jandh/fowey.htm jandh@globalnet.co.uk	122 514 Mar-Oct	200mtrs £18.50 D 1D 1T PRIV FACIL.
51	Mrs A Cottrell The Nook Guest House 10 North Street FOWEY PL23 1DD	01726 823070 mikecottrell@lineone.net		1 km £18.00 O D 2D 2F ALL ES
52	Mr & Mrs Rogers Quayside House POLRUAN PL13	01726 870377		500mtrs PD £20.00 O D PL KT 3D[3] 1T
52	Mrs P Moore Chyavallon Landaviddy Lane POLPERRO PL13 2RT	01503 272788 01503 272788		350mtrs £18.00 O D PL CP DW 2D 1T ALL ES
52	Mrs P Wilcox The Watchers The Warren POLPERRO PL13 2RD	01503 272296 01503 272296 www.polperro.org		On path £19.00 O D PL DW DW by Arrang. 2D 1T ALL ES
53	Mrs McQueen Penvith Barns ST MARTIN-BY-LO PL13 1NZ	01503 240772 01503 240772 anne@cornwallexplore.co.uk	283 541	1500mtrs PD £17.00 O D EM PL CP LSP DW 2D 1T 1F ALL ES
53	Mr M Neaves Schooner Point 1 Trelawney Terrace WEST LOOE PL13 2AG	01503 262670 melv.neaves@tinyworld.co.uk	Feb-Nov	150mtrs £14.00 D PL CP 3D[1] 2S 1F[1]

Sect.	Name and Address	Tel. No. Fax. No. Web / Email	Map Reference Opening Times	Distance from Path Starting Price Facilities Accommodation
53	Mr & Mrs R Manser Halcyon Station Road LOOE PL13 1HN	01503 264169	254 537	100mtrs O D PL CP LSP 2D[2]
53	Mr & Mrs C Eveleigh Grasmere St Martins Road EAST LOOE PL13 1LP	01503 262556	254 544	400mtrs £15.00 O D EM PL CP 3D[1] 2F[2]
53	Mr & Mrs A Fish St John's Court East Cliff EAST LOOE PL13 1DE	01503 262301 01503 262301 www.stjohnscourtlooe.tripod.com stjohnscourt@looecornwall.freeserve.co.uk		On path £17.50 O D PL DW KT 4D[4] 1T[1] 1S 1F[1]
53	Mr E Mawby Marwinthy Guest House East Cliff EAST LOOE PL13 1DE	01503 264382 smoothhound/looe/hotels eddie.mawby @tinyonline.co.uk	256 533	On Path £17.00 O D DW 3D[2] 1T 1F
53	Mr & Mrs J Jenkin Sea Breeze Lower Chapel Street EAST LOOE PL13 1AT	01503 263131 01503 263131 www.cornwallexplore.co.uk/seabreeze johnjenkin@sbgh.freeserve.co.uk	256 351	100mtrs £16.00 O D PL DW 4D[3] 1T
54	Mrs P Rowlandson Blue Haven Hotel Looe Hill SEATON PL11 3JQ	01503 250310 www.smoothhound.co.uk/hotels/bluehaven.html bluehaven@btinternet.com		300mtrs £20.00 O D EM PL CP DW EM PL DW by arrange. 3D[2] 1T[1] 1S 1F[1]
54	Mr & Mrs G L Burton The Barn CAIR DEVIOCK DOWNDERRY PL11 3DN	01503 250545 Mobile 0850 223548 glbremovals@brethemail.net	313 555	1km PD O D CP LSP DW KT 3D
54	Mr D Maynard The Inn On The Shore Seafront DOWNDERRY PL11 3JY	01503 250210	314 539	800 mts O D EM PL CP LSP 2D 2T 1F ALL ES
54	Mrs Thatcher & Mrs Salte Bay View DOWNDERRY PL11 3LE	01503 250162		300mtrs £17.50 O D PL CP LSP 2D 1S PRIVATE FACIL
54	Mrs A J Harvey The Bungalow Cliff Road PORTWRINKLE PL11 3BY	01503 230334	355 541 April to Oct	On Path £15.00 D PL CP 1D 1T
54	Mrs K Ridpath Fir Cottage LOWER TREGANTLE CRAFTHOLE PL11 3AL	01752 822626 01752 822626		200 mtrs PD £17.50 O D EM PL CP LSP DW KT 1D 1T 2F
54	Mrs P Wilton Penmillard Farm RAME NR CAWSAND PL10 1LG	01752 822215 01752 822454 www.penmillard.co.uk stay@penmillard.co.uk		1 kms £25.00 O D CP 2D 1T ALL ES
54	Finnygook Inn CRAFTHOLE PL11 3BQ	01503 230338 www.finnygook.co.uk		200mtrs £25.00 O D EM PL CP LSP DW 5D ALL ES
55	Mr & Mrs A Fidler Rame Barton RAME CAWSAND PL10 1LG	01752 822789 01752 822789	425 492 Jan to Oct	800mtrs £20.00 D EM PL CP LSP DW 1T[1]

Sect.	Name and Address	Tel. No. Fax. No. Web / Email	Map Reference Opening Times	Distance from Path Starting Price Facilities Accommodation
55	Mr C Collins Avon House Garrett Street CAWSAND PL10 1PB	01752 822229 collins@cawsand.f9.co.uk	435 502	500 mtr £14.00 D PL CP LSP DW 2D[1] 2S
55	Mrs D Goodwright Clarendon Garrett Street CAWSAND PL10 1PD	01752 823460	435 502	On Path £17.00 O D PL 1D 1T 1S
55	Mr D Riggs The Halfway House Inn Fore Street KINGSAND PL10 1NA	01752 822279 01752 823146 www.connexions.co.uk/halfway/		500mtrs £26.00 O D EM PL CP LSP DW 3D 1S 1T 1F ALL ES
55	Mr & Mrs C E Taylor The Haven Market Street KINGSAND PL10 1ND	01752 823860		On path £17.00 O D PL 1D 1T 1S
55	Mr & Mrs A Ogilvie Algoma, The Green KINGSAND TORPOINT PL10 1NH	01752 822706 www.crabpot.co.uk alan@aogilvie.freeserve.co.uk	434 506	10 mts PD £20.00 O D PL LSP KT 1D 1F ALL ES
55	Mr A Ogilvie Algoma The Green KINGSAND PL10 1NH	01752 822706 alan@aogilvie.freeserve.co.uk	434 506	25 mtrs £20.00 O EM DW 1D 1F ALL ES
55	Mr A Bartlett Friary Manor Hotel MAKER HEIGHTS KINGSAND PL10 1JB	01752 822112 friaryman@aol.com		1KM £29.00 OO EM PL CP DW KT 3D[2] 1T 3F[3]
56	Mr & Mrs D Nicholson Admirals Rest Hotel 64 Durnford Street PLYMOUTH PL1 3QN	01752 224306 01752 226111 admiralsresthotel@lineone.net		On Path £18.00 O D EM PL CP LSP DW 3D 2T 1S 3F[1]
56	Mrs J Moulds Berkeley's of St James 4 St James Place East PLYMOUTH PL1 3AS	01752 221654 017522 221654 www.smoothhound.co.uk/hotels/berkely2.html		on path £20.00 O D PL CP 3D[2] 1S[1] 1F[1]
56	Mr & Mrs T.J. Tregidgo Sea Breezes 28 Grand Parade PLYMOUTH PL1 3DJ	01752 667205 01752 667205	478 537	5 mtrs £15.00 O D EM PL CP LSP DW 2D[2] 2T[1] 1S 2F
56	Mrs J Turner Rusty Anchor 30 Grand Parade PLYMOUTH PL1 3DJ	01752 663924 01752 663924		£16.00 O D PL CP DW 1D[1] 2T[1] 2S 4F[3]
56	Messrs J Lovell & A Pascoe Plymouth Backpackers Hotel 172 Citadel Road PLYMOUTH PL1 3DB	01752 225158 01752 207847		On Path PD £8.50 O D CP LSP Also 1 Female En Suite Dorm sleeps 6 3D 8 DORMS(SLEEP 2-8)
56	Mrs M Emery Acorns & Lawns Guest House 171 Citadel Road PLYMOUTH PL1 2HY	01752 229474 01752 229474		100mtrs £14.00 O D PL 6D[3] 4T[2] 2S 2F[1]
56	Mrs C M Hawton Edgcumbe Guest House 50 Pier Street West Hoe PLYMOUTH PL1 3BT	01752 660675 01752 666510 www.hawton.clara.net hatwon@clara.co.uk		20 mts £18.00 O D PL CP DW 4D[3] 3T[2] 2S 2F[1]

Sect.	Name and Address	Tel. No. Fax. No. Web / Email	Map Reference Opening Times	Distance from Path Starting Price Facilities Accommodation
56	Mr S Jones The Old Pier Guest House 20 Radford Road West Hoe PLYMOUTH PL1 3BY	01752 268468 www.oldpier.co.uk enquire@oldpier.co.uk	472 537	100 mts £16.00 O D PL 2D[1] 1T 1S 1F
56	Mrs Jan Rayne The Boringdon Arms TURNCHAPEL NR PLYMOUTH PL9 9TQ	01752 402053 01752 481313 bori@boringdon-arms.demon.co.uk	495 531	5 mtrs PD £16.00 O D EM PL CP DW 3D 1T 2F[1]
57	Mr & Mrs D F Kaye Seascape 20 Beach View Crescent PLYMOUTH PL9 0HJ	01752 863595 01752 862800 seascape@totalise.co.uk	500 mtrs PD £17.50 O D PL CP LSP KT 1D[1]	
57	Heybrook Bay Private Beach Road HEYBROOK BAY NR PLYMOUTH PL9 0BS	01752 862345	496 488	On path £18.00 O D PL CP LSP DW 4D 2T
57	Mr & Mrs A J Farrington Bay Cottage 150 Church Road WEMBURY PL9 0HR	01752 862559 01752 862559 the fairies @ aol.com	520 485	200 mtrs £26.00 O D PL CP LSP DW 2D(2) 2T(1) 1S
57	Mrs M R Denby Knoll Cottage 104 Church Road WEMBURY PLYMOUTH PL9 0LA	01752 862036	523 489	500 mts £18.00 O D EM PL CP LSP 2D[2] 1S
57	Mrs J Mills Willowhayes Ford Road WEMBURY PL9 0JA	01752 862581	524 495	2 kms D CP DW 2D[1] 1T 1S
57	Mrs P M Cane Venn Farm BRIXTON PL8 2AX	01752 880378 01752 880378		4.8 kms PD £18.00 O D CP LSP 1D[1] 1T 1S 1F
58	Mrs J D Johnson Crown Yealm NEWTON FERRERS PL8 1AW	01752 872365 01752 872365	25 Oct-25 Sept	2.5kms £20.00 D PL CP DW 1D 1T 1F
58	Mrs J Cross Wood Cottage Brigend NEWTON FERRERS PL8 1AW	01752 872372 jillx@wdcott.freeserve.co.uk	555 482	on path £20.00 O D EM PL CP DW KT PD 2D 1T[1] 1F[1]
58	Mrs A Hill Rowden House Stoke Road NOSS MAYO PL8 1JG	01752 872153 www.rowdenhouse.co.uk enquire@rowdenhouse.co.uk	555 472	500mtrs £20.00 O D PL CP LSP DW KT PD 2T 1F
58	Mrs B Sherrell Brookindale NOSS MAYO PL8 1EN	01752 872665	547 475	1.2kms £18.00 D PL CP LSP 2D 1T
58	Mrs J Rogers Higher Shippen WORSWELL BARTON NOSS MAYO PL8 1HB	07152 872977		800 mtrs PD £18.50 O D PL CP LSP 1D 1F
58	Mrs J Stockman Bugle Rocks, The Old School BATTISBOROUGH HOLBETON PL8 1JX	01752 830422 01752 830558	601 473	500 mtrs £25.00 O D PL CP LSP DW 2D[1]

Sect.	Name and Address	Tel. No. Fax. No. Web / Email	Map Reference Opening Times	Distance from Path Starting Price Facilities Accommodation
58	Miss F Kempt West Hanover Lodge HOLBETON PL8 1JN	01752 830582	617 502 Easter-Oct	4.5kms PD £17.00 D CP PD 1D(1)
58	Miss L Price Mildmay Colours Inn HOLBETON PLYMOUTH PL8 1NA	01752 830248 01752 830432		2 kms £30.00 O D EM PL CP DW 3D 3T 2F ALL ES
58	Mrs L Wallis Windlestraw Penquit ERMINGTON PL21 OLU	01752 896237 01752 896237 wallispenquit@beeb.bet	646 544	2kms PD £20.00 O D PL CP LSP KT Will PD Yealm Erme Avon 1T 1S
58	Mrs P J Brunskill Cliff Path RINGMORE NR KINGSBRIDGE TQ7 4HR	01548 810654	651 456	800 mtrs £16.00 O D PL CP LSP 1T
58	Mrs I Dodds Ayrmer House RINGMORE NR KINGSBRIDGE	01548 810391		1.2kms £22.00 O D PL CP LSP 2D[2] 1T
58	Mr M Walker Blackadon Barns NR IVYBRIDGE PL22 0HB	01752 897034 www.blackadonbarns.co.uk mwalkone@aol.com		PD £17.00 O D EM PL CP LSP DW KT 4D[4] 4T[3]
58	Mrs C Walsh Folly Foot CHALLABOROUGH BIGBURY-ON-SEA TQ7 4JB	01548 810036	652 447 Mar-Oct	50 mtrs PD £20.00 D PL CP LSP KT 2D[1] 1S 1F[1]
58	Mr & Mrs M A Farrell Warren Cottage Marine Drive BIGBURY-ON-SEA TQ7 4AS	01548 810210 01548 810210	650 444	On path PD £18.00 O D EM PL CP LSP KT 1T 1S
58	Mrs J Hughes Warren Point Marine Drive BIGBURY-ON-SEA TQ7 4AS	01548 810616	649 445 Apr-Dec	On Path £22.50 D PL CP LSP KT 1D 1T 1S 1F PRIV. BATH
58	Mrs R van der Heiden Avonlea 3 Folly Hill BIRBURY-ON-SEA TQ7 4AR	01548 810926 01548 810926 hansudheiden@eurobell.co.uk		20 mts £25.00 O D PL CP 2D[1] 1T 1S
58	Ms U Phelan Lincombe BIGBURY-ON-SEA TQ7 4BD	01548 810426 Mobile 07971 227451 tuphelan@clara.co.uk	669 454	2km PD £22.50 O D CP LSP DW KT 2D 1T ALL ES
59	Mrs P Rowland Heron House Hotel THURLESTONE SANDS TQ7 3JY	01548 561308/561600	677 413	On Path £55.00 O D EM PL CP LSP 11D 7T 1S ALL ES
59	Mr & Mrs J Litchfield Beacon Point Hotel THURLESTONE SANDS TQ7 3JY	01548 561207	676 411	10mtrs £18.00 O D EM PL CP DW 3D[3] 1T[1] 3F[1]
59	Mrs T Wilson 2 Horswell Cottages SOUTH MILTON TQ7 3JU	01548 561328	619 423	1.5 kms PD £18.00 O D EM PL CP KT 1D 1T

Sect.	Name and Address	Tel. No. Fax. No. Web / Email	Map Reference Opening Times	Distance from Path Starting Price Facilities Accommodation
59	Mr & Mrs L Clarke Hope Cove Hotel HOPE COVE TQ7 3HH	01548 561233 01548 561233	Easter to Oct	50mtrs £24.50 D EM PL CP LSP 5D 2T ALL ES
59	Mr & Mrs C Barclay The Sand Pebbles Hotel Grand View Road HOPE COVE KINGSBRIDGE TQ7 3HF	01548 561673		250 mtrs £25.00 D EM PL CP DW 9D 3T ALL ES
59	Mrs Jea Guymer Cove Cottage HOPE COVE TQ7 3HG	01548 561446 01548 561446		100 mtr £14.00 D CP LSP DW 1D 1T 1S
59	Mr & Mrs N P Daly Rose Cottage GALMPTON NR KINGSBRIDGE TQ7 3EU	01548 561953 01548 561953 www.rosecottagesalcombe.co.uk	689 409	1.45kms £20.00 O D EM CP 2D 1T ALL ES
60	Mr & Mrs R Petty-Brown Rocarno Grenville Road SALCOMBE TQ8 8BJ	01548 842732 rocarno@c.s.com	736 389	500mtrs £19.50 O D PL LSP DW 1D 1T ALL ES
60	Mr & Mrs A Axtell Amalfi Grenville Road SALCOMBE TQ8 8BJ	01548 842155 01548 843720 b-and-b.amalfi@virgin.net	736 389	1 km £19.50 O D CP 2D 2T ALL ES
60	Mr & Mrs A J Bouttle Torre View Hotel Devon Road SALCOMBE TQ8 8AJ	01548 842633 01548 842633 bouttle@torreview.eurobell.co.uk	735 385 March to Oct	500 mtrs £28.00 D EM PL CP 2D 1T 2S 1F
60	Mrs N Carter Karenza Grenville Road SALCOMBE TQ8 8BJ	01548 843422 01548 843422 karenza@salcombe-devon-fsnet.co.uk		2km £18.00 O D EM PL CP DW KT PD 1D[1] 2F
60	Mrs J Dean Furzehill Moult Rd SALCOMBE TQ8 8LG	01548 843319 01548 843319		500mtrs £21.00 D PL CP LSP 1D[1] 1T[1] 1F BUNKROOM
60	Mr & Mrs P Towner Lyndhurst Hotel Bonaventure Road SALCOMBE TQ8 8BG	01548 842481 01548 842481 lyndhot.salc@tesco.net		400 mtrs £23.00 O D CP 4D 2T 2F ALL ES
60	Mr & Mrs P A Thomas Beadon Farmhouse Beadon Road SALCOMBE TQ8 8LX	01548 843020		1km £30.00 O D PL CP LSP KT 1D 1T 1F ALL ES
60	Mr & Mrs R Vaughan Trennels Hotel Herbert Road SALCOMBE TQ8 8HR	01548 842500 www.btinternet.com/~r.vaughn/trennels-hotel trennels_hotel@btinternet.com	Mar-Oct	900mtrs £22.00 CP 5D ALL ES
60	Mrs E M Weymouth Motherhill Farm Main Road SALCOMBE TQ8 8NB	01548 842552 01548 842552 djw@dweymouth.fsnet.co.uk	730 393 Easter-Oct	1.5 kms £17.00 D CP 1D 1T 1S 1F
60	Mr P Howard Allenhayes Allenhayes Road SALCOMBE TQ8 8HU	01548 843546	388 738	200 mtrs PD £20.00 O D CP KT 2D 1T ALL ES

Sect.	Name and Address	Tel. No. Fax. No. Web / Email	Map Reference Opening Times	Distance from Path Starting Price Facilities Accommodation
61	Mr & Mrs N Alen Ashleigh House Ashleigh Road KINGSBRIDGE TQ7 1HB	01548 852853 www.ashleigh-house.co.uk reception@ashleigh-house.co.uk	731 439	6 kms PD £20.00 O D EM PL CP DW KT 5D 2T 1F ALL ES
61	Mr & Mrs D Griffiths Meadow Barn High House EAST PORTLEMOUT TQ8 8PN	01548 843085 dcgriffiths@portables1.ngfl.go	759 378 Feb to Oct	500mtrs £20.00 D EM PL CP LSP KT PD 1D 1T
61	Mr & Mrs M Mitchelmore Sunnyside EAST PRAWLE TQ7 2BY	01548 511387	Feb-Dec	PD £16.00 D CP LSP KT PD 1D 1T 2S
61	Mrs J Foss Down Farm START POINT KINGSBRIDGE	01548 511234 01548 511234	806 377 16 Jan-14 Dec	600mtrs £18.00 D CP LSP 1D[1] 1T
61	Mrs P Wolstenholme Widget NORTH HALLSANDS NR KINGSBRIDGE TQ7 2EX	01548 511110		50 mts PD £20.00 O D PL CP LSP KT 2D[1] 1T
61	Mr & Mrs G Chivers The Cricket Inn BEESANDS TQ7 2EN	01548 580215 01548 580215	879 403	50mtrs O D EM PL CP LSP DW 1D 1T 1F ALL ES
61	Mrs L Rogers Higher Beeson House BEESON KINGSBRIDGE TQ7 2HW	01548 580623 01548 580623 Mobile-07977 905836 crogersbeeson@tinyworld.co.uk	810 406	1km PD £27.50 O D CP LSP KT 2D[2]
61	Mr & Mrs BSmith Waterside TORCROSS KINGSBRIDGE TQ7 2TQ	01548 580280 01548 580280 www.watersidehouse.com waterside.house@virgin.net	824 421 Mar-Nov	On path £19.00 O PL CP 3D[2] 1T[1] 1S 1F[1]
61	Mr & Mrs R Rose-Price Startlea House TORCROSS KINGSBRIDGE TQ7 2TQ	01548 580724 www.startlea.co.uk Rose-Price@startlea.co.uk	823 422	5 mts £22.50 O D CP 2D 1T ALL ES
62	Mrs V A Mercer Old Walls SLAPTON NR KINGSBRIDGE TQ7 2QN	01548 580516	822 449	1 km PD £18.00 O D PL DW KT 1T 2F[2]
62	Ms L Meir & Ms V Blake The Roundhouse SLAPTON TQ7 2PN	01548 580019	821 451	800 mtrs £20.00 O D PL CP 2D
62	Mrs S Hutchinson Sloutts Farm House SLAPTON TQ7 2PR	01548 580872 01548 580872		1km £25.00 D EM PL CP 3T[3]
62	Mr B Wood & Mr Colin Smith The Slide House Hynetown Road, STRETE DARTMOUTH TQ6 ORS	01803 770378 01803 770197 106461.3324@compuserve.com	Feb-Nov	On Path PD £35.00 D CP LSP KT 2D 1T ALL ES
62	Mrs S Leach Sunny Banks Guest House 1 Vicarage Hill DARTMOUTH TQ6 9EW	01803 832766 01803 832766 www.sunnybanks.com sue@sunnybanks.com	Closed Jan	1 km £20.00 D PL CP DW 5D[4] 2T[2] 1S 2F[2]

Sect.	Name and Address	Tel. No. Fax. No. Web / Email	Map Reference Opening Times	Distance from Path Starting Price Facilities Accommodation
62	Mrs J Makepeace Skerries STRETE NR DARTMOUTH TQ6 0RH	01803 770775 01803 770950 jamskerries@rya-online.net		PD £20.00 O D PL CP KT 2D 1T ALL ES
62	Mrs J Wright Camelot 61 Victoria Road DARTMOUTH TQ6 9RX	01803 833805	875 514	£17.00 O D CP 2D 1T 1F ALL ES
62	Mrs A Cardwell The Maitland 28 Victoria Road DARTMOUTH TQ6 9SA	01803 835854	875 513	2.4 kms £16.00 O D CP 2D[2] 1T 1S
63	Mr & Mrs L Congdon Carlton House Higher Street KINGSWEAR TQ6 0AG	01803 752244		100 mtrs £15.00 O D PL DW 3D 1T 1S 1F
63	Mr & Mrs P Hancock Melville Hotel 45 New Road BRIXHAM TQ5 8NL	01803 852033	March to Dec	500 mtrs £16.00 D EM PL CP 4D[3] 2T[1] 3S 1F[1]
63	Mr & Mrs T J Boulton Sampford House 57/59 King Street BRIXHAM TQ5 9TH	01803 857761 01803 857761		50 mtrs £17.50 O D PL CP DW 5D 1T ALL ES
63	Mr I Hayhurst Richmond House Hotel Higher Manor Road BRIXHAM TQ5 8HA	01803 882391 01803 882391		400mtrs £18.00 O D PL DW 4D 1T 1F ALL ES
63	Mr&Mrs T Boulton Sampford House 57/59 King Street BRIXHAM TQ5 9TH	01803 857761 01803 857761 carole@boulton.fsbusiness.co.uk		50mtrs £17.50 O D EM PL CP DW 4D 1T 1F ALL ES
64	Mrs P Kingdon Bruce Lodge Guest House 2 Elmsleigh Road PAIGNTON TQ4 5AU	01803 550972 01803 550972 www.torbay.gov.uk/accom/business.pages/brucelo roger.kingdon@lineone.net	891 610 Easter-Sept	500mtrs £15.00 D PL CP 2D 2T 1S 1F
64	Mrs R Leysinger Cedar Court 3 St Matthews Road TORQUAY TQ2 6JA	01803 607851	903 634	700 mts £20.00 O D EM PL CP 5D 3S 2F ALL ES
64	Mrs J Hodgson Torquay Backpackers 119 Abbey Road TORQUAY TQ2 5NP	01803 299924 torquay.backpackers@btinternet		1km £6.00 O D CP LSP DW 1D 8 DORMS
64	Ansteys Cove Hotel 327 Babbacombe Road TORQUAY TQ1 3TB	01803 293674 01803 211150 www.torquaydevon.com info@torquaydevon.com		On Path £21.00 O EM CP LSP 6D 4T 1S 1F ALL ES
65	Ms J Hobday Beech Close Guest House 53 Babbacombe Road BABBACOMBE TQ1 3SN	01803 328071		100 mtrs £16.00 O D PL CP LSP 4D[1] 1S
65	Mr D.A Day Sunray Hotel Aveland Road BABBACOMBE TQ1 3PT	01803 328285 sunrayhotel@sunrayhotel.eurobell.co.uk		2.5kms PD £15.00 O PL CP DW KT 1T 1S 1FALL ES

Sect.	Name and Address	Tel. No. Fax. No. Web / Email	Map Reference Opening Times	Distance from Path Starting Price Facilities Accommodation
65	Mr T P Pinder Birch Tor 315 Babbacombe Road TORQUAY TQ1 3TB	01803 292707 01803 292707 www.members1.visualcities.com/b-and-b/index.html terry@birchtor.worldonline.co.uk	932 648	50 mts £15.00 O EM PL CP DW KT 3D[1] 1T 1S 1F
65	Mr & Mrs K A James Suite Dreams Hotel Steep Hill MAIDENCOMBE TQ1 4TS	01803 313900 01803 313841 suitedreams@suitedreams.co.uk		200 mtr £20.50 O D CP DW 6D 3T 3F ALL ES
65	Mrs B Cook Green Willow Stoke Road MAIDENCOMBE TORQUAY TQ1 4TN	01803 329764 cook@greenwillow.freeserve.co.uk		1km PD £15.00 O PL CP 1T
65	Mrs D Sibthorp The Beehive Steep Hill MAIDENCOMBE TORQUAY TQ1 4TS	01803 314647	927 687	250mtrs £18.00 O D CP LSP 1D 1T ALL ES
65	Mr & Mrs K Underwood Glenside Hotel Ringmore Road SHALDON TORQUAY TQ14 0EP	01626 872448		600 mtrs £20.00 O D EM PL CP DW 4D[4] 3T[3] 1S
65	Mr & Mrs A D Mohan Chelsea Cottage 45 Fore Street SHALDON TORQUAY TQ14 0EA	01626 873824		 £21.00 O PL DW 3D ALL ES
66	Mr & Mrs J New Lalla Rookh Guest House 1 Bitton Avenue TEIGNMOUTH TQ14 8HD	01626 779653	937 731	1 km from ferry £14.50 O D 2D 1T 1S
66	Mr M Valentine Valentine Guest House 1 Glendaragh Road TEIGNMOUTH TQ14 8PH	01626 772316 01626 772316		200 mtrs £16.50 3D 1T ALL ES
66	Mrs A Ferris The Blenheim 1 Marine Parade DAWLISH EX7 9DJ	01626 862372		10mts £21.50 O D PL CP DW 3D 3T 3S 3F ALL ES
66	Mr & Mrs M Hayes The Old Vicarage STARCROSS EX6 8PX	01626 890206 01626 890206 maggie@theoldvicarage.clara.co.uk		On path £20.00 O D CP LSP 3D[2] 2T[1]
66	Mrs T Weeks Eastdon Farm Linhay Eastdon, Warren Road NR STARCROSS EXETER EX6 8RH	01626 891377	977 799	100 mts £19.00 O D PL CP LSP DW 1D[1]
66	Mrs M Lambert Wixels Ferry Road TOPSHAM EX3 0JH	01392 876785		On path £16.00 O D CP LSP 1D
66	Mr & Mrs G Parkin 131 Victoria Road EXMOUTH EX8 1DR	01395 269222	995 805	50mtrs O D PL CP 2D 1T 1F

Sect.	Name and Address	Tel. No. Fax. No. Web / Email	Map Reference Opening Times	Distance from Path Starting Price Facilities Accommodation
66	Mr & Mrs D M Palfreman The Barn Hotel EXMOUTH EX8 2DF	01395 224411 01395 225445	014 801	100 mtrs £30.00 EM PL CP LSP 4D 1T 2S 4F ALL ES
66	Mrs P M Garwood St Aubyns 11 Hartley Road EXMOUTH EX8 2SG	01395 264069		1km £17.00 O D PL CP LSP DW 3D 1T 1S 1F
66	Ms A Jones Sholton Guest House 29 Morton Road EXMOUTH EX8 1BA	01395 277318	999 807	100 mtrsPD £17.00 O D PL CP DW 6D[3] 2T[2] 1S 2F[2]
67	Mrs S Freeman 10 Knowle Village BUDLEIGH SALTER EX9 6AL	01395 445807	050 825	1.5km £18.00 O D PL CP LSP DW PD 1D 1T 1S
67	Mrs H.J. Simmons Chapter House 6 Westbourne Terrace BUDLEIGH SALTER EX9 6BR	01395 444100		100mtrs £20.00 O D PL CP DW 1D[1] 1T 1S 1F[1]
68	Mrs D Lee Cheriton Guest House Vicarage Rd SIDMOUTH EX10 8UQ	01395 513810 01395 513810 www.smoothhound.co.uk su9129@eclipse.co.uk		800mtrs PD £16.00 O D EM PL CP LSP DW KT advance notice for dogs 4D 2T 2S 2F ALL ES
68	Mr M C Penaluna Canterbury Guest House Salcombe Road SIDMOUTH EX10 8PR	01395 513373 cgh@eclipse.co.uk	127 878	600 mtr £16.00 O EM PL CP DW KT 3D 2T 3F ALL ES
68	Mrs Capon 1 Elim Villas Peaslands Road SIDMOUTH EX10 9BG	01395 577500	126 883	1km PD £15.00 O D PL CP LSP DW 1D 1T 1S 1F
68	Mrs L Lever Larkstone House 22 Connaught Road SIDMOUTH EX10 8TT	01395 514345		500 mtrs £17.00 O D CP DW 1D 1T[1] 1S
68	Mrs J Young Avalon Guest House Vicarage Road SIDMOUTH EX10 8UQ	01395 513443 www.avalonsidmouth.co.uk owneravalon@aol.com		500mtrs £20.00 O D EM CP EM not peak season 4D 1T ALL ES
68	Mr & Mrs P Scorey Cranmere House 2 Fortfield Place SIDMOUTH EX10 8NX	01395 513933		200 mtrs £18.50 O D CP 2D[2] 2T 2S 1F[1]
68	Mr & Mrs D Haslam Bramley Lodge Guest House Vicarage Road SIDMOUTH EX10 8UQ	01395 515710 haslam@bramleylodge.fsnet.co.uk		750mtrsPD £18.50 O D EM PL CP DW KT 1D[1] 1T[1] 3S[1] 2F
68	The Manager The Royal York & Faulkner Hotel Esplanade SIDMOUTH EX10 8AZ	Free 0800 220714 01395 577475 www.royalyorkhotel.net yorkhotel@eclipse.co.uk	Feb-Dec	500 mts £28.50 D EM PL CP DW 9D 30T 22S 7F
68	Mr T Eardley High Creek Trow SALCOMBE REGIS SIDMOUTH EX10 0PB	01395 577678 t.eardley@talk21.com	156 894	1 km PD £20.00 O D EM PL CP LSP KT 1D 1F ALL ES

Sect.	Name and Address	Tel. No. Fax. No. Web / Email	Map Reference Opening Times	Distance from Path Starting Price Facilities Accommodation
69	Mr & Mrs G Van Den Broeck Chapel House BRANSCOMBE SEATON EX12 3AY	01297 680520	192 886	500 mtrs £25.00 O D PL CP DW 1D 1T 1F
69	Mr & Mrs R Hart Hole Mill BRANSCOMBE EX12 3BX	01297 680314 www.users.globalnet.co.uk/~branscombe/hole1.htm	192 895	2kms £18.50 O D CP LSP DW PD 2D 1T
69	Mrs R Harding High House Barline BEER EX12 3LS	01297 20325 thehardings@connectfree.co	225 892	500 mtrs PD £15.00 O D EM PL CP DW KT 1T 1F
69	Mr & Mrs P R Manning Pendennis South Down Road BEER EX12 3AE	01297 23395	228 889 Mar-Sept	on path £18.00 D EM PL CP LSP 3D[2] 3T[1] 2S 1F
68	Mr & Mrs B Rosewarne Sea Glimpses Burrow Road SEATON EX12 2NF	01297 22664	250 899	300 mts £17.00 O D PL CP LSP 1D 1T
69	Mr & Mrs P R Webber The Tors Guest House 55 Harbour Road SEATON EX12 2LX	01297 20531		£20.00 O PL CP 2D[1] 1T[1] 1S 1F
69	Mrs E D Jordan Lyndhurst Manor Road SEATON EX12 2AQ	01297 23490		800 mtr £16.00 O D CP DW 2D 1T 1S
70	Ms M Bolton Cliff Cottage Tea Garden Cobb Road LYME REGIS DT7 3JP	01297 443334 merry@cliffcottage.fsbusiness.co.uk	Easter to Nov	25 mtrs £20.00 D EM PL CP DW 2D[2] 1T 1S 1F[1]
70	Mr & Mrs S Bales Coverdale Guest House Woodmead Road LYME REGIS DT7 3AB	01297 442882 01297 444673	338 924	450 mtr £22.50 D PL CP LSP DW 4D 2T 1S 2F ALL ES
70	Mr & Mrs P A Brittain Lydwell House Lyme Road LYME REGIS DT7 3TJ	01297 443522 lydwell@brittain16.fsbusiness.co.uk	330 931	1 km £22.00 O D EM PL CP 1D 1T 1S 2F ALL ES
71	Mrs R Appleton The Granary Hook Farm, Gore Lane LYME REGIS DT7 3UU	01297 442801 www.hookfarm-uplyme.co.uk	323 929 Easter-Dec	1.5 kms £20.00 D CP LSP 2F[2]
72	Mr K A Baylis Seatown Cottage SEATOWN NR BRIDPORT DT6 6JT	01297 489027 01297 489027 keith@seatown.co.uk	420 919	100 mtrs £22.50 O D PL CP KT PD 1D 1T 1S
72	Mr & Mrs N Whittaker Seatown House SEATOWN BRIDPORT DT6 6JU	01297 489417 01297 489151 www.guardhouse.co.uk nigelwhitt@aol.com		2 S/C COTTAGES AVAILABLE
72	Mr & Mrs J Goodfellow Park Farmhouse Main Street CHIDEOCK DT6 6JD	01297 489157 01297 481762 parkfarmhouse@freeuk.com	426 928	1500 mtrs £20.00 O D PL CP LSP DW 3D 1T 2F

Sect.	Name and Address	Tel. No. Fax. No. Web / Email	Map Reference Opening Times	Distance from Path Starting Price Facilities Accommodation
72	Mr & Mrs R Harvey Betchworth House CHIDEOCK DT6 6JW	01297 489478		1.6kms £18.00 O D PL CP LSP 2D[2] 2T[2] 1S 1F[1]
72	Mrs V Vallard Egdon Third Cliff Walk WEST BAY BRIDPORT DT6 4HX	01308 422542		50 mtr £20.00 O D CP DW 1D 2T
72	Mr & Mrs R P Hansowitz Cranston 27 Church Street BRIDPORT DT6 3PS	01308 456240	467 927	1.5 kms PD £18.00 O D PL CP LSP DW KT 3D[2] 3T[2] 3S[2] 1F[1]
72	Mr A Hardy Britmead House West Bay Road BRIDPORT DT6 4EG	01308 422941 01308 422516 www.britmeadhouse.co.uk britmead@talk21.com	465 913	£22.00 O D PL CP DW KT 3D 2T 2F ALL ES
72	Mrs G R Bramah 143 Victoria Grove BRIDPORT DT6 3AG	01308 456617	467 934	3km PD £18.00 O D CP LSP KT 1T
73	The Proprietor The Burton Cliff Hotel BURTON BRADSTOC DT6 4RB	01308 897205 01308 898111 www.burtoncliffhotel.com.uk		on path £21.00 O D EM PL CP DW KT PD 7D(4) 8T(6) 3S(1)
73	Mr & Mrs G D Parr Chesil Coppice WEST BEXINGTON DORCHESTER DT2 9DD	01308 897351 01308 897390		£15.00 D EM PL CP LSP 1F
73	Mr & Mrs P Millard Blegberry Swyre Road WEST BEXINGTON DT2 9DD	01308 897774 01308 898300 paddymillard@freezone.co.uk	532 872	500 mts PD £20.00 O D CP LSP KT 1D 1F PRIV FACIL.
73	Mrs M Harman Linton Cottage ABBOTSBURY DT3 4JL	01305 871339 www.lintoncottage.co.uk queenbee@abbotsbury.co.uk		1km £25.00 O D PL CP LSP 3D(3)
73	The Swan ABBOTSBURY			1km O EM PL CP LSP DW 3D[3] 2T[1]
73	Mr & Mrs F Harber The Keep Back Street ABBOTSBURY DT3 4JP	01305 871294 mayling.thirlaway@which.net	578 854	50mtrs £18.50 O D CP LSP KT 1D(1) 2S
73	Mrs P Crockett 21 Rodden Row ABBOTSBURY DT3 4JL	01305 871465 01305 871465	855 579 7 Jan-10 Dec	750mtrs £17.50 D PL CP LSP 1D 1T
74	Mrs J Baker Aveswood 5 Bramdon Lane PORTESHAM DT3 4HG	01305 871413	603 857	800 mts PD O D PL CP LSP KT 1D 1T
74	Mrs A Martin The Old Fountain 36 Front Street PORTESHAM DT3 4ET	01305 871278 01305 871278	603 860	2 kms PD £18.00 O D PL CP LSP KT 1D 1T

Sect.	Name and Address	Tel. No. Fax. No. Web / Email	Map Reference Opening Times	Distance from Path Starting Price Facilities Accommodation
74	Mrs P Westcott Stonebank 14 West Street CHICKERELL DT3 4DY	01305 760120 01305 760871 www.stonebank-chickerell.co.uk sww@stonebank-chickerell.co.uk	643 807 Apr-Sept	2 kms £22.50 D PL CP 2D ALL ES
75	Mr & Mrs Lees 47 New Street Easton PORTLAND DT5 1HG	01305 822879		500mtrs £14.00 O PL CP LSP DW 1D 1T 1F
75	Mr D Fox The Pulpit Inn PORTLAND DT5 2JT	01305 821237		on path £20.00 O D EM CP LSP 3D 1S
76	Mrs S A Greenwood Goldcroft Guest House 6 Goldcroft Avenue WEYMOUTH DT4 0ET	01305 789953 gold@goldcroft6.freeserve.co.u	675 795	800 mtrs £20.00 O D EM PL CP LSP 2D 1T 3F
76	Mrs Harvey Florian 59 Abbotsbury Road WEYMOUTH DT4 0AQ	01305 773836 01305 750160		500 mtrs £18.00 O D EM PL CP 2D[2] 2T[2] 1S[1] 2F[2]
76	Mrs M Wakefield Anchorage 23 Stavordale Road WEYMOUTH DT4 0AB	01305 785719 01305 771501 anchorage.rod@zetnet.co.uk	674 788	700 mtrs £18.00 O D CP LSP 3D 1T 1F ALL ES
76	Westwey Hotel 62 Abbotsbury Road WEYMOUTH	01305 784564 dave@westwey.demon.co.uk		£18.50 O D EM CP 6D 5T 2S 1F ALL ES
76	Mrs G Blackshaw The Pebbles Guest House 18 Kirtleton Avenue WEYMOUTH DT4 7PT	01305 784331 01305 784695		1.6 kms PD £15.00 O D EM PL CP LSP DW KT 3D[3] 2T[1] 1S 1F[1]
76	Ms J Coxhill Southbrook Preston Road OVERCOMBE DT3 6PU	01305 832208 01305 832208		£18.00 O D PL CP DW 5D[3] 2T[1] 2S 1F
76	Mrs K Legg Rosedale Church Lane OSMINGTON DT3 6EW	01305 832056	Mar-Nov	on path D CP LSP 2D(1) 1T[1]
76	Mrs J Ravensdale Elads-Nevar West Road WAREHAM BH20 5RZ	01929 400467	824 806	800 mtrs £16.00 O D PL CP DW 1D 1T 1F
76	Mr & Mrs R J Foote Lulworth Cove Hotel WEST LULWORTH BH20 5RQ	01929 400333 01929 400534 lulworthcove@saqnet.co.uk		2 mtr £25.00 O E EM PL CP LSP DW 14D[12] 2F[2]
76	The Shirley Hotel 01929 400167 WEST LULWORTH NR WAREHAM BH20 5RL	01929 400358 www.shirleyhotel.co.uk durdle@aol.com	824 806 Feb-Nov	400mtrs £35.00 D EM PL CP DW 9D 4T 1S 1F ALL ES
76	Mr & Mrs J Payne Mill House Hotel Lulworth Cove WEST LULWORTH BH20 5RQ	01929 400404 01929 400508 www.millhousehotel.tripod.com dukepayne@hotmail.com	Jan-Mid Dec	On Path £28.50 D PL CP LSP 6D 1T 2F ALL ES

Sect.	Name and Address	Tel. No. Fax. No. Web / Email	Map Reference Opening Times	Distance from Path Starting Price Facilities Accommodation
76	Mrs C Miller Cromwell House Hotel WEST LULWORTH BH20 5RJ	01929 400253 01929 400566 www.lulworthcove.co.uk catriona@lulworthcove.co.uk		on path £30.00 D EM PL CP LSP DW 7D 5T 2S 3F ALL ES
76	Mr & Mrs P Brachi West Coombe Farmhouse COOMBE KEYNES WAREHAM BH20 5PS	01929 462889 01929 405863 www.westcoombefarmhouse.co.uk west.coombe.farmhouse@barclays.net	842 842	4km £25.00 O D PL CP PD 1D[1] 1T 1S
76	Mr & Mrs R T Cooper April Thatch COOMBE KEYNES LULWORTH COVE BH20 5PP	01929 463412 www.aprilthatch.co.uk admin@aprilthatch.co.uk	842 843	4.8kms PD £20.00 O D PL CP LSP KT 2D[1] 1T[1] 1S
77	Mr M Francis East Burton House WOOL WAREHAM BH20 6HE	01929 463857 01929 463026 www.eastburton.fra-yellow.com mikef@fdn.co.uk	870 834	3km PD £23.00 O D PL CP LSP KT 2D 1T
77	Mrs A Hole Kimmeridge Farm House KIMMERIDGE BH20 5PE	01929 480990	916 799	400mtrs £21.00 O D EM PL CP LSP 2D 1T ALL ES
77	Mrs E Braisby Blackmanston Farm STEEPLE KIMMERIDGE BH20 5NZ	01929 480743 01929 480743	916 808	1.5km £20.00 O D EM PL CP LSP DW KTPD 2D[1] 2T[1] 2S 1F[1]
78	Mrs G Hole Bradle Farm CHURCH KNOWLE KIMMERIDGE BH20 5NU	01929 480712 01929 481144 www.smoothhound.co.uk/hotels/brundle.html hole.bradle@farmersweekly.net	930 805	PD £22.00 O D PL CP LSP 2D 1T ALL ES
78	Mr & Mrs I Taylor The Haven WORTH MATRAVERS BH19 3LF	01929 439388 taylorhaven@talk21.com	976 777	1.5 kms PD £21.00 O D PL CP DW KT 1D 1T[1]
78	Mrs S Amos Dorest's West Country B&B 12 Rempstone Road SWANAGE BH19 1DW	01929 423271		2km £19.50 O D PL CP 2D 2T 2F ALL ES
78	Mr & Mrs C Davison Penny Farthings 124 Kings Road West SWANAGE BH19 1HS	01929 422256 hibike@globalnet.co.uk	023 790	800 mtrs PD £19.00 O D PL CP DW 2D[2] 1T[1] 1S
78	Mr & Mrs A Preston Sunny Bay 17 Cluny Crescent SWANAGE BH19 2BP	01929 422650 gillgc@aol.com		200mtrs £17.00 O D CP 1D 1T 1F[1]
78	Mrs E Hine Perfick Piece Springfield Road SWANAGE BH19 1HD	01929 423178 01929 423558	028 788	400mtrs £14.00 O D EM PL CP DW 1D 1T 1F[1]
78	The Amberlea Hotel 36 Victoria Avenue SWANAGE BH19 1AP	01929 426213	026 792	£16.00 O EM PL CP 5D 1T 2F ALL ES
78	Mr & Mrs M S Cooper Sunny South 118 Kings Road West SWANAGE BH19 1HS	01929 422665 www.sunnysouth.btinternet.co.uk SunnySouth@btinternet.com	023 790	812 mtr PD £15.00 O D PL CP KT 2D[2] 1T

Sect.	Name and Address	Tel. No. Fax. No. Web / Email	Map Reference Opening Times	Distance from Path Starting Price Facilities Accommodation
78	Mr & Mrs Ford The Eversden Hotel 5 Victoria Road SWANAGE BH19 1LY	01929 423276 01929 427755 www.eversden-hotel.co.uk		1km £23.00 D EM PL CP 5D[5] 1T[1] 1S 5F[5]
79	Mrs J Small 11 Durlston Point 78 Park Road SWANAGE BH19 2AE	01929 421717 je.small@virgin.net	033 782	200 mts PD £20.00 O D EM PL CP LSP KT 1D[1] 1T
79	Mr & Mrs M J Morris Rousemount 167 Bournemouth Road POOLE BH14 9HT	01202 7321384		PD £20.00 O D CP PD 2D[1] 1T 1S
79	Mrs North The Laurels 60 Britannia Road POOLE BH14 8BB	01202 265861 thelaurelsbandb.freeservers.com martin@thelaurelspoole.freeserve.com	033 913	1km £18.00 O D CP 1D 1T 1S 1F ALL ES

CAMPSITES

A list of campsites has been prepared in path order.

The following letter code is used;

T	= Toilets	S	=	Showers
G	= Grocery Shop	CP	=	Car Parking
LSP	= Long Stay Parking	LY	=	Laundry
O	= Open All Year	DW	=	Dogs Welcome
KT	= Kit Transfer	PD	=	Pick Up/Drop

KT - Kit Transfer. A service being offered by some of our accommodation providers is to transfer your kit to your next accommodation. This could prove useful to you. Naturally a fee may be levied for this service.
Distance from Path. Please remember these are only approximate and may not be accurate.
PD - Pick Up/Drop. This code appears following the distance from the path and denotes a facility whereby your host is prepared to collect and return you to the coast path within reasonable distance. No fee should be charged for this service.

The part of the address in CAPITALS is an aid to location; it does not signify the postal town. The extreme left-hand column refers to the appropriate section in the 'Trail Description'; we feel it may help you to find addresses quickly. The amount quoted gives an **indication of the starting rate** per night, and may well rise. If working on a tight budget, it is best to ask first.

Individuals - but we stress **not parties** - usually find no problem in obtaining leave to camp away from official camp sites if they request permission to do so. In fact, our correspondence has many examples of extra kindnesses extended by farmers and others to campers. We would, however, very much emphasize the requesting of permission first. It would be so easy for the thoughtlessness of a few to undo the good relationships of many others built up over some years.

This list is thin in many areas. Suggestions for inclusions in future lists will always be welcome. Information of any new sites should be addressed to the Administrator.

Sect.	Name and Address	Tel. No. Fax. No. Email Web	Map Ref. Distance from Path	Facilities Starting Price Opening Times
1	Mr P R Weaver Sparkhayes Farm Camp Site Sparkhayes Lane PORLOCK TA24 8NE	01643 862470	446 469 on path	O T S LY G CP LSP DW £4.00 Apr to Oct
2	Sunny Lyn Camp & Caravan Site LYNBRIDGE LYNTON TR12 6SD	01598 53384	719 485 800 mts	T S LY G CP DW Mar-Dec
3	Mr & Mrs T Greenaway Newberry Farm Touring Caravans & Camping Woodlands COMBE MARTIN EX34 OAT	01271 882334 01271 882880	574 470 200 mts	T S LY CP £6.50 Easter - End Oct
4	Mr & Mrs D S Dovey Hele Valley Holiday Park HELE BAY ILFRACOMBE EX34 9RD	01271 862460 01271 867926 holidays@helevalley.co.uk www.helevalley.co.uk	600 mts	T S LY G CP LSP DW KT £6.00 Apr-Oct
4	Mr D L Wassell Big Meadow Camp Site WATERMOUTH ILFRACOMBE EX34 9SJ	01271 862282	558 483 On path	T S LY G CP LSP DW KT Easter-Oct
4	Mrs J M Barten Little Meadow Caravan & Camping Site Lydford Farm ILFRACOMBE EX34 9SJ	01271 862222 info@little.meadow.co.uk www.little.meadow.co.uk	400 mts	T S CP DW £5.00 Easter-Sept
8	Ruda Holiday Park CROYDE BAY BRAUNTON EX33 1NY	01271 890671 01271 890656 enquiries@ruda.co.uk www.ruda.co.uk	438 397 50 mts	T S LY G CP LSP £6.00 Mar-Oct
8	Mrs Stansmore Chivenor Cross Caravan Park BARNSTAPLE EX31 4BN	01271 812217 01271 812644	100 mts PD	T S LY G CP DW £6.00 15 Mar-15 Nov
8	Midland Caravan Park Braunton Road BARNSTAPLE	01271 343691 01271 326355 www.midlandpark.co.uk	533 346 1.6 kms	T S LY G CP LSP DW £8.00 Mar-Nov
10	Mr R Croslegh Steart Farm Touring Park Horns Cross BIDEFORD EX39 5DW	01237 431836	356 229 1 km	T S LY CP LSP DW £5.00 Easter-30 Sept
11	Mrs H Davey Stoke Barton Farm STOKE HARTLAND EX39 6DU	01237 441238	234 246 800 mts	T S CP LSP DW KT Tearoom on site Easter - End Sept £3.50
12	Bude Holiday Park Maer Lane BUDE	01288 355955 01288 355980 enquiries@budeholidaypark.co.uk www.budeholidaypark.co.uk	208 085 200 mts	T S LY G CP DW £5.50 Apr - Sept
12	Mr & Mrs J M Cloke Upper Lynstone Camping & Caravan Park BUDE EX23 0LP	01288 352017 01288 359034 reception@upperlynstone.co.uk www.upperlynstone.co.uk	205 053 100 mts	T S LY G CP DW £7.00 Easter - Oct

Sect.	Name and Address	Tel. No. Fax. No. Email Web	Map Ref. Distance from Path	Facilities Starting Price Opening Times
12	Wooda Farm Caravan & Camping Park Wooda Farm BUDE EX23 9HJ	01288 352069 01288 355258 enquiries@wooda.co.uk www.wooda.co.uk	 229 078 3kms	T S LY G CP LSP £7.50 Apr to Oct
13	Mrs J Onions Coxford Meadow St Gennys CRACKINGTON HAVEN EX23 0NS	01840 230707 01840 230451	 161 967 1 km PD	T S CP LSP DW £3.00 Easter - Oct
13	Mrs S Weller Hentervene Camping & Caravan Park CRACKINGTON HAVEN EX23 0LF	01840 230365	 155 944 3.2 kms	O T S LY G CP LSP DW £4.50 Open All Year
15	Mr & Mrs R L Wickett Bossiney Farm Caravan & Camping Park BOSSINEY TINTAGEL PL34 0AY	01840 770481 01840 770025	 067 888 200mtrs	T S LY G CP DW April to Oct
15	Mr & Mrs M Francis The Headland Caravan & Camping Park Atlantic Road TINTAGEL PL34 0DE	01840 770239 01840 770925 headland.cp@virgin.net www.headlandcp-tintagel.co.uk	 056 888 300mtrs	T S LY G CP LSP DW £7.00 Easter to Oct
17	Mrs R Harris South Winds Camping & Caravan Park 01208 862080 POLZEATH PL27 6QU	01208 863267 www.rockinfo.co.uk	 948 790 on path	T S LY CP LSP DW £10.00 Mar to Sept
17	Mr R Harris Tristram Caravan & Camping Park POLZEATH PL27	01208 862215 01208 862086 www.rockinfo.co.uk	 948 790 on path	T S LY G CP LSP DW £10.00 Mar to Nov
18	Dennis Cove Campsite Dennis Cove PADSTOW	01841 532349 PL28 8DR	 920 745 500 mts	T S LY DW £4.40 Apr - Sept
20	Carnevas Farm Holiday Park PORTHCOTHAN BAY PL28 8PN	01841 520230 01841 520230	 862 728 800mtrs	T S LY G CP DW £5.50 1 Apr to 31 Oct
20	Mr P Langmaid Mother Iveys Bay Caravan Park TREVOSE HEAD PADSTOW PL28 8SL	01841 520990 01841 520550 info@motheriveysbay.com www.motheriveysbay.com	 865 756 on path	T S LY G CP DW £6.00 31 Mar to 31 Oct
21	The Warden The Camping & Caravan Club Site TREGURRIAN NEWQUAY TR8 4AE	01637 860448 www.campingand caravanningclub.co.uk	 853 654 800 mts	T S LY G CP DW Non members from £4.30 Mar-Sept

Sect.	Name and Address	Tel. No. Fax. No. Email Web	Map Ref. Distance from Path	Facilities Starting Price Opening Times
23	Perranporth Tourist Park Budnick Road PERRANPORTH	01872 572174	758 544 1 km	T S LY G CP LSP DW Easter-Sept
24	Ms J. Sawle Beacon Cottage Farm Touring Park Beacon Drive ST AGNES TR5 ONU	01872 552347/553381	705 505 400mtrs	T S LY G CP LSP DW £5.00 Apr to oct
24	Mr M Ellis & Ms T Makinson Mayo Blue Hills Touring Park CROSS COMBE ST AGNES	01872 552999 01872 552999	730 520 On Path	T S LY G CP LSP DW KT Good Friday-Sept
25	Mr J Barrow Rosehill Touring Park PORTHTOWAN TRURO TR4 8AR	01209 890802 johnbarrow@compuserve.com www.rosehillcamping.co.uk	693 473 800 mts	T S LY G £7.50 Apr-End Oct
26	Mr H Williams & Son Magor Farm Caravan Site TEHIDY Portreath	01209 713367 632 427	15mtrs	T S LY CP LSP DW £6.00 Apr - Oct
28	Mr M Osborne Trevalgan Family Camping Park ST IVES TR26 3BJ	01736 796433 01736 796433 trevalgan@aol.com www.trevalganholidayfarm.co.uk	490 402 400mtrs	T S LY G CP LSP DW 1 May to 30 Sept
30	Mr J Boyns Levant House Camp Site TREWELLARD PENDEEN TR19 7SX	01736 788795	375 337 500mtrs	T S CP LSP DW £2.50 1 Apr to 31 Oct
30	Kelynack Caravan & Camping Park KELYNACK Penzance	01736 787633 01736 787633 steve@kelynackholidays.co.uk	372 301 1.5kms PD	T S LY G CP LSP DW PD £3.00 Also Small Bunk Barn avail
30	Mr P Eachus Trevaylor Camp Site BOTALLACK PENZANCE TR19 7PU	01736 787016	370 328 500 mts	T S LY G CP DW £6.00 Apr to Oct
31	Mr T Ellison Whitesands Lodge Lands End Backpackers SENNEN TR19 7AR	01736 871776 01736 871776 info@whitesandslodge.co.uk www.whitesandlodge.co.uk	366 264 400 mts	O T S LY CP DW £6.00 Open All Year
33	Mr J Hall Treen Campsite TREEN NR PENZANCE TR19 6LF	01736 810526	392 228 90 mts	T S G CP LSP DW £5.00 end Mar - end Oct
34	Mr & Mrs Robbins Bone Valley Holiday Park Heamoor PENZANCE TR20 8UJ	01736 360313	462 318 2kms	T S G CP LY £4.50 1 Mar- 7 Jan
35	Mr Laity Wheal Rodney Gwallon MARAZION TR17 0HL	01736 710605	1.2 kms	T S LY CP LSP DW £5.50 1 Apr to 31 Oct

Sect.	Name and Address	Tel. No. Fax. No. Email Web	Map Ref. Distance from Path	Facilities Starting Price Opening Times
36	Mrs W Rowan Lower Pentreath Caravan & Camp Site PRAA SANDS PL20 9TL	01736 763221	300 mts	T S CP LSP DW £6.00
38	Mr M Bolton Criggan Mill MULLION COVE TR12 7EU	01326 240496 info@crigganmill.co.uk www.crigganmill.co.uk	667 180 200 mts	T S LY CP KT £6.50 Easter - End Oct
38	Mr A B Thomas Tenerife Farm Caravan & Camping Park Predannack MULLION TR12 7EZ	01326 240293 01326 240293	672 166 800 mts	T S LY CP LSP DW £6.00 Easter to Oct
39	Mr & Mrs R H Lyne Henry's Campsite Caerthillian Farm THE LIZARD TR12 7NX	01326 290596 01326 290080	SW125701 500mtrs PD	O T S G CP LSP DW KT £5.00 Open all year
40	Mr & Mrs K G Bonser Silver Sands Holiday Park Gwendreath KENNACK SANDS TR12 7LZ	01326 290631 01326 290631 silversands@aol.com www.ukparks.co.uk	729 169 1km	T S LY CP DW £5.50 May to Sept
40	T Gibson Gwendreath Farm Caravan Park KENNACK SANDS HELSTON TR12 7LZ	01326 290666 tom.gibson@virgin.net www.tomandlinda.co.uk	729 168 1km	T S LY G CP DW £5.30 Easter to Oct
40	Mrs M Mita Little Trevothan Caravan & Camping Park COVERACK	01326 280260 01326 280260 trevothan@connexions.co.uk www.connexions.co.uk/trevothan/index.ht	770 180 1 km	T S LY G CP LSP DW £4.00 Apr-Oct
41	Mrs P Hosking Gear Farm ST MARTIN HELSTON TR12 6DE	01326 221364	723 249 4.5 kms PD	T S G CP LSP DW KT £5.00 Easter-Oct
42	Mr & Mrs A J Jewell Pennance Mill Farm Chalet & Camping MAENPORTH FALMOUTH TR11 5HJ	01326 312616 01326 317431	791 307 800 mts	T S LY G CP LSP DW £6.50 Easter to Oct
44	Mr & Mrs V Barry Treloan Coastal Farm PORTSCATHO TRURO TR2 5EF	01872 580989/580899 01872 580989 holidays@treloan.freeserve.co.uk www.coastalfarmholidays.co.uk	874 348 300 mtrs PD	O T S LY G CP LSP DW KT £5.50 Open All Year
47	Dr J Whetter Trelispen Camping Park GORRAN HAVEN	01726 843501 01726 843501 trelispen@care4free.net	005 421 750 mts	T S LY £7.00 Apr to Oct
47	Mrs M Parkhouse Treveor Farm GORRAN ST AUSTELL PL26 6LW	01726 842387 01726 842387	987 418 1.6 kms	T S LY CP DW £6.00 Apr - Oct
50	Mr J Taylor Carlyon Bay Camping Park Cypress Avenue CARLYON BAY PL25 3RE	01726 812735 01726 815496 jeffst@globalnet.co.uk www.carlyonbaycamping.co.uk	053 525 200 mtrs	T S LY G CP DW £5.00 Easter to Oct

Sect.	Name and Address	Tel. No. Fax. No. Email Web	Map Ref. Distance from Path	Facilities Starting Price Opening Times
51	Penhale Caravan & Camping FOWEY PL23 1JU	01726 833425 01726 833425 penhale@farmersweekly.net	103 526 2 kms	T S LY G CP LSP DW £5.00 Apr-Sept
53	Tencreek Caravan Park LOOE PL13 2JR	01503 262447 01503 262760 tencreek@aol.com www.tencreek.co.uk	234 525 On path	O T S LY G CP LSP DW £7.50 Open All Year
53	Mr & Mrs R Haywood Talland Barton Caravan Park TALLAND BAY NR LOOE PL13 2JA	01503 272715 01503 272224	515 234 100 mts	T S LY G CP LSP DW £3.00 Apr-Oct
58	Mr J Tucker Mount Folly Farm BIGBURY ON SEA TQ7 4AR	01548 810267 01548 810267	661 447 on path	O T CP LSP DW £3.50 Open All Year
59	Mr P Higgin Karrageen Camping Site BOLBERRY NR KINGSBRIDGE TQ7 3EN	01548 561230 01548 560192 phil@karrageen.co.uk www.karrageen.co.uk	689 394 1.2 kms	T S LY G CP DW £7.00 15 Mar to 15 Nov
60	Mrs S M Squire Higher Rew Camping Park MALBOROUGH KINGSBRIDGE TQ7 3DW	01548 842681 01548 843681	714 382 1.5 kms	T S LY G CP LSP DW £5.00 Easter-End Oct
60	Mr & Mrs B Sweetman Sun Park Caravan & Camping SOAR MILL COVE NR SALCOMBE TQ7 3DS	01548 561378 01548 561378	1200 mts	T S LY DW £6.00 Easter - Sept
61	Mr & Mrs J Bradney Old Cotmore Farm Caravan & Camping Park STOKENHAM TORCROSS TQ7 2LR	01548 580240 01548 580875	804 415 1 km	T S LY G CP LSP DW £6.50 15 Mar to 15 Nov
66	Mr A Jeffery Lady's Mile Touring & Camping Park Week Lane DAWLISH EX7 0LX	01626 863411 01626 888689 www.ladysmile.co.uk	968 784 500mtrs	T S LY G DW £7.00 Mid Mar to Oct
67	Ladram Bay Holiday Centre LADRAM BAY BUDLEIGH SALTERTON EX9 7BX	01395 568398 01395 568338 welcome@ladrambay.co.uk	096 854 60mtrs	T S LY G CP DW 1 Apr to 30 Sept
68	Mr & Mrs D Franks Oakdown Caravan Park Weston SIDMOUTH EX10 0PH	01297 680387 01297 680541 oakdown@btinternet.com www.bestcaravanpark.co.uk	167 902 2 kms	T S LY CP DW £7.75 Apr to Oct
69	Mr D. Boyce Salcombe Regis Caravan & Camping Park SALCOMBE REGIS SIDMOUTH EX10 0JH	01395 514303 01395 514303 info@salcombe-regis.co.uk www.salcombe-regis.co.uk	151 892 1.5kms	T S LY G CP LSP DW £7.00 15 Apr - 28 Oct
69	Mr J M Salter Manor Farm Camping & Caravan Site Seaton Down Hill SEATON EX12 2JA	01297 21524	1km	T S LY DW £8.00 15 Mar to 31 Oct

Sect.	Name and Address	Tel. No. Fax. No. Email Web	Map Ref. Distance from Path	Facilities Starting Price Opening Times
69	Mr R K Webber Axmouth Camping Site Axe Farm SEATON EX12 4BG	01297 24707 axe.farm@ic24.net www.axefarm.co.uk	256 911 1 km	T S G CP LSP DW £6.00 Mid Mar-Mid Oct
70	Mr G Appleton Uplyme Touring Park Hook Farm Gore Lane LYME REGIS DT7 3UU	01297 442801 www.hookfarm-uplyme.co.uk	323 929 1.5 kms	O T S LY G CP LSP DW £7.00 Open all Year
71	Mr R Loosmore Manor Farm Holiday Centre CHARMOUTH DT6 6QL	01297 560226 www.manorfarmholidaycentre.co.uk	368 937 500mtrs	O T S LY G CP LSP DW £8.00 Open All Year
72	Mr & Mrs M Cox Golden Cap Holiday Park SEATOWN BRIDPORT DT6 6JX	01308 422139 01308 425672	424 919 100mtrs	T S LY G CP DW 17 Mar to 5 Nov
72	Mr & Mrs M Cox Highlands End Holiday Park EYPE BRIDPORT	01308 422139 01308 425672 highlands@wdlh.co.uk www.wdlh.co.uk	450 910 100 mts	T S LY G CP DW Mar to Nov
72	Mr K G Mundy Eype House Caravan & Camping Park EYPE NR BRIDPORT DT6 6AL	01308 424903 01308 424903 www.eypehouse.co.uk	446 912 100mtrs	T S LY G CP LSP DW £8.00 Easter to Oct
73	Mr R Condliffe Freshwater Beach Holiday Park BURTON BRADSTOCK NR BRIDPORT DT6 4PT	01308 897317 01308 897336 freshwater@fhbp.co.uk www.fhbp.co.uk	898 479 200mtrs	T S LY G DW £8.50 17 Mar - 12 Nov
76	Mrs A MacMorran Durdle Door Holiday Park LULWORTH COVE WEST LULWORTH BH20 5PU	01929 400200 01929 400260 durdledoor@lulworth.com www.lulworth.com	811 808 on path	T S LY G DW £5.00 1 Mar-31 Oct
78	Toms Field Campsite Toms Field Road SWANAGE BH19 3HN	01929 427110 01929 427110	995 785	T S G CP LSP LY DW £3.00 Mid Mar to Oct
78	Ulwell Cottage Caravan Park ULWELL SWANAGE BH19 3DG	01929 422823 01929 421500 www.ulwellcottagepark.co.uk	3 kms	T S LY G CP DW 1 Mar - 7 Jan
79	Mrs S Howell Huntick Farm Caravan Park Huntick Road LYTCHETT MATRAVERS POOLE BH16 6BB	01202 622222 01202 620501 PD		T S CP LSP KT 1 Apr-31 Oct

YOUTH HOSTEL ASSOCIATION

There is an amazing variety of youth Hostels along the South West Coast Path, 23 in total and all offering comfortable, friendly accommodation. Prices start from £5.15 per night, including bed linen, the use of self-catering kitchens, drying rooms and cycle sheds. The YHA is a membership organisation, however non-members are welcome to join on arrival at the hostel. Membership (£5.50 Under 18, £11 Adult per annum) enables you to take advantage of the 5000 Youth Hostels world wide, regular member's magazine 'Triangle', annual YHA Accommodation Guides and discounts at YHA Adventure Shops and local tourist attractions. YHA annual membership costs are currently under 18 - £6.25, adult - £12.50 and family (2 adults & 2 children) - £25.00. The meals are excellent value, at around £3.40 for breakfast, Packed Lunches £2.70 to £3.50 and Evening Meals £4.00 - £4.60.

Book directly with the Youth Hostel of your choice of for further assistance, please contact English Regions Office, P O Box 11, Matlock, Derbyshire, DE4 2XA. Telephone 01629 825850, fax 01629 824571 or email Englishregions@YHA.org.uk, or why not visit their website at www.YHA.org.uk

Prices range from £4 to £9.75 for bed and bed linen, but please remember to check with each individual hostel before booking.

YOUTH HOSTELS

Minehead Youth Hostel Alcombe Combe	MINEHEAD	TA24 6EW	Tel: 01643 702595	GridRef: 973 442	
Lynton Youth Hostel Lynbridge	LYNTON	EX35 6AZ	Tel: 01598 753237	GridRef: 720 487	
Elmscott Youth Hostel Hartland	BIDEFORD	EX39 6ES	Tel: 01237 441367	GridRef: 231 217	Self Catering only
Boscastle Youth Hostel Palace Stables	BOSCASTLE	PL35 0HD	Tel: 01840 250287	GridRef: 096 915	
Tintagel Youth Hostel Dunderhole Point	TINTAGEL	PL34 0DW	Tel: 01840 770334	GridRef: 047 881	Self Catering only
Treyarnon Bay Youth Tregonnan Treyarnon	PADSTOW	PL28 8JR	Tel: 01841 520322	GridRef: 859 741	
Perranporth Youth Hostel Droskyn Point	PERRANPORTH	TR6 0GS	Tel: 01872 573812	GridRef: 752 544	Self Catering only
Land's End Youth Hostel Letcha Vean	ST JUST	TR19 7NT	Tel: 01736 788437	GridRef: 364 305	
Penzance Youth Hostel Castle Horneck Alverton	PENZANCE	TR20 8TF	Tel: 01736 362666	GridRef: 457 302	
Coverack Youth Hostel Park Behan School Hill	HELSTON	TR12 6SA	Tel: 01326 280687	GridRef: 782 184	
Pendennis Youth Hostel Pendennis Castle	FALMOUTH	TR11 4LP	Tel: 01326 311435	GridRef: 823 319	
Boswinger Youth Hostel Boswinger	St Austell	PL26 6LL	Tel: 01726 843234	GridRef: 991 411	
GORRAN Golant Youth Hostel Penquite House Golant	FOWEY	PL23 1LA	Tel: 01726 833507	GridRef: 118 557	
Plymouth Youth Hostel Belmont House Belmont Place	PLYMOUTH	PL3 4DW	Tel: 01752 562189	GridRef: 461 555	
Salcombe Youth Hostel Overbecks Sharpitor	SALCOMBE	TQ8 8LW	Tel: 01548 842856	GridRef: 728 374	
Maypool Youth Hostel Maypool House Galmpton	BRIXHAM	TQ5 0ET	Tel: 01803 842444	GridRef: 877 546	
Exeter Youth Hostel 47 Countess Wear Road	EXETER	EX2 6LR	Tel: 01392 873329	GridRef: 942 897	
Beer Youth Hostel Bovey Combe Townsend	SEATON	EX12 3LL	Tel: 01297 20296	GridRef: 223 896	
Litton Cheney Youth Hostel Litton Cheney	DORCHESTER	DT2 9AT	Tel: 01308 482340	GridRef: 548 900	Self Catering only, no smoking
Lulworth Cove Youth School Lane WEST LULWORTH	Wareham	BH20 5SA	Tel: 01929 400564	GridRef: 832 806	
Portland Youth Hostel Hard House Castle Road	PORTLAND	DT5 1AN	Tel: 01305 861368		
Swanage Youth Hostel Cluny Crescent	SWANAGE	BH19 2BS	Tel: 01929 422113	GridRef: 031 785²	

TOURIST INFORMATION CENTRES

MINEHEAD	17 Friday Street		TA24 5UB	Phone: 01643 702624	Fax: 01643 707166
LYNTON	Town Hall	Lee Road	EX35 6BT	Phone: 01598 752225	Fax: 01598 752755
COMBE MARTIN	Sea Cottage	Cross Street	EX34 0DH	Phone: 01271 883319	Fax: 01271 883319
ILFRACOMBE	The Promenade		EX34 9BX	Phone: 01271 863001	Fax: 01271 862586
WOOLACOMBE	Red Barb Cafe Car Park	Barton Road		Phone: 01271 870553	Fax:
BRAUNTON	The Bakehouse Centre	Caen Street	EX33 1AA	Phone: 01271 816400	Fax: 01271 816947
BARNSTAPLE	36 Boutport Street		EX31 1RX	Phone:01271 375000	Fax: 01271 374037
BIDEFORD	Victoria Park	The Quay	EX39 2QQ	Phone: 01237 477676	Fax: 01237 421853
BUDE	Visitor Centre	The Crescent	EX23 8LE	Phone: 01288 354240	Fax: 01288 355769
PADSTOW	Red Brick Building	North Quay	PL28 8AF	Phone: 01841 533449	Fax: 01841 532356
NEWQUAY	Municipal Offices	Marcus Hill	TR7 1BD	Phone: 01637 871345	Fax: 01637 852025
PERRANPORTH	Beiners Arms Hotel			Phone: 01872 573368	Fax:
PENZANCE	Station Road		TR18 2NF	Phone: 01736 362207	Fax:
FALMOUTH	28 Killigrew Street		TR11 3PN	Phone: 01326 312300	Fax: 01326 313457
FOWEY	4 Custom Hill House		PL23 1AB	Phone: 01726 833616	Fax: 01726 833616
ST IVES	The Guildhall	Street an Pol	TR26 2DT	Phone: 01736 796297	Fax: 01736 798309
LOOE	The Guildhall	Fore Street	PL13 1AA	Phone: 01503 262072	Fax: 01503 265426
PLYMOUTH	Island House	9 The Barbican	PL1 2LS	Phone: 01752 304849	Fax: 01752 257955
SALCOMBE	Council Hall	Market Street	TQ8 8DE	Phone: 01548 843927	Fax: 01548 842736
DARTMOUTH	The Engine House	Mayors Avenue	TQ6 9YY	Phone: 01803 834224	Fax: 01803 835631
KINGSBRIDGE	The Quay			Phone: 01548 853195	Fax: 01548 854185
BRIXHAM	The Old Market House	The Quay	TQ5 8TB	Phone: 01803 852861	Fax:
TORQUAY	Vaughan Parade		TQ2 5JG	Phone: 01803 297428	Fax:
PAIGNTON	The Esplanade		TQ4 6BN	Phone: 01803 558383	Fax: 01803 551959
TEIGNMOUTH	The Den	Sea Front	TQ14 8BE	Phone: 01626 779769	Fax: 01626 779770
DAWLISH	The Lawn		EX7 9EL	Phone: 01626 863589	Fax:
EXMOUTH	Alexandra Terrace		EX8 1NZ	Phone: 01395 222299	Fax:
BUDLEIGH SALTERTON	Fore Street		EX9 6NG	Phone: 01935 445275	Fax:
SIDMOUTH	Ham Lane		EX10 8XR	Phone: 01395 516441	Fax: 01395 516441
SEATON	The Underfleet		EX12 2TB	Phone: 01297 21660	Fax: 01297 21689
LYME REGIS	Guildhall Cottage	Church Street	DT7 3BS	Phone: 01297 442138	Fax: 01297 443773
BRIDPORT	32 South Street		DT6 3NQ	Phone: 01308 424901	Fax: 01308 421060
WEYMOUTH	King's Statue	The Esplanade	DT4 7AN	Phone: 01305 785747	Fax: 01305 788092
SWANAGE	The White House	Shore Road	BH19 1LB	Phone: 01929 422885	Fax: 01929 423423
WAREHAM	Trinity Church	South Street	BH20 4LU	Phone: 01929 552740	Fax: 01929 554491
POOLE	Tourism Centre	The Quay	BH15 1HE	Phone: 01202 253253	Fax: 01202 684531

SOUTH WEST COAST PATH ASSOCIATION - HISTORY

We are sometimes asked what we have done and we set out below some of the things in which we have been involved in one way or another. We do as well send a steady flow of reports on path deficiencies, both as regards maintenance and the route of the path to the local authorities and the Countryside Agency.

1973 Official Formation in May.
Attendance Cornish Opening at Newquay.
Comments to Sports Council on proposed Countryside Park at Northam Burrows.
First Information Sheets produced.

1974 Evidence submitted to Mr Yepp for his report to the Countryside Commission on Long Distance Footpaths.
We welcomed Devon N.F.U. representation on our Committee.
Attendance at South Devon and Dorset Opening in September at Beer.
Registration as a Charity.
First Description issued.

1975 Mark Richard's book 'Walking the North Cornwall Coastal Path' published - a work in which we may fairly say we played a part.
Clematon Hill, Bigbury, small new section of Coast Path agreed at SWWA's instigation.
Article on SWW in 'Rucksack'.
Attendance at Opening of so-called Exmoor Coastal Path.
Bideford Public Enquiry - successful opposition to Golf Course on the Coastal Path at Abbotsham.
Hartland Point Success at last in getting path south from Hartland Point over Blagdon and Upright Cliffs. Walk over new Lulworth Range Walk.

1976 First Footpath Guide issued.
Thurlestone Diversion opposed.
Evidence submitted to House of Commons Expenditure Committee Environment sub-committee.
North Cliffs Improvements between Portreath and Hayle secured, thanks to National Trust.
Public Enquiry with R.A. at Kingswear on the section Kellys Cove to Man Sands.
Consulted by Devon County Council on path at Watermouth and Dorset County Council about Abbotsbury.
Goodbye to our first Chairman, Mr Walter - we lose a tower of strength.

1977 SWWA mentioned in the YH. Handbook.
Publications of Letts Guides in three volumes. The first satisfactory books to whole path in which we can say our information helped a little.
Attendance at Coverack Youth Hostel official opening.
Evidence presented to Lord Porchester's Exmoor Study.
Badges produced.
Evidence given to Devon County Council for Taw/Torridge Estuary Survey.

1978 First Printed Footpath guide.
Attendance at Westward Ho! Somerset/North Devon Opening.
Dean Quarry, St Keverne, Cornwall Opposition to diversion.
Pentewan Lack of Path submitted to Local Ombudsman.
Hartland New path seaward of Radar Station obtained, thanks to South West Way Association.

1979 Evidence given at Public Enquiries at Abbotsbury and Lulworth Cove.
Submission to Mr Himsworth for his report on Areas of Outstanding Natural Beauty.
First printed News Letters and Descriptions, and the first illustrated description.
Pine Haven to Port Quin gap submitted to Local Ombudsman.
Assistance to Letts for their Guide reprint.

1980 Result of 1976 Public Enquiry at Kingswear published.
Discussion Dean Quarry, St Keverne, Cornwall.
Dialogues with Countryside Commission about path deficiencies.
Alternative coastal path open Glenthorne Estate, Somerset and we submit proposals for rerouting in Exmoor National Park.
St Loy, Cornwall Special report submitted.

Attendance at Widmouth Head, North Devon, Public Enquiry.
Opinions expressed to Department of Environment on draft 'Wildlife and Countryside Bill'.

1981 Annual Guide 'State of the Path' section improved.
Attendance at second Kingswear Public Enquiry.
Countryside Commission decide that path wardenship will be greatly extended.
Duckpool, North Cornwall Bridge provided.
Path improvements at Watermouth; Braunton to Barnstaple; Dean Quarry; Clematon Hill; Bigbury; Mothecombe and Maidencombe.

1982 Wardenship of coastal path in Cornwall completed.
Further openings at: Cleave Farm in North Cornwall, Pentewan with its unfortunate execution and Mount Edgecombe in South Cornwall, Higher Brownstone Farm, Kingswear and a short section west of Berry Head in South Devon.
Agreement was also reached for a high tide route at Mothecombe in South Devon.
The 1982 Guide incorporates a new `Itinerary Suggested' section.

1983 Opening of the Widmouth Head section in North Devon and a second long section in South Devon between Kingswear and Man Sands.
Crackington Haven, North Cornwall Major improvements to the Path on the western side.
Cornwall's 10th Anniversary Walk.

1984 **New Section** A new section of the Path opened on the east bank of the mouth of the River Dart close to Kingswear and giving access to Mill Bay Cove and a splendid stretch of coastal walking.
Trebarwith Strand to Backways Cove in North Cornwall A coastal route opened.

1985 **Culbone - Foreland Point** The alternative coastal path at the Glenthorne Estate was waymarked as the official route, which is a great improvement.
Pinehaven - Port Quin (North Cornwall) The new path was opened and is a vast improvement, although the substantial fence and barbed wire detracts from the scene.

1986 **Minehead to Porlock Weir** New alternative path between North Hill and Hurlstone Point signposted and waymarked.
Black Head, Cornwall Now purchased by the National Trust.

1987 **Barnstaple/Bideford/Northam** The new route completed along the railway lines and open.
Bude Attendance at Public Enquiry to prevent development adjacent to footpath.
Chynhalls Point Coast path moved to seaward of hotel.
Branscombe Attendance at Public Enquiry to urge true coast path instead of inland route. Preferred route adopted.
Bidna/Northam Owing to breach in sea wall an acceptable diversion is negotiated.

1988 **Woody Bay to Trentishoe** Devon County Council adopts our recommended, nearer the coast route as the official coast path.

1989 **Culbone** On site exploration with Countryside Commission and Exmoor National Park Authority to discover an acceptable alternative to the long unnecessary Culbone diversion.
Chynhalls Cliff On site exploration for a more coastal trail.
Fire Beacon Point/Pentargon Cornwall County Council installs grand new path.
Wembury Attend public meeting at Down Thomas to successfully oppose erection of locked gates across Coast Path by Royal Navy.
Strete Gate/Warren Cove Attend public meeting and give evidence to support proposals by Countryside Commission and Devon County Council for an improved and more true coast path.

1990 **Membership** Now over 1000.

1991 **Buckator** At our request Cornwall County Council re-route official path around the headland.
Worthy/Culbone On site explorations for a preferable diversion to that proposed by Exmoor National Park Authority.
Strete Gate/Warren Cove Continuing our strong argument with Devon County Council for a coast path.
Lyme Regis Continued pleas to Dorset County Council to reinstate the coast path along the golf course.
We estimate the Coast Path to be about 613 miles (982 km) long.

1992 **Watcombe and Maidencombe** Our recommended route put in by Devon County Council.
Worthygate Wood Our suggested path installed by National Trust.
Commenced discussions with Countryside Commission to examine sections of coast suitable for 'Set Aside'.

1993 **Foreland Point** Successful opposition to an application to close path on west side.
Buck's Mills Success with our request for a coast path avoiding the holiday complex.
Port Quin Our suggested path is installed by National Trust.
Write and produce the `trail description' in this book the 'Other Way Round'.

1994 Invited by the Countryside Commission to become a member of the South West Coast Path Steering Group to review the management of our Coast Path.
Association acquires a computer.

1995 Membership reaches 2,000
Culbone section re-opened by Exmoor National Park.
Strete Gate/Warren Point - continuous pressure causes Devon County Council to explore again for a route that will provide an acceptable coast path.
Continuing involvement in the 'Coast Path Project'.
Association details on the Internet. See Web address on page 2.

1996 Path descriptions for the whole SWW written and printed.
Continuing involvement in the coast path project and production of the strategy document.
Lyme Regis - Golf Course Route reinstated by Dorset County Council.
Strete Gate/Warren Point - Devon County Council decides to install our preferred route but rejected by Countryside Commission.

1997 **Red River at Gwithian** A new footbridge put in by Cornwall County Council.
The SWCP Project published its strategy for the future management of the Coast Path.
The Association becomes a member of the SWCP Management Group.

1998 Our Silver Jubilee Year (25 years old). Application made, jointly with R.A. to Minister for the Environment requesting he use his powers to create a coast path between Strete Gate and Warren Point. Application refused.
Mountbatten Point, Plymouth opened as a coast path.
Jennycliff Plymouth City Council installs an off-road coast path.
South West Way Association launches its Silver Jubilee Appeal to raise funds towards markers at each end of the coast path.
South West Way Association produces a Development Plan for the next three years.

1999 Name changed to South West Coast Path Association.
Membership Secretary becomes known as Administrator.
Publications Officer appointed.   Membership passes 3,000.
Continued involvement with celebratory markers at each end of the coast path.
A history of the coast path written and published.

2000 Global Positioning reveals the length of the Coast Path (1014 km - 630 miles) - it is Britain's only National Trail to exceed 1000 km.
Strete Gate / Warren Point - South West Coast Path Team undertakes a complete review of this section.
St German's Beacon - progress made in realising an acceptable Coast Path.
Crock Pits - Exmoor National Park installs a coastal route sought by us for many years.
Revised Path Descriptions now produced in-house.

OFFA'S DYKE PATH - A MONUMENTAL TRAIL

Walkers on the Offa's Dyke Path glimpse the sea only twice as they progress from Sedbury Cliffs on the Severn estuary to Prestatyn on Liverpool Bay, or vice versa. In between their first and last day, however, they pass through a very varied landscape as they follow the approximate historic border of England and Wales. Unspoilt moorland, rolling hills and farmland are crossed by the path between the tourist areas of the Wye Valley and the North Wales coast. Across the plains of Gwent, over the Black Mountains, the river valleys of Radnor, the Severn and Dee valleys, the limestone hills round Llangollen and the Clwyddian ridges; the list of varied attractions is long. For nearly half the route, the Offa's Dyke ancient monument is a silent companion, sometimes almost eroded away, but at others an impressive 6 1/2 yards (6 metres) from ditch to the bank top as the earthwork rolls across the hills of the Clun area. Many ancient hill-forts, castles and abbeys lie on or near the route whose 177 miles (285 km) can be covered in a week, although most visitors will prefer a longer period in which to absorb its varied attractions.

Offa's Dyke Association was formed in 1969 as a pressure group to press for the establishment of the trail. When the route was officially opened in 1971, the Association continued its voluntary work by providing information services to walkers in the form of 'strip maps', route notes, guide books and its 'Where to Stay' accommodation and camping booklet. Pressure group activities continued to ensure the maintenance of the route, as its system of volunteers watched over lengths of the path.

Since 1982 the trail has been maintained by a professional service for which the Association lobbied. This has developed into the 'Offa's Dyke Management Service' financed by the Countryside Council for Wales and the Countryside Agency through Powys and Shropshire County Councils. ODA helps this body, with whom it shares premises at the recently opened Offa's Dyke Centre at Knighton, whilst also continuing to support walkers, run the Knighton TIC, and provide educational services based on the Offa's Dyke Interpretive Exhibition.

For details of membership and services offered, contact Offa's Dyke Association (SW), Knighton, Powys, LD1 1EN. Tel: 01547 528753. E-mail oda@offasdyke.demon.co.uk

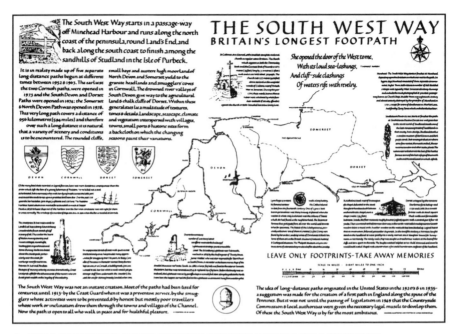

A CALLIGRAPHIC MAP OF THE SOUTH WEST COAST PATH

This quality produced calligraphic map of the South West Coast Path, Britain's longest footpath was designed, illustrated and written by James Skinner of Gloucester. He is a keen rambler and member of a number of walking organisations including the South West Coast Path association, the Backpackers Club and the Ramblers Association.

James, and his wife Linda have spent many holidays walking this coastal path - experiencing at first hand the incredible diversity of scenery. The South West Coast Path passes through five areas of outstanding natural beauty, numerous heritage coasts, through wild isolated countryside, across high cliffs and wide estuaries - yet touching small villages, towns and popular resorts.

The printed calligraphic map has been written entirely by hand complemented by fine pen and ink drawings illustrating many of the sights to be found whilst walking the path.

The **COLOUR** indicating the relief of the peninsular was achieved through using professional quality colour pencils. James has been interested in calligraphy since the mid-1980's when he attended a local summer school. More recently he has completed a full-time professional course in Calligraphy and Book-binding at Digby Stuart College, London. At present, James teaches the craft to adults at a variety of centres in his home county and the South West of England. This calligraphic map would make a superb gift, or an ideal memento for anyone having walked part or all of the path.

Overall size (approximately): 560mm deep x 760mm wide.

Image size : 464mm deep x 6 75mm wide.

ALL PRICES ARE INCLUSIVE OF POSTAGE AND PACKING
Calligraphic Map:- LAMINATED : UNLAMINATED - suitable for framing UK £8.95 USA $21;
other overseas countries £12.50 (payable by sterling draft drawn on a London bank).
Allow 28 days for delivery. Please make cheques payable to James Skinner and send to:
James Calligmphy Services 49 Appleton Way Hucclecote.
GLOUCESTER GL3 3RP England.

INTRODUCTION TO THE SOUTH WEST COAST PATH ASSOCIATION

Whilst walking the path, or on any other occasion, should you meet someone interested in this book, the Association, or the coast path, do not worry if no one has a pencil and paper - just tear off one of these:

-- ----

The South West Coast Path Association was formed 28 years ago to promote the interest of users of our coast path. We continue to press the authorities to maintain it properly and to complete the path. We produce guide books which are issued to members and can be purchased through the Administrator.

Administrator, Sarah Vincent, 25 Clobells, South Brent, Devon. TQ10 9JW
Tel / Fax: (01364) 73859, e-mail: coastpath.swcpa@virgin.net

Secretary, Eric Wallis, Windlestraw, Penquit, Ermington, Devon, PL21 OLU (01752 896237), e-mail: wallispenquit@beeb.net

-- ----

The South West Coast Path Association was formed 28 years ago to promote the interest of users of our coast path. We continue to press the authorities to maintain it properly and to complete the path. We produce guide books which are issued to members and can be purchased through the Administrator.

Administrator, Sarah Vincent, 25 Clobells, South Brent, Devon. TQ10 9JW
Tel / Fax: (01364) 73859, e-mail: coastpath.swcpa@virgin.net

Secretary, Eric Wallis, Windlestraw, Penquit, Ermington, Devon, PL21 OLU (01752 896237), e-mail: wallispenquit@beeb.net

--✂----

The South West Coast Path Association was formed 28 years ago to promote the interest of users of our coast path. We continue to press the authorities to maintain it properly and to complete the path. We produce guide books which are issued to members and can be purchased through the Administrator.

Administrator, Sarah Vincent, 25 Clobells, South Brent, Devon. TQ10 9JW
Tel / Fax: (01364) 73859, e-mail: coastpath.swcpa@virgin.net

Secretary, Eric Wallis, Windlestraw, Penquit, Ermington, Devon, PL21 OLU (01752 896237), e-mail: wallispenquit@beeb.net

--✂----

The South West Coast Path Association was formed 28 years ago to promote the interest of users of our coast path. We continue to press the authorities to maintain it properly and to complete the path. We produce guide books which are issued to members and can be purchased through the Administrator.

Administrator, Sarah Vincent, 25 Clobells, South Brent, Devon. TQ10 9JW
Tel / Fax: (01364) 73859, e-mail: coastpath.swcpa@virgin.net

Secretary, Eric Wallis, Windlestraw, Penquit, Ermington, Devon, PL21 OLU (01752 896237), e-mail: wallispenquit@beeb.net